NEW TOWN
Union Infirmary
Coverley Fields
Church
School
Pavilion Theatre
MET. DIST. JOINT RY.
HOSPITAL
Medical College
FIELDGATE STREET
CHARLOTTE STREET
MOUNT STREET
GREEN STREET
NOTTINGHAM PLACE
MYRDLE STREET
FORDHAM STREET
PARFETT STREET
GREENFIELD STREET
WALDEN STREET
UNION ROW
HOLLOWAY ST.
COKE STREET
Brewery
Goods Depot
BATTY STREET
FAIRCLOUGH STREET
LIZ STRIDE
CHRISTIAN STREET
JAMES STREET
WILLIAM STREET
ELLEN STREET
BOYD STREET
MARYANN STREET
GOWER'S WALK
Wool Warehouse
RICHARD STREET
TRAMWAY

ONE-ARMED JACK

UNCOVERING THE REAL JACK THE RIPPER

Sarah Bax Horton

Michael O'Mara Books Limited

First published in Great Britain in 2023 by
Michael O'Mara Books Limited
9 Lion Yard
Tremadoc Road
London SW4 7NQ

A CIP catalogue record for this book is available from the British Library.

This product is made of material from well-managed, FSC®-certified forests and other controlled sources. The manufacturing processes conform to the environmental regulations of the country of origin.

ISBN: 978-1-78929-516-0 in hardback print format
ISBN: 978-1-78929-536-8 in trade paperback format
ISBN: 978-1-78929-517-7 in ebook format

1 2 3 4 5 6 7 8 9 10

Jacket design: Natasha Le Coultre
Designed and typeset by Design23
Cover picture credits: London Metropolitan Archives (City of London); © The British Library Board. All rights reserved. With thanks to The British Newspaper Archive (www.britishnewspaperarchive.co.uk)
Maps: OS data © Crown copyright 2023

Printed and bound by CPI Group (UK) Ltd, Croydon, CR0 4YY

www.mombooks.com

CONTENTS

This book is dedicated to my great-great-grandfather,
H Division Sergeant Harry William Garrett

INTRODUCTION

The continuing fascination of the Jack the Ripper case relies on its mystery; seemingly unsolvable; its perpetrator unidentifiable; his motive unmentionable. It invokes our deep-seated fear of the unknown, a paralysing inability to make use of our logic or senses. Characterized as the 'Nemesis of Neglect'[1] against a backdrop of social depravation, this unearthly figure made no noise and left no trace. His murders were senselessly brutal, featuring throat-cutting, abdominal mutilations and the removal of body parts. One hundred and thirty-five years later, we continue to debate who he was, and even whether he is a figment of our collective imaginations, with random crimes pieced together to create a serial killer.

Yet Criminal Investigation Department (CID) Chief and Secret Service officer Robert Anderson claimed in his memoir not only that the case had been solved, but 'there was no doubt whatever as to the identity of the criminal'.[2] Unwilling to name Jack the Ripper in public, owing to Scotland Yard's code of confidentiality and the risk of a libel action, he was not alone in his conviction. Surviving indiscretions from his colleagues, Ripper hunter Inspector Donald Swanson among them, allude to a Polish Jew, a true East Ender, against whom insufficient evidence could be brought, but who was admitted to Stepney Workhouse, and Stone and Colney Hatch Lunatic Asylums.

Testifying to the close collaboration between the Metropolitan and the City of London Police Forces, the latter also knew this man, claiming to have chased him from the scene of Kate Eddowes' murder,

Mitre Square, and run surveillance operations against him hoping to catch him red-handed. The joint efforts of both Forces identified Jack the Ripper and removed him from the streets, although not in time to save the life of his final victim, Mary Jane Kelly.

Several of the officers who worked on the Jack the Ripper investigation – called 'one of the most ignominious police failures of all time'[3] – later reflected on its challenges:

> That a crime of this kind should have been committed without any clue being supplied by the criminal, is unusual, but that five successive murders should have been committed without our having the slightest clue of any kind is extraordinary, if not unique, in the annals of crime …[4]

> No one ever saw the Whitechapel murderer; many homicidal maniacs were suspected, but no shadow of proof could be thrown on any one …[5]

> What makes it so easy for him … is that the women lead him, of their own free will, to the spot where they know interruption is least likely. It is not as if he had to wait for his chance; they make the chance for him.[6]

None of these statements is entirely correct. The Ripper left physical clues behind him after the murder of Kate Eddowes. He discarded a torn piece of her apron in a doorway on his escape route afterwards. Chalked up on the wall above it was the complaint, its exact spelling and wording the subject of later dispute: The Juews [*sic*: Jews] are the men that will not be blamed for nothing.[7] Since termed the Goulston Street 'graffito', it was washed off before the photographer arrived, in a hasty decision by Metropolitan Police Commissioner Sir Charles Warren and H Division's Superintendent Arnold. A photographic record could have been used to identify the murderer, by comparing his handwriting against anonymous correspondence claiming to be written by the Ripper, and in the case of One-armed Jack, his signature on his religious and civil marriage certificates.

Of the six murders considered in this analysis to be perpetrated by the Ripper, four involved eyewitness reports of a man interacting with his victims minutes before their deaths. A male was seen and heard soliciting Annie Chapman outside 29 Hanbury Street before she was killed in its back yard. On the night of the 'double event', when two women were killed in swift succession, Elisabeth Stride had a night out with a man who was described by several eyewitnesses, one of whom sold him a bag of black grapes. Less than an hour later, three passers-by saw Kate Eddowes pressed up against a man who might have been Stride's earlier date, standing near an entrance to Mitre Square. And neighbours and acquaintances of Mary Jane Kelly witnessed her socializing with more than one man on the night of her death, the last of whom killed her.

They might not all have seen the same individual, but those people described whom they saw: a man of medium height and build, between 5 foot 5 and 5 foot 8 in. tall, stout and broad-shouldered. Aged between thirty and forty, he had a full face, dark hair, a moustache and possibly a beard. His clothing was shabby-genteel, or shabby chic, typically a dark jacket or coat and trousers, with a bowler hat or peaked cap. He spoke colloquial English, with one witness referring to his mild voice.

There was disagreement about whether his complexion was dark or fair, and whether or not he was foreign, meaning Jewish, as were most of the non-native inhabitants of Whitechapel. Puzzling disparities emerged: to some, he looked as rough as a sailor, and to others, a respectable clerk. Several witnesses perceived the identifying characteristics of a stiff arm, or stiff knees, not bending as he walked or ran. Despite fears of reprisals, all but a minority of witnesses willingly attended identity parades, and testified at inquests about whom they saw.

The victims, keen to solicit a client to pay for their bed and board, were remarkably relaxed as they engaged with their killer. Annie Chapman was leaning with one arm against the house shutters, as her killer stood opposite her, both talking loudly. Even after her murder, when it was widely known that a serial killer was active in their immediate area, his next victims continued to give him their trust. The man seen with Elisabeth Stride was hugging and kissing her at a pub, treating her to grapes in the street, yet later punched her to the ground. Kate Eddowes was standing so close to her interlocutor that she had her hand on his chest. They were not arguing, but talking quietly. Mary Jane Kelly had two paying customers on the night of her death. The second chatted sociably to her as they walked to her room, supplying her with the handkerchief that she lacked. If this was the same man, the Ripper, those women did not fear him, and willingly took him somewhere more private to be alone.

On what might be called the 'long list' of potential Rippers is Hyam Hyams, a Polish Jew who, in April 1889, was brought to Colney Hatch Lunatic Asylum 'in restraint' (a straitjacket) and admitted as a 'very violent and threatening'[8] dangerous lunatic suffering from epileptic mania. His mental and physical decline coincided with the Ripper's killing period. It escalated between his breaking his left arm in an accident or attack in February 1888 and his permanent committal in September 1889, and that escalation path matched the increasing violence of the murders. Hyams was an alcoholic who suffered from delusions, insanity and mania. He was particularly violent after his severe epileptic fits, which explains the periodicity of the murders.

Initially focused on his wife – whom he repeatedly assaulted and twice attacked with a weapon – and her alleged infidelities, his homicidal mania could have spread to the women on the streets. He demonstrated the criminal motivation suggested by police, as 'a misogynist, who at some time or another had been wronged by a woman'.[9] Being diagnosed with a venereal disease might have fuelled that belief. A local man, it is arguable whether he did in fact pass unnoticed on the streets, or whether his epileptic fits, alcoholism and episodes of *delirium tremens* (alcohol withdrawal syndrome), caused more remarkable behaviour. A close fit to the physical descriptions and psychological profiles, misidentified by previous researchers, and mistaken for other same-named East End residents, Hyam Hyams has never before been fully explored as a Ripper suspect. To protect the confidentiality of living individuals, two of the Colney Hatch Asylum files on patients including Hyams were closed to public view until 2013 and 2015.[10]

Once he was detained for being what was termed a 'wandering lunatic' and committing two non-fatal attacks, his wife took responsibility for providing information to Infirmaries and Asylums, and visiting him there. Although she confirmed his assaults on her, and her periodic fear of him, she spoke of her 'kind, industrious'[11] husband with compassion. With the possible exception of individual members of the local Jewish community, among them a crucial eyewitness, there was no conspiracy to keep him free. Yet the weighty responsibility of causing a man like Hyams to be hanged was ducked by the crucial eyewitness, and possibly others. Owing to insufficient evidence, whoever the Ripper was, he was not arrested for his crimes.

It was a living nightmare for the police who worked on the Whitechapel Murders, as the Jack the Ripper case was called before a journalist coined his nickname. The perpetrator could have been anyone in the East End's overcrowded, disorderly streets. As the Ripper investigation gathered pace, always a step behind the killer it chased, the streets of Whitechapel, and the City of London, or 'Square Mile' to its west, were flooded with hundreds of policemen from the Metropolitan and City Forces.

Among them was my police ancestor Harry Garrett, led by uncanny timing to Whitechapel's Leman Street station in January 1888.[12] He had already served fifteen years in the Metropolitan Police's R Division (Greenwich), based at its station in Lee Green. A temporary promotion to Acting Sergeant in the summer of 1887, during Queen

Victoria's Golden Jubilee, led to his promotion to Sergeant at the end of that year. In those fifteen years, he established a career and lifestyle that were an appreciable improvement on working as a cobbler in his home town of Sittingbourne in Kent. All men were transferred to a new Division on promotion, to establish their authority at a more senior rank. Whitechapel must have been quite a shock after Greenwich, although Garrett had received more than one kicking from roughs resisting arrest at Woolwich Docks.

Leman Street police station, where he was based, became the headquarters of the Ripper investigation. From May 1891, Garrett, his wife and young family 'lived in' at the station's newly refurbished premises, where their youngest child Norah May was the first baby to be born.[13] None of the surviving records link him directly to the case, but all men in H Division contributed to the huge police effort against the first modern serial killer. Jack the Ripper was undoubtedly his and his colleagues' greatest adversary in a career lasting twenty-three years. When Garrett retired in 1896, his pension form described him as 5 foot 8¾ in. tall, with fair hair, blue eyes, a fair complexion and no 'marks or infirmities'.[14] That description, and the neat copper-plate handwriting of his signature, left scant traces of his personality.

Policemen in those days had only a truncheon, a whistle and a bull's-eye lantern to defend themselves and signal for help. Their presence on the streets neither acted as a deterrent nor caught the murderer red-handed. The Ripper was not endowed with super-powers, or the wealth and connections that could manoeuvre him out of trouble. He was just lucky, operating on his own turf with a strong instinct for self-preservation. And, somehow, he was a grey man, invisible, over whom the eyes of passers-by grazed and moved on.

The Ripper's victims are known today as the 'canonical five', a grouping that refers to their widely acknowledged status as women killed by the Ripper. A sixth, Martha Tabram, was probably the Ripper's first victim, and lodged within two minutes' walk of Hyams' home. Much has been made of what The Five – Mary Ann 'Polly' Nichols, Annie

Chapman, Elisabeth Stride, Kate Eddowes and Mary Jane Kelly – had in common. Like Martha Tabram, they were termed 'unfortunates', casual street-walkers who sold sex for money to supplement what they earned from cleaning or hawking minor necessities on the streets, such as needles and thread. They were not vagrants killed while sleeping rough. In the hours before their murders, most of them went out to solicit clients, some even telling their associates of their intentions. Most of them were seen with a man in the hours, even minutes, before their murders. Destitution caused them to be risking their lives on the streets of Whitechapel late at night looking for trade, even as the tally of murders increased.

The downfall of each of the women ran along similar lines, no less shocking for its predictability. After leaving a home that was respectable if unhappy, any woman of limited means had equally limited options. She was soon in the workhouse, or a dosshouse known as a common lodging house, crowded with prostitutes, thieves and tramps who had nowhere else to go and whose fee of fourpence a night was hard-earned.

Each woman owned nothing more than the dirty old clothes she stood up in, and the useful odds and ends in her pockets. She might take up with another man, but he would not pay her way. She had to earn her living somehow, selling oddments on the street, and even her body. A dram of gin helped her to forget her former role in life as a daughter, wife or mother. Soon, she was drinking the fourpence that should pay for her bed, and sleeping rough. She would die on those streets, but not of natural causes. The murderer of these women could not have chosen more defenceless victims.

These six victims shared acquaintances and punters at locations familiar to them all: the lodging houses, shelters, pubs and shops to the north and south of Whitechapel Road. At least one of them, Elisabeth Stride, knew her killer. But any of them might have seen his face before, as a local drinker and gambler. Fatally, between August and November 1888, each woman found herself in the wrong place at the wrong time, and fell into the wrong company.

1

WHITECHAPEL'S VICE AND VILLAINY

'The question of identity is a question involving the most profound panic – a terror as primary as the nightmare of the mortal fall.'

FROM *The Devil Finds Work* BY JAMES BALDWIN

It is a subject of speculation whether the Ripper might have been caught if he had been operating in Westminster rather than Whitechapel: 'A district which, even before the advent of Jack the Ripper … had a reputation for vice and villainy unequalled anywhere in the British Isles.'[1] The Metropolitan Police H Division covered 1.5 square miles of Whitechapel and Spitalfields as part of an alphabetically named series stretching over the metropolis within a fifteen-mile radius of Charing Cross. Its divisional boundary ran from the City in the west to Regent's Canal in the east, stopped at its south by the River Thames. It covered Spitalfields in a northern extension up to Hackney Road, ceding ground on its irregular north-eastern border to Bethnal Green's J Division.

Encompassing 'the whole of the poorest districts of the East-end',[2] the area was densely populated with occupants of slum dwellings and common lodging houses, their numbers swelled by transient workers around the docks. Contemporary commentators called it a 'sink'[3] or 'black spot'[4] that was 'inhabited by a mainly criminal population'.[5] Straddling either side of the major thoroughfare, Commercial Street was 'the wicked quarter-mile',[6] a lattice of roads including Dorset

Street, Flower and Dean Street, and Thrawl Street. It was 'a den of thieves'[7] notorious for fights and muggings, where policemen patrolled in pairs for their own safety. The Ripper's victims paid by the night at the local lodging houses, and the last, Mary Jane Kelly, was killed in a rented room on Dorset Street.

Robust H Division detectives called a posting to the district of Whitechapel, 'the best in which to test the worth of a fledgling constable'.[8] A police presence on the streets was essential to deter and detect crime, with the objective of catching a villain in the act. There was a strong reliance on the use of physical and circumstantial evidence, witness testimony and informants. Published descriptions of victims and villains, posters, handouts and door-to-door inquiries were used to solicit cooperation from members of the public, whose favourable response was not guaranteed.

The Police Commissioner's annual review of 1888 cited the Whitechapel Murders as one of two operational priorities which

> necessitated the concentration in particular localities of large bodies of police, and such an increase of force in one quarter of the metropolis, it must be remembered, is only procurable by diminishing the number of men in other divisions … Any additional drain on its resources leads to diminished protection against, and consequent increase of crime … There is great need for a very considerable augmentation.[9]

H Division itself was regularly augmented over the period of the Ripper killings, both by uniformed men on the beat and by plain-clothes detectives.

In addition to resourcing issues, the police had few tools and techniques to assist them in solving crimes. Forensic science did not yet extend to fingerprinting and distinguishing ABO blood types, although photography was increasingly used in the identification of corpses, and to preserve the details of crime scenes. Footprints could be measured and preserved in plaster of Paris, and the perambulating wheels that were used to regulate the length of police beats also measured the distances between crime scenes and criminal haunts. Under Metropolitan Police Commissioner Sir Charles Warren's direction, police experimented with the use of bloodhounds to track murderers and locate body parts. The so-called canine sleuths were not used for the Ripper case, although police delayed forcing an entry into Mary Jane Kelly's lodgings in the hope of their arrival.

One of the policemen who worked on 'the great man-hunt',[10] and felt sickened by the sight of the victims' remains, was Walter Dew. An H Division Detective Constable, ultimately promoted to Chief Inspector, in his memoir he defended the police's inability to secure an arrest, stating that the best men were deployed, who gave their total commitment to the case:

> I feel I must say some words in defence of the police – of whom I was one – who were severely criticized for their failure to hunt down the wholesale murderer …
>
> Failure it certainly was, but I have never regarded it other than an honourable failure … Looking back to that period, and assisted in my judgment by the wideness of my experience since, I am satisfied that no better or more efficient men could have been chosen.[11]

Dew commended the 'Big Three' detectives from Scotland Yard who led the Ripper investigation. Chief Inspector Henry Moore 'was a huge figure of a man, as strong minded as he was powerful physically. He had much experience behind him, and was in every way a thoroughly reliable and painstaking officer.'[12]

The second officer in Dew's line-up was Inspector Frederick Abberline, 'portly and gentle speaking. The type of police officer – and there have been many – who might easily have been mistaken for the manager of a bank or a solicitor. He also was a man who had proved himself in many previous big cases … No question at all of Inspector Abberline's abilities as a criminal hunter.'[13]

Both Abberline and Moore dedicated hours of their own time to the investigation, and used their own money to pay vulnerable women, without respectable homes, to stay safe. In the words of the former:

> Many a time, even after we had carried our inquiries as far as we could – and we made out no fewer than 1600 sets of papers respecting our investigations – instead of going home when I was on duty, I used to patrol the district until four or five o'clock in the morning, and, while keeping my eyes wide open for clues of any kind, have many and many a time given those wretched homeless women, who were Jack the Ripper's special prey, fourpence or sixpence for a shelter to get them away from the streets and out of harm's way.[14]

The third man was Inspector Walter Andrews, 'a jovial, gentlemanly man, with a fine personality and a sound knowledge of his job'.[15] Although he had a senior role supervising parts of the investigation, Andrews featured neither in the surviving papers on the Whitechapel Murders files, nor as a commentator on the case. Press reporting indicates that, during 1888, he travelled widely on 'Secret Service' work, including to Canada.

Dew concluded: 'These three men did everything humanly possible to free Whitechapel of its Terror. They failed because they were up against a problem the like of which the world had never known, and I fervently hope, will never know again.'[16]

While observing that 'the higher police authorities in ignoring the power of the Press deliberately flouted a great potential ally, and indeed might have turned that ally into an enemy',[17] Dew opposed the 'equally undeserved'[18] criticism experienced by his seniors, Commissioner Sir Charles Warren and Criminal Investigation Department (CID) Chief Robert Anderson.

Warren was appointed Commissioner in 1886 after a successful career as a soldier-archaeologist. His approach to policing was heavily influenced by the Army way of doing things, and a desire to lead from the front, creating what was termed 'the General and his blue Army'.[19] Warren's strong will and lack of finesse caused friction with the Home Secretary Henry Matthews, and ultimately led to his resignation within three years. He was in no doubt as to the gravity of the threat posed by the Ripper, reporting to the Home Office in mid-October 1888, 'I look upon this series of murders as unique in the history of our country, and of a totally different character ... in a totally different category.'[20] Warren publicly defended the police handling of the case: 'Every single idea was investigated ... People talk as if nothing had been done,'[21] but he made no conjecture about who the killer was.

Warren's successor, James Monro, had extensive knowledge of the Ripper series of murders, holding several police and Home Office roles between 1884 and 1890, including head of Special Branch. Beyond a passing observation that the Ripper was a 'sexual maniac',[22] he too refrained from pinpointing a suspect.

Robert Anderson, who in addition to being the CID Chief was also an Assistant Commissioner of the Metropolitan Police, was a former barrister turned Home Office adviser on political crime, cover for his activities as a Secret Service officer. A self-described 'anglicised Irishman of Scottish extraction',[23] he was a wily operator, working with Monro, his predecessor as CID Chief, to stop the Fenian bombing campaign on the British mainland in the 1880s. Anderson's covert skills in agent handling and surveillance operations served him well when he turned detective. His memoir *The Lighter Side of My Official Life*, published in 1910, revealed that the identity of the Whitechapel Murderer was known to the police.

According to Anderson, and at least one of his brother officers, Jack the Ripper was a Polish Jew, a true East Ender, who, according to the Secret Service convention of 'need to know', remained unnamed. He was positively identified by a reluctant witness, who refused to testify against him in court. Although his crimes could not be evidenced, he was neutralized by his admission to an asylum. Anderson's memoir contained sufficient information about the unnamed suspect to suggest that it might be possible to identify him.

Dew also gave credit to Inspector Edmund Reid, a CID officer seconded to H Division. Like his seniors, Reid was dedicated to catching the Ripper and 'never went to bed or took off his clothes for three weeks at a stretch, in order that the instant information arrived of any new crime he might get on the track of the criminal'.[24] An amateur balloonist and magician, Reid had used his untiring ingenuity to try 'every means of discovering or entrapping the murderer, among the measures he adopted being indiarubber soled boots for the policemen, detectives disguised as women, and finally the formation of a complete police cordon round the area haunted by the man …'[25]

Reid was the right-hand man of H Division's highly popular Superintendent Thomas Arnold, who served his entire career in the East End and deferred his retirement in the hope of solving the Whitechapel Murders. On his retirement in 1893, Arnold said of the case, 'I can assure you that no stone was left unturned by the police in endeavouring to detect the criminal,'[26] adding: 'This had been a terrible time when a great cloud hung over Whitechapel, and without the support of the people of the district he did not think he could have stood it.'[27] Arnold had been heavily criticized for erasing a significant clue, a piece of writing on a wall in Goulston Street, chalked up after the murder of Kate Eddowes. He feared reprisals against Jewish stallholders at the nearby Petticoat Lane Market, as it was rumoured that the Ripper was a Jew.

Several of these key figures later had their views about the case published in press interviews and memoirs. Moore stated: 'So far as I could make out, he was a mad foreign sailor, who paid periodical visits to London on board ship. He committed the crimes and then went back to the ship, and remembered nothing about them …'[28]

Abberline based his assessment on the eyewitness accounts: 'He was a foreign-looking man, but that, of course, helped us little in a district so full of foreigners as Whitechapel … The people who allege that they saw Jack the Ripper at one time or another, state that he was a man about 35 or 40 years of age.'[29]

Reid had his own theory:

> My opinion is that the perpetrator of the crimes was a man who was in the habit of using a certain public-house, and of remaining there until closing time. Leaving with the rest of the customers, with what soldiers call 'a touch of delirium triangle' [a slang term for *delirium tremens*], he would leave with one of the women.
>
> My belief is that he would in some dark corner attack her with the knife and cut her up. Having satisfied his maniacal blood-lust he would go away home, and the next day know nothing about it.[30]

Walter Dew disagreed with Reid, proposing that, as the Ripper habitually carried a knife, his crimes were premeditated. He speculated about the killer's 'powers of fascination', and why his victims trusted him:

> There must have been something about him which inspired immediate confidence in those he selected as his victims.
>
> These poor women knew better than anyone else the grave risks they ran in associating at this time with strange men. This danger to themselves must ever have been uppermost in their minds. Yet they accepted the man's advances seemingly without question.
>
> *How was he able so readily to allay their fears?*
>
> Is the explanation the more simple one that the man in appearance and conduct was entirely different from the popular conception of him?[31]

Was he, as Dew suggested, 'a man of prominence and good repute locally?'[32] or, descending a level in the social pecking order, the familiar face of someone who lived and worked in Whitechapel or Spitalfields, went down the pub, and hung around on street corners? Dew conjectured about the identity of Jack the Ripper: 'Why not a butcher, or a slaughterman, or even the proprietor of an East End stall?'[33]

Whoever he was, the police had a huge number of suspects to discount. Although the police papers on many of the Jack the Ripper suspects were lost or weeded out as inessential in the 1970s and '80s, parts were transcribed by Paul Bonner, a BBC reporter. Bonner's accompanying note reads: 'Many men, at least 100 in the file, were taken to police stations just for carrying black bags, having foreign accents, accosting women, or talking about the "Ripper" in pubs, but then released on being able to prove their identity.'[34] The black bag was a red herring, an accessory carried by at least two men who were investigated by police, then released.

As Inspector Moore indicated in a post-retirement interview, an overstretched Force had difficulty in managing the public response:

> The police were handicapped in their work. It was almost impossible to get anything like a trustworthy statement while every crank in England was sending postcards or writing on walls. The class of woman we had to deal with have told any number of stories for a shilling …
>
> If we had tried to keep under observation the persons we were told were 'Jack the Ripper', we should have needed every soldier in the British Army to become a detective …[35]

Eleven days after the murder of Annie Chapman, on 19 September 1888, Commissioner Sir Charles Warren submitted a status report to Home Secretary Henry Matthews:

No progress has yet been made in obtaining any definite clue to the Whitechapel murderers [*sic*]. A great number of clues have been examined & exhausted with out finding any thing suspicious.

A large staff of men are employed and every point is being examined which seems to offer our prospect of a discovery.

There are at present three cases of suspicion.

1. The lunatic Isensmith [*sic*], a Swiss arrested at Holloway – who is now in an Asylum at Bow & arrangements are being made to ascertain whether he is the man who was seen on the morning of the murder in a public house by Mrs. Fiddymont.

2. A man called Puckeridge [*sic*] was released from an asylum on 4 August. He was educated as a Surgeon – has threatened to rip people up with a long knife. He is being looked for but cannot be found as yet.

3. A Brothel Keeper who will not give her address or name writes to say that a man living in her house was seen with blood on him on morning of murder. She described his appearance & said where he might be seen – when the detectives came near him he bolted, got away & there is no clue to the writer of the letter.

All these three cases are being followed up & no doubt will be exhausted in a few days – the first seems a very suspicious case, but the man is at present a violent lunatic.

I will say tomorrow if any thing turns up about him.

Moreover the reporters for the press are following our detectives about everywhere in search of news & cross examine all parties interviewed so that they impede police action greatly – they do not however as yet know of the cases 2 & 3.[36]

The first suspect on Warren's list, Jacob Isenschmid, was in his early forties, a Swiss-born resident of North London. Following Annie Chapman's murder, his landlord had raised concerns to two doctors about him being 'a butcher and a lunatic', and having 'frequently been absent from home at early morning'.[37] On 11 September, Doctors Cowan and Crabb reported Isenschmid to the Y Division police at Holloway. Police kept watch on the lodgings of both Isenschmid and his estranged wife Mary Ann until the following day, when Isenschmid was admitted to Grove Hall Lunatic Asylum in Bow.[38] At a previous stay at Colney Hatch Lunatic Asylum, he was found to be 'very violent'.[39]

Mary Ann Isenschmid told police that on Sunday 9 September, the day after Chapman's murder, her husband had visited her lodgings in her absence and taken some clothing. He was in the habit of carrying around large butchers' knives. She said:

> I do not think my husband would injure anyone but me.
> I think he would kill me if he had the chance.
> He is fond of other women.
> He used to frequent a Public House kept by a 'German' named Gerkinger [*sic*] in Wentworth Street Whitechapel.
> He is known as the mad butcher.[40]

The publican of the City of Norwich pub, at 61 Wentworth Street, was a German, Frederick Gehringer. Within walking distance of all of the Whitechapel Murders locations, Wentworth Street ran between Middlesex Street, also known by its archaic name of Petticoat Lane, and Brick Lane. Near Wentworth Street's junction with George Yard, where Martha Tabram was killed, the pub was exactly the type of venue where the killer might meet his victims.

Inspector Abberline reported that detailed inquiries were under way while Isenschmid was detained at Bow's Grove Hall Lunatic Asylum:

> Although at present we are unable to procure any evidence to arrest him with the murders he appears to be the most likely person that has come under our notice to have committed the crimes and every effort will be made to account for his movements on the dates in question …
>
> He is now detained at Bow … and from his description he is believed to be identical with the man seen in the Prince Albert P.H. [public house] Brushfield St Spitalfields with blood on his hands at 7am on the morning of the murder of Annie Chapman.[41]

The Prince Albert pub, also known as the 'Clean House', was within ten minutes' walk of 29 Hanbury Street. The man described in Abberline's report arrived at the pub approximately an hour after Chapman's murder. The Prince Albert's barwoman Hannah Fiddymont, her friend Mary Chappell, and a neighbour Joseph Taylor, reported the visit of a strange customer with a streak of blood under his right ear, and dried blood between the fingers of his hand:

> The man was rather thin, about 5 ft. 8 in. high, and apparently between 40 and 50 years of age. He had a shabby genteel look, pepper and salt trowsers [*sic*] which fitted badly, and dark coat.
>
> His eyes were as wild as a hawk's.
>
> The man walked … holding his coat together at the top. He had a nervous and frightened way about him.
>
> He wore a ginger-coloured moustache and had short sandy hair.[42]

The Medical Superintendent of Grove Hall Asylum, Canadian-born Doctor William Julius Mickle, initially denied police access to Isenschmid, saying that this could 'not be done at present with safety to his patient'.[43] A noted authority on brain and nervous disorders, he aimed to 'seek where possible a material cause of mental disorders'.[44] Although Fiddymont was mentioned in the press as participating in identity parades for other suspects,[45] there is no record of whether or not she was able to identify the man as Isenschmid. The latter was 'well nourished and powerfully built',[46] not matching the description of a thin man. Even if Fiddymont had identified Isenschmid, no direct connection could have been drawn to the Chapman murder.

Isenschmid remained under continuous supervision at the Lunatic Asylums at Grove Hall, Banstead and Colney Hatch, from 12 September 1888 until 19 May 1890, when he was assessed to have 'recovered'.[47] After 30 September 1888, the night of the double event, his confinement led him to be eliminated from further investigation. From 15 October 1891 onwards, he was repeatedly admitted to, and discharged from, Colney Hatch Lunatic Asylum,[48] and he died there on 8 March 1910.[49]

The second suspect on Warren's list, Oswald Puckridge, was a chemist and *accoucheur*, the male equivalent of a midwife. City of London Police Chief Sir Henry Smith, formerly a Major, wrote in his memoir that he alerted Warren to an unnamed Ripper suspect.[50] Surviving City of London Police files prove that this suspect was Puckridge, detailing dates and times in which he was followed from his lodgings at Rupert Street to various locations around London.[51] The timing of Puckridge's stay at Hoxton House Lunatic Asylum in Shoreditch, between 6 January and 4 August 1888,[52] meant that he was released immediately before the Ripper started to kill. Smith stated, however, that 'he proved an alibi without the shadow of doubt'.[53]

The third suspect on the Metropolitan Police Commissioner's list, proposed by an anonymous female brothel keeper, remains unidentified. He was one of hundreds of men reported to police owing to bloodstained hands or clothing, or otherwise suspicious behaviour.

Another senior Metropolitan policeman to expound his views on the subject, Assistant Commissioner of the CID Melville Macnaghten, took up his post as Robert Anderson's deputy in June 1889. Known even to the newest recruit as 'Mac', he was 'a man of action' whose 'house in the West End was never closed to the men who worked with him'.[54] Although he missed the peak of the Ripper investigation, Macnaghten made several well-considered observations about the case in a confidential report for Scotland Yard dated 1891.[55] The purpose of his report was to demonstrate that the recently detained Thomas Hayne Cutbush was not the Whitechapel Murderer, and that there were more credible suspects.

Aged only twenty-three in 1888, Cutbush had worked as a door-to-door salesman in the East End. At that time, he had contracted syphilis.[56] Not then under police investigation, Cutbush was charged over two years later with malicious wounding and an attempted wounding, having stabbed the buttocks of two young women. Considered 'Not in a fit state of Mind to Plead',[57] he was detained at Her Majesty's Pleasure in Broadmoor until his death in 1903.[58]

Macnaghten was unable to relate Cutbush's proclivities to the Whitechapel Murders, commenting:

> It will be noticed that the fury of the mutilations increased in each case, and, seemingly, the appetite only became sharpened by indulgence. It seems, then, highly improbable that the murderer would have suddenly stopped in November '88, and been content to recommence operations by merely prodding a girl behind some 2 years & 4 months afterwards.
>
> A much more rational theory is that the murderer's brain gave way altogether after his awful glut in Miller's Court [the location of Mary Jane Kelly's murder], and that he immediately committed suicide, or, as a possible alternative, was found to be so hopelessly mad by his relations, that he was by then confined in some asylum.[59]

He considered that the canonical five were the 'only' victims of the Ripper. His view of the double event is widely held, namely that the killer was disturbed when killing Elisabeth Stride, and 'nondum satiatus [not yet satisfied], went in search of a further victim whom he found at Mitre Square'.[60]

Macnaghten listed 'the cases of three men' as specific examples of more compelling suspects than Cutbush.

> (1) A Mr M. J. Druitt, said to be a doctor & of good family, who disappeared at the time of the Miller's Court murder, & whose body (which was said to have been upwards of a month in the water) was found in the Thames on 31st. Decr., or about 7 weeks after that murder. He was sexually insane and from private inf. I have little doubt but that his own family believed him to have been the murderer.
>
> (2) Kosminski, a Polish Jew, & resident in Whitechapel. This man became insane owing to many years indulgence in solitary vices. He had a great hatred of women, specially of the prostitute class, & had strong homicidal tendencies; he was removed to a lunatic asylum about March 1889. There were many circumstances connected with this man which made him a strong 'suspect'.
>
> (3) Michael Ostrog, a Russian doctor, and a convict, who was subsequently detained in a lunatic asylum as a homicidal maniac. The man's antecedents were of the worst possible type, and his whereabouts at the time of the murders could never be ascertained.[61]

Born in 1857 in Dorset, a surgeon's son, Montague John Druitt was a highly educated, well-dressed gentleman. His mother suffered from mental health problems, dying in 1890 at Chiswick's Manor House Asylum.[62] The case for Druitt being the Ripper is weak, relying on the facts that he lived in the City of London from 1885 onwards, and killed himself in early December 1888, within weeks of the murder of Mary Jane Kelly. Aged thirty-one, he left a suicide note addressed to his brother saying that he felt that he was going mad, like their mother, before drowning himself in the River Thames. Macnaghten's claim that he was 'sexually insane', offering a credible motivation for the Ripper murders, has not been substantiated.

The second suspect, mentioned only by the surname Kosminski, has never been firmly identified. A possible match is Aaron Kosminski,[63] a hairdresser who lived at addresses off Whitechapel Road at Sion Square, Fieldgate Street and Greenfield Street.[64] Not only were these within walking distance of the canonical five murder locations, but the last two addresses were extremely close to Berner Street,[65] where Elisabeth Stride was killed. Born in 1865 in Klodawa (Klodiva) in central Poland, Kosminski is believed to have emigrated to London in 1880/81 with his two sisters and their husbands in order to join their brother, a London tailor.

On Saturday 12 July 1890, Aaron Kosminski was admitted to Mile End Old Town Workhouse on the grounds of his being '2 years insane', dating his mental health issues back to the summer of 1888. He was discharged three days later 'in care of brother'. On his next admission to the workhouse in February 1891, Kosminski was certified insane and transferred to secure premises at Colney Hatch Lunatic Asylum, where he remained until 19 April 1894. He was reported to have threatened to kill his sister with a knife, and to be delusional, being 'guided and his movements altogether controlled by an instinct that informs his mind; he says that he knows the movements of all mankind'.[66]

It is of some significance that, two years later, he was transferred to Leavesden County Asylum near Abbots Langley in Hertfordshire. Leavesden housed patients who required a lower level of supervision than at Colney Hatch. Despite having made a threat to kill, Kosminski was assessed as neither epileptic, suicidal nor dangerous to others.

His asylum records stated that he had been suffering from 'mania' (a psychological condition involving periods of overactive and excited behaviour) and 'self-abuse' (masturbation) for a duration of six years, which would place the start of his mental illness at around 1885.[67] Kosminski was diagnosed with secondary dementia, and died in 1919 of gangrene of the left leg.[68]

Kosminski's age in 1888, twenty-three or twenty-four years old, was considerably younger than that suggested by eyewitness accounts of the Ripper, which typically placed him in his mid-thirties. He was reported to speak only German, which does not tally with witness accounts of the Ripper speaking fluent, colloquial English to his victims. And not considered to be dangerous, Kosminski exhibited little violent behaviour other than a verbal threat to kill. Those factors all make it unlikely that Aaron Kosminski was Jack the Ripper, though we must acknowledge that he might not be the 'Kosminski' meant by Macnaghten.

The third man on Macnaghten's list, Michael Ostrog, was a thief and fraudster with multiple convictions for theft and defaulting on his bail. A Polish Jew who claimed to be a surgeon, at the age of fifty-four in 1888[69] he was too old to match the eyewitness descriptions of the Ripper. At 5 foot 11 in., he was also too tall.[70] Although he was committed to more than one Lunatic Asylum suffering from mania, he was never violent towards women nor did he have any connection to the Whitechapel area, let alone the notorious murders.

Moreover, he was almost certainly not at liberty, or even in the UK, for the duration of the Whitechapel Murders. On 10 March 1888, Ostrog was released from Banstead's Surrey Pauper Lunatic Asylum;[71] however, on 26 July he was arrested for theft in Paris. He probably remained in French custody between his arrest date and his conviction on 14 November, when he received a two-year prison sentence.[72]

Another suspect investigated by the contemporary police was the shadowy 'Leather Apron'. A local criminal only known by that nickname had been terrorizing the local prostitutes with violence and extortion. Like the Ripper himself, Leather Apron proved impossible to identify, and might even have been a mythical character, or the conflation of multiple men. First mentioned in a Ripper context after the murder of Polly Nichols, a man known as 'Leather Apron' was alleged to have 'more than once attacked unfortunate and defenceless women. His dodge is ... to get them into some house on the pretext of offering them money. He then takes whatever little they have and "half kills" them in addition.'[73] That type of apron, which he allegedly always wore, was not a unique identifier, being used in many trades as a protective garment.

The hunt for Leather Apron began in earnest after Annie Chapman's murder, when an actual leather apron was found in the back yard at the crime scene, 29 Hanbury Street. It had been left hanging up to dry, and belonged not to the killer, but to the landlady's son, John Richardson, a cabinet maker.[74] Although he had visited the back yard shortly before Chapman's murder, Richardson was discounted by the police as being either Leather Apron or the murderer. Named individuals who also came under police scrutiny as Leather Apron included Isenschmid, who was supposedly known by that name among the women of Holloway, and a boot-finisher called John Pizer.

On Monday 10 September 1888, Pizer, a Polish Jew aged thirty-five, was arrested by an efficient H Division officer, Sergeant William Thick, who was convinced that Pizer had been known by that nickname for several years. Pizer was temporarily staying with family at 22 Mulberry Street, near St Mary's Church in Whitechapel. He was discovered to have a firm alibi for the morning of Chapman's murder, and was able to testify at the inquest into her death in order publicly to exonerate himself.[75] That was the end of Leather Apron, man or myth, although it is debatable whether the 'harmless'[76] Pizer was the person referred to by East Enders as a violent pimp.

Demonstrating the formidable effort that went into the investigation after Chapman's murder, the police had a number of other suspects lined up. William Henry Piggott was a local man in his early fifties, who was arrested in Gravesend on the following day. A ship's cook, his loose talk about women in Whitechapel, together with an injury to one of his hands, caused a pub landlady to send for the police.[77]

Inspector Abberline escorted Piggott back to Whitechapel, to take part in an identity parade with witnesses including Fiddymont, on the off chance that he might be identical with her strange, wild-eyed customer.

> At a quarter past two the prisoner was placed among a number of other men, and Mrs Fiddymont and other witnesses, who had noticed the mysterious customer at the Prince Albert Tavern, were called in, and one after another inspected the row of men drawn up before them. To the great disappointment of the police not one of the witnesses was able to identify Pigott [*sic*] as the man wanted, and the authorities were for the moment at a loss to know what to do with their prisoner, whom they once more handed over to [divisional police surgeon] Dr. Phillips.
>
> That gentleman, as the result of further inquiry and examination, arrived at the conclusion that Pigott [*sic*] was not in his right mind, and gave a certificate to that effect. Armed with this document the police removed the man to the lunatic ward of the workhouse, preliminary to his removal to an asylum. He is under close observation, as his condition is not incompatible with the development of homicidal mania.[78]

Stepney Workhouse records state that Piggott was suffering from *delirium tremens*, and that, having recovered, he was released from its infirmary on 9 October.[79] That date, falling after the double event, suggests that Piggott was no longer of interest to the police.

In 1903, the retired Abberline stated in a newspaper interview that he suspected Severin Klosowski, alias George Chapman, of being Jack the Ripper.[80] A Polish Jew who under his pseudonym claimed to be American, Klosowski had recently been hanged for committing two murders by poisoning. Congratulating the detective who had brought him to justice, Abberline observed: 'I have been so struck with the remarkable coincidences in the two series of murders, that I have not been able to think of anything else for several days past … You've got the Ripper at last!'[81] Klosowski had arrived in England from Prague in June 1887, and had in 1890 lodged in George Yard,[82] where Martha Tabram was killed. Despite those coincidences of timing and location, he did not match the Ripper's profile. Eyewitness accounts placed the Ripper as a man in his mid-thirties, while Klosowski was aged twenty-two in 1888, and he used a very different method of killing.

Another American suspect named by a senior Metropolitan policeman was the eccentric Doctor Francis Tumblety. John Littlechild was a retired Detective Chief Inspector, who in 1913 wrote a letter mentioning Tumblety as a Ripper suspect, calling him 'an American quack' who was a 'frequent visitor to London'.[83] An eccentric fifty-six-year-old physician, Tumblety came to the attention of the Metropolitan Police in November 1888, after the murder of Mary Jane Kelly. In activities unrelated to the Whitechapel Murders, he was charged with eight counts of gross indecency, and indecent assault with force and arms against four men.[84] When bailed, he escaped via France to New York.[85] His age, nationality, red walrus moustache and flamboyant dress are among many factors that would have been noticed by witnesses, and therefore eliminate him as a credible candidate.

In that letter, Littlechild made a closing reference to Jack the Ripper's identity. Referring to an unnamed man proposed by CID Chief Robert Anderson, Littlechild commented that Anderson only 'thought he knew'.[86] Within a decade of his retirement, in 1910, Anderson published his memoir, opening with the statement that its content was sanitized: 'I cannot even now write about the Secret Service, or police work in London, save with much reserve and under definite restraints.'[87] Yet Anderson went on the record to state that the case of Jack the Ripper had been solved. He described a suspect, whom he declined to name publicly, in sufficient detail to enable his possible identification by a later researcher. *One-armed Jack* proposes that Anderson's suspect was Hyam Hyams, and that far from ending in failure, the huge surge of effort by the Metropolitan and City Police Forces not only identified but neutralized that most notorious of serial killers.

2

HUNTING CID CHIEF ROBERT ANDERSON'S SUSPECT

'When you have eliminated all which is impossible, then whatever remains, however improbable, must be the truth.'

FROM *The Case-Book of Sherlock Holmes*
BY SIR ARTHUR CONAN DOYLE

Eminent physicians drew their own conclusions about who Jack the Ripper was, contradicting each other as they vied to define the unknown assailant. Psychiatrist Doctor Forbes Winslow, who offered his services to both the Metropolitan and City Police to identify the Ripper,[1] opined, 'The murderer is a homicidal monomaniac [obsessive] of infinite cunning.'[2] Was he a criminal mastermind, whose meticulous operational planning enabled him to elude the police? Or was a second commentator, the highly reputable physician Sir James Risdon Bennett, more accurate in stating that the Ripper was mentally disturbed, unpredictable and visibly incapable of behaving normally: 'A man suffering from acute mania to whom the ordinary rules of motive and procedure do not apply. His infirmity would be obvious to almost every person with whom he came into contact.'[3]

In November 1888, after the final Ripper murder of Mary Jane Kelly, acutely aware of the escalation in the killings' ferocity, Robert Anderson commissioned senior police surgeon and forensic expert Mr Thomas Bond to produce a profile of the serial killer. Bond was tasked to review the medical notes on all of the canonical five victims, starting with Polly Nichols, and reach conclusions that would assist the police investigation. His analysis validated the grouping of the canonical five murders, and directed the police towards the type of criminal who committed them:

> 1. All five murders were no doubt committed by the same hand. In the first four the throats appear to have been cut from left to right. In the last case owing to the extensive mutilation it is impossible to say in what direction the fatal cut was made, but arterial blood was found on the wall in splashes close to where the woman's head must have been lying.
>
> 2. All the circumstances surrounding the murders lead me to form the opinion that the women must have been lying down when murdered and in every case the throat was first cut.
>
> 3. In the four murders of which I have seen the notes only, I cannot form a very definite opinion as to the time that had elapsed between the murder and the discovering of the body. In one case, that of Berner's [*sic*] Street [Elisabeth Stride], the discovery appears to have been made immediately after the deed – in Buck's Row[4] [Polly Nichols], Hanbury Street [Annie Chapman], and Mitre Square [Kate Eddowes] three or four hours only could have elapsed. In the Dorset Street[5] Case [Mary Jane Kelly] … one or two o'clock in the morning would be the probable time of the murder.
>
> 4. In all the cases there appears to be no evidence of struggling and the attacks were probably so sudden and made in such a position that the women could neither resist nor cry out. In the Dorset Street case the corner of the sheet to the right of the woman's head was much cut and saturated with blood, indicating that the face may have been covered with the sheet at the time of the attack.

5. In the first four cases the murderer must have attacked from the right side of the victim. In the Dorset Street case, he must have attacked from in front or from the left, as there would be no room for him between the wall and the part of the bed on which the woman was lying. Again, the blood had flowed down on the right side of the woman and spurted onto the wall.

6. The murderer would not necessarily be splashed or deluged with blood, but his hands and arms must have been covered and parts of his clothing must certainly have been smeared with blood.

7. The mutilations in each case excepting the Berner's [*sic*] Street one were all of the same character and shewed clearly that in all the murders, the object was mutilation.

8. In each case the mutilation was inflicted by a person who had no scientific nor anatomical knowledge. In my opinion he does not even possess the technical knowledge of a butcher or a horse slaughterer or any person accustomed to cut up dead animals.

9. The instrument must have been a strong knife at least 6 inches long, very sharp, pointed at the top and about an inch in width. It may have been a clasp knife, a butcher's knife or a surgeon's knife. I think it was no doubt a straight knife.

10. The murderer must have been a man of physical strength and of great coolness and daring. There is no evidence that he had an accomplice. He must in my opinion be a man subject to periodical attacks of Homicidal and erotic mania. The character of the mutilations indicates that the man may be in a condition sexually, that may be called satyriasis [hypersexuality or compulsive sexual behaviour]. It is of course possible that the Homicidal impulse may have developed from a revengeful or brooding condition of

> the mind, or that Religious Mania may have been the original disease, but I do not think either hypothesis is likely.
>
> The murderer in external appearance is quite likely to be a quiet inoffensive-looking man probably middle-aged and neatly and respectably dressed. I think he must be in the habit of wearing a cloak or overcoat or he could hardly have escaped notice in the streets if the blood on his hands or clothes were visible.
>
> 11. Assuming the murderer to be such a person as I have just described he would probably be solitary and eccentric in his habits, also he is most likely to be a man without regular occupation, but with some small income or pension. He is possibly living among respectable persons who have some knowledge of his character and habits and who may have grounds for suspicion that he is not quite right in his mind at times. Such persons would probably be unwilling to communicate suspicions to the Police for fear of trouble or notoriety, whereas if there were a prospect of reward it might overcome their scruples.[6]

Bond's analysis crossed a strong man 'of great coolness and daring' with a 'quiet inoffensive-looking man'.[7] Which word-portrait best described the killer? In support of the police investigation, Bond's key recommendation was to offer a reward to encourage the man's family or fellow lodgers to report him. He presumed that the Ripper's protectors were motivated by money.

A hundred years after the Whitechapel Murders, US special agent and criminal profiler John E. Douglas conducted a behavioural analysis of the Ripper based on Federal Bureau of Investigation (FBI) methodology. He classified the killer as a white male in the age bracket of twenty-eight to thirty-six, an East Ender from a dysfunctional family. Douglas went further than Bond in outlining the unidentified subject's family background and formative years, suggesting that he originated 'from a family with a domineering mother and weak, passive, and/or absent father':

> As a result, he failed to receive consistent care and contact with stable adult role models and became detached socially with a diminished emotional response towards others …
>
> As he grew older, his fantasy developed a strong component that included domination and mutilation of women … For employment, he would have sought a position where he could work alone and vicariously experience his destructive fantasies … as a butcher, mortician's helper, hospital or morgue attendant …
>
> He was paranoid and carried one or more knives with him in case of attack. This paranoid-type thinking would have been in part justified because of his poor self-image. He might have had some physical abnormality, scarring or speech problem that he perceived as psychologically crippling. He was not adept at meeting people socially, and most of his relationships would have been with prostitutes. Due to … the absence of treatment for venereal diseases, he may have been infected, which would have further fuelled his hatred and disgust for women …
>
> He would have been perceived as a quiet, shy loner, slightly withdrawn, obedient and fairly neat and orderly in appearance …[8]

This profile included the likelihood of the Ripper living or working in the Whitechapel area, where he might have drunk in the local pubs. The location of the first murder would be close to either his home or workplace. It also speculated that the Ripper was either unmarried, or that a previous marriage to an older woman had not lasted for long. Significant points of difference from Bond's analysis are the level of anatomical knowledge and knife skills held by the killer, and his poor self-image, perhaps reinforced by a physical disability.

Co-edited by John E. Douglas, the *Crime Classification Manual* places serial killers into three categories: organized, disorganized and mixed (offenders who exhibit organized and disorganized characteristics). Disorganized serial killers such as the Ripper, making 'frenzied, out-of-control overkills', have the following characteristics:

> [They are] usually far more impulsive, often committing their murders with a random weapon available at the time, and usually do not attempt to hide the body. They are likely to be unemployed, a loner, or both, with very few friends. They often turn out to have a history of mental illness, and their *modus operandi* or lack thereof is often marked by excessive violence and sometimes necrophilia or sexual violence.
>
> Disorganized serial killers have been found to have a slightly lower mean IQ than organized serial killers, at 92.8 [between 90 and 110 is considered average].[9]

Such a killer is an opportunist, likely to commit at least one murder extremely close to his home, and he might be drawn back to the scenes of his killings, or to visit the graves of his victims. A disorganized serial killer is likely to leave the crime scene, 'spontaneous and disarrayed, with a great deal of physical evidence'.[10] That description best fits the room where Mary Jane Kelly was murdered, although without advanced forensics the Whitechapel police were unable to exploit the traces left by the Ripper using finger- or hand-print identification, and DNA profiling.

There is considerable consensus that Kelly's murder was the Ripper's last. Serial killers stop for several reasons. They can be arrested for murder or a lesser charge; they can become debilitated or hospitalized; they can die of natural or violent causes, including suicide; they can find another outlet, such as sexual substitution; or they can experience a significant life event such as marriage, leading to a change in habit and behaviour. Given the almost-monthly periodicity between his kills, by the end of 1888, some barrier or life change must have halted him.

After Robert Anderson's retirement, his memoir outlined his own conclusions about the identity of Jack the Ripper. Personally assigned to the investigation from early September 1888, while 'suffering from the strain of long and anxious work'[11] after the Fenian bombing campaign, Anderson spent a week at Scotland Yard before leaving for a month's rest in Switzerland. His timing was less than ideal, as his sick leave started the day after the Chapman murder. Following the double event, he was recalled to London by the Home Secretary.

Anderson's opening claims were bold, if not sensational:

> One did not need to be a Sherlock Holmes to discover that the criminal was a sexual maniac of a virulent type; that he was living in the immediate vicinity of the scenes of the murders; and that, if he was not living absolutely alone, his people knew of his guilt, and refused to give him up to justice.
>
> During my absence abroad the Police had made a house-to-house search for him, investigating the case of every man in the district whose circumstances were such that he could go and come and get rid of his blood-stains in secret. And the conclusion we came to was that he and his people were certain low-class Polish Jews; for it is a remarkable fact that people of that class in the East End will not give up one of their number to Gentile justice.
>
> And the result proved that our diagnosis was right on every point. For I may say at once that 'undiscovered murders' are rare in London, and the 'Jack-the-Ripper' crimes are not within that category. And if the Police here had powers such as the French Police possess, the murderer would have been brought to justice.[12]

Envious of the powers of the French police, he made specific reference to their latitude: 'It sometimes happens that the murderer is known, but evidence is wholly wanting. In such circumstances the French Police would arrest the suspected person, and build up a case against him at their leisure, mainly by admissions extracted from him in repeated interrogations.'[13]

By contrast, in the UK, duress could not be used, and the police were unable to search private properties prior to arrest: 'No law hinders a police officer from going into a private house or private grounds to arrest a criminal. But the law gives him no right to enter for the investigation of the crime and the securing of evidence that may lead to the detection of the criminal.'[14]

Anderson made clear that the Ripper had not written what is commonly known as the 'Dear Boss' letter. Dated 25 September 1888 and addressed to the Central News Agency, it was two pages of red ink that claimed to be written by the murderer. One of hundreds of hoax letters or more genuine denunciations proposing the names of suspicious individuals for investigation, its signature was the first use of the nickname 'Jack the Ripper'. Anderson went into print to state that the letter was not a clue to the killer's identity, but one of many hoaxes written by a journalist, presumably to generate sales: 'Scotland Yard can boast that not even the subordinate officers of the department will tell tales out of school, and it would ill become me to violate the unwritten rule of the service. So I will only add here that the 'Jack-the-Ripper' letter which is preserved in the Police Museum at New Scotland Yard is the creation of an enterprising journalist.'[15]

Anderson ended his argument by explaining the ongoing need for secrecy about the identities of both the journalist and the Ripper, and introducing a key witness who was able to identify the Ripper, but who refused to testify against him in court:

> Having regard to the interest attaching to this case, I am almost tempted to disclose the identity of the murderer and of the pressman who wrote the letter above referred to. But no public benefit would result from such a course, and the traditions of my old department would suffer. I will merely add that the only person who had ever had a good view of the murderer unhesitatingly identified the suspect the instant he was confronted with him; but he refused to give evidence against him.

> In saying that he was a Polish Jew I am merely stating a definitely ascertained fact. And my words are meant to specify race, not religion. For it would outrage all religious sentiment to talk of the religion of a loathsome creature whose utterly unmentionable vices reduced him to a lower level than that of the brute.[16]

Anderson was referring to a specific individual, whose identity was known to him. His phrasing that the police 'diagnosis' was proved right validates the accuracy of Bond's profiling. The police had a firm suspect as Jack the Ripper, who was under active investigation but against whom a solid prosecution case could not be constructed. The question remains of how and when they detected him. September 1888 must have been too early for a discovery of the suspect, during the house-to-house searches after the murder of Annie Chapman. But was the identification of the Ripper as late as November, after the final murder of Mary Jane Kelly, or earlier, after September's 'double event' surfaced a significant volume of information about the killer, including a key eyewitness sighting?

In a footnote, Anderson expanded upon the fate of the prime suspect as the Ripper, and the behaviour of the key eyewitness who might have convicted him: 'When the individual whom we suspected was caged in an asylum, the only person who had ever had a good view of the murderer at once identified him, but when he learned that the suspect was a fellow-Jew he declined to swear to him.'[17] Anderson gave the suspect's admission into an unspecified asylum as the reason why the crimes ended when they did, and in another published article, wrote that the perpetrator started to kill when 'the mania seized him'.[18] His explanations provided a start and an end point, but no explanation of the intervals between the serial attacks. He also noted, 'there was no doubt whatever as to the identity of the criminal'.[19] If there were no doubt as to the Ripper's identity, with that firm belief dating from 1888 or 1889, it might be possible to identify him today.

Anderson provided some interesting commentary on the subject of evidence. In a newspaper interview dated 1908, he was quoted as saying that two clues had been obliterated before the police were able to assess them:

> In two cases of that terrible series there were distinct clues destroyed – wiped out absolutely – clues that might very easily have secured for us proof of the identity of the assassin.
>
> In one case it was a clay pipe. Before we could get to the scene of the murder the doctor had taken it up, thrown it into the fire-place and smashed it beyond recognition.
>
> In another case there was writing in chalk on the wall – a most valuable clue; recognised as belonging to a certain individual. But before we could secure a copy, or get it protected, it had been entirely obliterated ...[20]

The second clue refers to the Goulston Street graffito, while the first clue was a clay pipe that was found under the body of another Whitechapel prostitute, Alice Kinsey or McKenzie, only to be accidentally broken by a doctor's assistant at the mortuary, and its shards swept away. A woman of a similar profile to the Ripper victims, her unsolved murder, in July 1889, was presumed by Anderson in an apparent self-contradiction to be 'by another hand'.[21]

Former City Commissioner Sir Henry Smith and Jewish representatives were among those who disagreed with Anderson's assertion that the killer was protected by his fellow Jews. Such helpers would risk being classed as 'accessories after the fact ... liable to penal servitude for life'.[22] Moreover, in Smith's view, 'the writing on the wall' after the double event 'probably was written – to throw the police off the scent, to divert suspicion from the Gentiles [people who were not Jewish] and throw it upon the Jews'.[23]

In a press article, Anderson repeated and expanded upon his previous comments:

> Curiously enough, there was, so far as we know, only one man who was able to identify Jack the Ripper – to point him out and say, 'That's the murderer; I recognise him as the man.' This man, when he found out that the murderer was a Jew, immediately went back on what he had said – he refused to stand to the identification – and so nothing more could be done in the matter.
>
> The murderer was a sexual maniac of a very virulent type. He was a quiet and harmless individual in the ordinary way, but when the parosysms [*sic*: paroxysms, meaning attacks] came upon him his ferocity knew no bounds.
>
> We knew that the murderer must live within that area, and we felt further that either he was a man living by himself or that his people were hiding him, for he must have gone home drenched with blood. If you remember the murder [of Mary Jane Kelly] in Miller's Court you will recollect that the place where the body was found presented a terrible spectacle. Blood was splashed all over the walls. The murderer could not have escaped being smothered with blood.[24]

This additional information reinforces what was previously stated about the Jewish witness who would not testify at court, as well as that the killer was a sexual maniac and his residence was close to the crime scenes. It throws doubt on whether he was protected by his family, or whether he lived alone, which might be more likely given the extent of the blood in which he was 'drenched' or 'smothered'. And it provides greater detail about the man himself, 'a quiet and harmless individual in the ordinary way, but when the paroxysms came upon him his ferocity knew no bounds'. When highlighting the killer's paroxysms and mania, was Anderson offering up mere flowery descriptions or was this a medical condition involving periodic episodes of illness, even fits? If so, did the killer have an identifiable illness or set of illnesses?

Anderson's statements have been embellished by 'the Swanson marginalia', pencilled comments made by retired CID Superintendent

Donald Swanson on a presentation copy of Anderson's memoir gifted to him by the man himself, and with whom he maintained a lifelong friendship. Although he features extensively in the surviving police files on the Whitechapel Murders, Swanson was not mentioned by Dew as one of the leading officers on the case. 'A very capable officer',[25] he was placed in charge of the Whitechapel Murders investigation after the killing of Annie Chapman. As Swanson did not himself publish a memoir, his jottings, if genuine, are of considerable interest.

At the bottom of the page of Anderson's memoir, which ends with the words about a witness who 'refused to give evidence against him', Swanson pencilled in the following addition, confirming that the witness, like the Ripper, was a fellow Jew, 'because the suspect was also a Jew and also because his evidence would convict the suspect, and witness would be the means of murderer being hanged, which he did not wish to be left on his mind. DSS [Donald Sutherland Swanson]'.[26]

Swanson then added some further commentary, ran out of space and continued on an endpaper:

> And after this identification which suspect knew, no other murder of this kind took place in London after the suspect had been identified at the Seaside Home where he had been sent by us with difficulty in order to subject him to identification, and he knew he was identified. On suspect's return to his brother's house in Whitechapel he was watched by police (City CID) by day & night.
>
> In a very short time the suspect with his hands tied behind his back, he was sent to Stepney Workhouse and then to Colney Hatch and died soon afterwards – Kosminski was the subject – DSS[27]

The book itself has a solid provenance, having been passed down the Swanson family. Yet the authenticity of its marginalia has been questioned, not least the final mention of a suspect. Two family members first brought Swanson's commentary to public attention in

1981. The story did not fully hit the press until July 2006, when the family presented the book to Scotland Yard's Crime Museum.[28]

The marginalia was tested by two separate handwriting experts, who found similarities to known samples of Swanson's handwriting. The second analysis, dated 3 November 2006, by Doctor Christopher Davies, MA, D.Phil. (Oxon) of the Forensic Science Service London Laboratory, was able to 'support the proposition that Swanson wrote the questioned annotations ...'[29] Unlike Macnaghten's report, the words naming 'Kosminski' were pencilled in almost as an afterthought, and again proposed a suspect identified only by his surname. As Anderson did not name his Polish Jew, was his suspect also 'Kosminski', whether Aaron Kosminski or an unknown individual with the same surname? Or was he someone else?

A Polish Jew who fits the specific attributes listed by Anderson and Swanson is the previously unexplored Ripper suspect Hyam Hyams. A thirty-five-year-old local man, not only was he admitted to Stepney Workhouse, Stone and Colney Hatch Lunatic Asylums, but he also had severe mental and physical conditions that fuelled episodes of extreme violence. He first came to the attention of the authorities on 29 December 1888, when he was stopped by police as a 'wandering lunatic' on Leman Street.[30] Arrested under the Vagrancy Act of 1824, he was by order of a magistrate treated for *delirium tremens* at Stepney's Baker's Row Workhouse Infirmary for a fortnight between 29 December 1888 and 11 January 1889.[31] It was where Polly Nichols' body had been taken after her murder on Buck's Row.

Delirium tremens, caused by excessive alcohol consumption for a period of a month or longer, is characterized by episodes of confusion, hallucinations and seizures, which could exacerbate other serious medical conditions. At the time of his detention, Hyam Hyams had suffered from epilepsy for nine years, with fits that occurred every two months, followed by episodes of extreme violence. His wife Sarah Hyams added that he drank to excess, that his father died in a fit and his uncle was insane.

Sarah Hyams also informed the authorities that her husband had the delusion that she was unfaithful to him, with men including his own brothers. She said that she had suffered four miscarriages, and claimed sporadically to live in fear of her husband's violence.[32] The cause of her miscarriages and her husband's violence were not explicitly connected, but might have been. Her claims were backed up by his continuing aggression towards her in recorded incidents that were often driven by sexual jealousy. At liberty for less than three months, Hyam Hyams was arrested for assault in early April and readmitted to Stepney Workhouse. The stated reason was that, 'In attempting to strike his wife with a chopper he seriously injured his mother on the head.'[33]

Hyams' admission notes, partly written by chief medical officer Doctor Herbert Larder, are summarized as follows:

> The patient has been under my care on a previous occasion and was then very violent. He has been very violent and threatening since admission. Says the food is poisoned, and refuses to eat it. He has a very wild & excited manner. Imagines people are all against him. In my opinion he is a dangerous lunatic …
>
> Says his wife got him here to have him killed. Refuses his food and throws it all over the place.
>
> Form of disorder: Mania. Ep [epileptic mania][34]

On 15 April 1889, an order for his committal having been signed by Justice of the Peace Philip Meadows Martineau, Hyams was transferred from the workhouse to Colney Hatch Lunatic Asylum. In his medical records is one of three formal descriptions of him when in medical facilities, none of which mention that he had any facial hair. Sightings of men assumed to be the Ripper reported his facial hair ranging from having a beard, to only a moustache, to otherwise being clean-shaven. Hyams was described as:

> A fairly nourished Jew with dark brown hair which is turning grey and brown eyes. He is admitted in an excited condition, being noisy and very restless, and is brought to the Asylum in restraint.
>
> His statements are incoherent and he has a delusion as to poison being administered to him by his wife, to whom he acknowledges that he has been violent. He was admitted with bruises on the shins, abrasions to the back arms, and knees, and a deformity of the left elbow …
>
> Suspicious expression, manner uneasy. Is sullen and morose. States he has not been able to work much for past 14 months owing to injury to left arm by which he cannot completely bend or extend it. The injury was caused by kicking when on the ground and appears to consist of ununited fracture of olecranon [elbow] with forward dislocation of both bones. Irregularity in lower ¼ of radius apparently a badly united fracture.
>
> Does not bear much questioning. States his brothers have injured him by causing wife to be unfaithful to him. Is suspicious of wife and brothers … Wife states that patient has suffered from epilepsy for 9 years; fits occur every 2 months, & he is very violent afterwards; has drunk to excess; father died in a fit and uncle was insane.[35]

Hyams committed a further assault on his wife when she visited in May. Doctors noted his uncertain temper, and related his violence to his fits:

> **May 20.** Has been excited and irritable during the last few days: yesterday he had a fit and today, on his wife visiting him he assaulted her in a most violent manner, striking and scratching her face …
> **June 9.** Is now quieter and is resuming condition previous to last fit.
> **July 3.** Has been fairly quiet since last note, but his temper is very uncertain.

> **August 26.** Has been very well behaved since last note and has had no fit.
> **August 30.** Discharged.[36]

Liberated for only a week, he was arrested for a third time, for stabbing his wife in what was again termed an 'assault'. Sarah's injuries cannot have been severe, as she was able to provide information to the authorities about her husband's medical condition. Hyams spent two nights at the City of London Workhouse on Bow Road before being transferred to the Asylum at Stone near Dartford in Kent.[37] Hyams' admission record to Stone noted that he suffered from mania, with a query against the initials G.P. meaning General Paralysis, or syphilis. The supposed causes of his mania were threefold: epilepsy, drink and heredity, suggesting an inherited disorder.

Under the heading 'Delusions or other symptoms' were observations about his paranoia, delusions and periodic violence:

> Terror of the police who has charge of him: feared they were about to strike or kill him. Fancied people were watching him along the Street.
>
> [Reported] By the wife: the delusion that she is unfaithful: violence offered to her leading to constant fear of him at occasional times after he has had fits. These occur about every few months.[38]

A brief report into his 'Condition on Admission' observed that his physical health was good, while his mental health was changeable, and under observation: 'In good health. Heart and lung sounds as normal. He is very discontented and irritable, but is not excited at present nor does he express any delusions so far as can be ascertained. He has a healing suppurating sore on right arm and an old scar on right wrist. A few scratch marks over back.'[39]

The official return made to the Commissioner in Lunacy read:

'Is insane suffering from mania. Has the delusions mentioned in the Medical Certificate. Is very excitable, has fairly good health, the heart and lung sounds are normal. Has a slight hesitancy of speech. The left pupil acts sluggishly.'[40]

Extracts from his records at Stone demonstrate the fidelity of his wife despite his delusions and sporadic violence:

> **Sept 19.** He is irritable and threatening at times. Told reporter that his wife co-habited with a Dr Long who she induced to give him medicine and produce the fits which he suffers from: that she administers the medicine to him during the night, and that she gave him 'the bad disorder [meaning venereal disease]'. He has a small sore on his penis …
> **Oct 18.** Is beginning to occupy himself usefully and conducts himself well. He has an intense antipathy to his wife.
> **Nov 26.** Had a severe and well marked epileptic fit – the first since admission – today he has been quiet and not so well during the past two days. The convulsions attacked chiefly the right side.
> **Dec 13.** For a few days after the fit he was irritable most quarrelsome & inclined to be violent. He has again settled down to his usual mental condition.
> **Dec 16.** Had two fits two nights ago and on the occasion of a visit from his wife today he became acutely violent attacking the head attendant in the visiting room. Is to have Pot[assium] Brom[ide] [an anticonvulsant and sedative] …[41]

After almost four months at Stone, on 7 January 1890, Hyams was readmitted to Colney Hatch. The City of London handed him over to the care of the Metropolitan authorities with this file note: 'Having been made chargeable to Mile End Union he was this day transferred to Colney Hatch Asylum: Discharged as Not Improved.'[42] His asylum records continued to report his fluctuating mental state:

> His conduct is that of an insane person – he says that he is about to be killed, that his wife is unfaithful to him and has poisoned him.
>
> [His] Attendant, states that he is alternately singing and crying – hopes that God will soon take him. With difficulty induced to take his food.
>
> He is an Epileptic, the fits not occurring very frequently; when they are upon him he is exceedingly excited and violent. At present he is fairly quiet, but very bitter against his wife.[43]

Hyams would spend the rest of his life at Colney Hatch Asylum, where, as part of its regular record-keeping, his photograph was taken.

For a 2006 documentary, an efit (Electronic Facial Identification Technique) was produced on a computer program, based on the

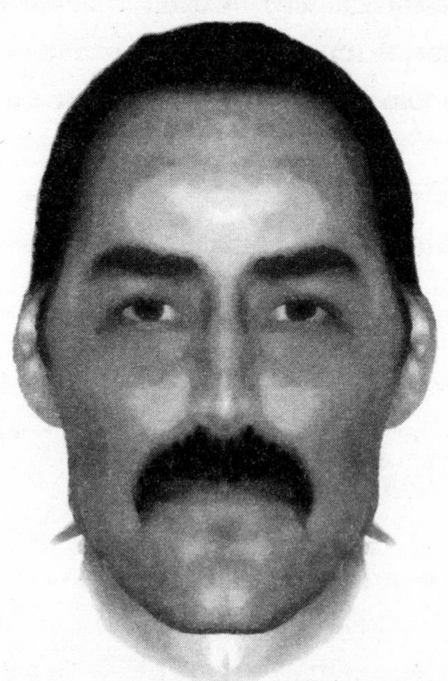

A computerized headshot of Jack the Ripper used contemporary accounts to produce a high-cheekboned, masculine image of the infamous murderer.

statements of people who believed they had seen Jack the Ripper.[44] It is the headshot of a distinctive-looking man aged between twenty-five and thirty-five, staring straight ahead with penetrating dark eyes. His face is long and tanned, with a square jaw and a large black moustache over firm lips. His nose is straight and neat, his ears set back, and his cheekbones are prominent. He looks strong, masculine and capable.

The Colney Hatch photograph of Hyam Hyams[45] taken in 1904 when he was fifty-one years old, and since colourized, presents a powerful contrast. His head is tilted to his left, displaying a neatly set-back ear, as his brown eyes look directly at the photographer's lens, wide and searching. Two frown lines sit between his slightly arched eyebrows, and beneath a high forehead. He has prominent cheekbones that run wide above rounded cheeks. His full beard and moustache are a brownish-grey, running to silver on his chin. He has a long low-bridged nose with a fleshy bobble at its tip, and a small mouth with pursed lips. Broad-shouldered, wearing a blue corduroy jacket and flannel waistcoat set off by a red neckerchief with a blue-and-white striped border, he looks completely harmless.

3

PROFILING JACK THE RIPPER

'To be ourselves we must have ourselves – possess, if need be re-possess, our life-stories.'

FROM *The Man Who Mistook His Wife for a Hat and Other Clinical Tales* BY OLIVER SACKS

Despite his unthreatening appearance, Hyams' medical notes from Colney Hatch Lunatic Asylum recorded fits and attacks of epileptic excitement 'when he is noisy, violent, and exceedingly filthy in his habits' alternating with periods when he was 'quiet and well behaved, clean and talks sensible'. His doctor, Cecil Fowler Beadles, noted that the patient remained well 'about a month and usually "off" for a fortnight but this has lasted a month'.[1] That periodicity is well matched to the lapses in time between the Ripper killings.

At Colney Hatch, Hyams' assaults on medical staff and fellow patients continued:

> Has been excited and violent after series of epileptic fits. Destroyed clothing, dangerous and threatening to others. Refused his food [sometimes saying it has been poisoned] and was fed with stomach pumps on several occasions. Is now becoming less excited and inclined to be depressed. Hardly speaks when addressed. Takes food now. Health fair …

> Has been fairly quiet for some weeks and went out to work [work therapy treatment], but two nights ago he had a fit, and yesterday and today he has been in a state of furious excitement: he suspects the medical officers of having an affection for his wife, and asks for a knife to kill himself …
>
> For several weeks past patient has been very quiet and well behaved, but yesterday he became very excited and incoherent, and tried to attack another Jewish patient, chasing him all round the airing court [exercise ground], under the delusion that he was in some way responsible for his detention …
>
> Demands his discharge in threatening manner … Remains in an excited and turbulent state, threatening and violent; often makes entirely unfounded charges against the attendants; has fits occasionally … Continues to be exceedingly excited and violent, attacking patients and attendants; paints the walls of his room with filth [excrement] and destroys his bedding.[2]

In August 1893, Hyams made a serious assault on one of his doctors:

> For the last few days he had been quiet and in one of his better behaved states. Today while one of the medical officers was passing through the ward, the patient came up behind him and attacked him with an instrument … causing a wound in M.O.'s [medical officer's] neck.
>
> The instrument it appears had been borrowed from another patient named Brimley and consisted of a sharpened steel, made by the latter patient apparently for quite innocent purposes … for several days after the 15th … remained in an excited state.
>
> **Aug 31.** Was only temporarily quiet, and has been excited and noisy up to the present time. When seen a couple of days ago, he glared and said 'I've done something better than you ever did,' pointing to his neck at the time.[3]

Hyams demonstrated a focus on his victim's neck, and gratification at causing a wound.

Sarah Hyams reported a serious injury experienced by her husband that affected his daily life and that he said left him 'not able to work much'.[4] Fourteen months previously, in approximately February 1888, Hyams had fractured his left elbow. The medical officer noted the injury, 'by which he cannot completely bend or extend it'.[5] That injury either hindered or prevented Hyams from carrying out his main trade as a cigar maker. The tools used by a cigar maker were a sharp knife, a gum pot and a board. It was a job that could be done by either gender, and it also required manual dexterity, speed and the use of two hands. However temporary, losing the full range of movement in his left hand was a serious impediment to any kind of manual work.

Hyams had an ununited fracture of the olecranon, a bony prominence at the elbow, on the upper end of the ulna, the larger and longer of the two bones in the forearm. He also had a forward dislocation of both bones and a noticeable irregularity in the lower quarter of the radius, the thicker and shorter bone, which was 'apparently a badly united fracture'.[6] The latter is a typical defence injury when warding off a blow.

His left arm was probably not splinted, as it did not heal properly. Physicians later called it 'a contracted elbow joint'.[7] Instead of offering a range of flexion up to 145 degrees, his elbow joint could not be extended further than 30 degrees. The injury would have healed to some extent within twelve weeks, but the pain and inflammation would have lasted for several months. Although not entirely useless, his left arm from elbow to wrist could not have moved flexibly, exerted significant pressure, or borne much weight. It is possible that the course of history would have changed if he had been left-handed, and rendered unable to wield a knife with force after his arm injury.

The Ripper's attacks were characterized by their rapid, sudden nature. His lightning-fast, blitz-style assaults were calculated to disable their victims by seizing their throats and causing hypoxia, or oxygen deprivation, then forcing them to the ground, on one occasion by a blow to the head, and cutting their throats. The women had no opportunity to cry out or fight back. Such attacks would enable a vulnerable man with a malfunctioning left arm to maintain physical control of potentially unpredictable situations.

Hyams suffered from the most severe form of epilepsy, described as the '*grand mal*', known today as 'tonic-clonic seizures', causing him to lose consciousness and any control of his bladder and bowels, and increasing his risk of erectile dysfunction. On his first admission to Colney Hatch Lunatic Asylum, his wife told medical staff that he had developed epilepsy nine years previously, dating back to approximately 1880.[8] His irregular lifestyle and alcohol abuse might have increased the occurrence and severity of his seizures. As epilepsy was a medical condition that was frequently feared and misunderstood, Hyams would have experienced social isolation. He and his family would have been stigmatized for his illness, his fits on the streets making him a freak show. Its genetic causes made it all the more unfair that he was visited with this condition, when his siblings were not.

Hyam Hyams was born and raised in the East End. His parents, Isaac Hyams and Rebecca Mordecai, were Ashkenazi Jews of Eastern European origin, whose ancestors had lived in England since at least the late 1790s. They married on 17 March 1853, at the Great Synagogue in the City of London's Duke's Place. Rabbi Aaron Levy Green, who in February 1851 was elected Second Reader of the Great Synagogue, performed the ceremony. Both illiterate, Isaac and Rebecca signed their marriage certificate with a cross.[9] Each stated their residence as 24 Love Court, a short street that ran parallel to Goulston Street on the edge of the parish of St Mary Whitechapel. The next street to the west, Middlesex Street, also known as Petticoat Lane, marked the border with the Portsoken district of the City of London. A 'general dealer' – the term for any kind of trader or shopkeeper – Isaac Hyams is likely to have sold oranges and lemons, one of the trades in commodities that was monopolized by Jews.

Rebecca was already pregnant with their first child, Hyam, who was born three months later on 16 June 1853, at 6 Crown Place, Aldgate.[10] My police ancestor Harry Garrett was born exactly six months later.[11] Crown Place was a stone's throw from Love Court, on the City side of the parish boundary. A residential street just to the east of Aldgate station and running north from 21 Aldgate High Street, its nearest modern-day equivalent is Blue Boar Alley. Aldgate station's other next-door neighbour was the Church of St Botolph without Aldgate.

Five more children followed after Hyam: Mark, Sarah, Lazarus, Priscilla and Lewis. The Hyams children probably attended the Jews' Free School in Bell Lane and, unlike their parents, could read and write. Although they would have spoken Yiddish at home, they were not 'foreign Jews' in the contemporary vernacular, meaning recent immigrants from Russia and Poland, but born Londoners. Familiar with the local Cockney dialect, they were able to navigate Whitechapel's web of streets and cut-throughs without a second thought.

Like their fellow East Enders, the Hyams family moved lodgings within a small radius, as their belongings were carried by barrow from one place to the next. On occasion the rented occupation of a house, or part of one, was passed between family members, or a family would move back to an address where they had previously lived.

All of the addresses occupied by the Hyams family were inside what was called the 'little district' of Petticoat Lane. Although it was renamed Middlesex Street, then, as now, the old name stuck. Also known as Rag Fair, Petticoat Lane Market was mainly a second-hand clothes market that was open every day, including Sundays. It dominated an area from Sandy's Row at its northern point down to Aldgate High Street, and spreading west into the City beyond Houndsditch.

Selling 'old black and satin waistcoats, old hats, second-hand caps, drawers, flannel waistcoats, men's stockings, women's stays [corsets], caps, stockings, petticoats, boots, shoes, &c.', it may have been where the Ripper's victims bought clothes, to be worn beyond their useful life. On a Saturday night in winter, with the Jewish Sabbath ending at sunset, lamps and candles were lit to 'produce a multiplicity of lights and shadows, which thrown and blended over the old clothes hanging up along the line of the street, cause them to assume mysterious and grotesque forms …'[12]

The market traders were mainly Jewish men, with some competition from the Irish, who while smoking their pipes would ply strangers with 'solicitations to buy'. Women and children sold old metal; 'dinner knives and forks, razors, pocket-knives, and scissors', all well-oiled, repaired, ground and polished. Everything was sold 'at the very lowest price', and food and drink were readily available, creating a peculiar savour of fried fish, meat and onions, hot potatoes, pickles, steam puddings, and oranges and lemons.[13]

On 23 October 1860, Hyam's maternal uncle Lewis Mordecai, a general dealer aged thirty-seven, was admitted to Colney Hatch Lunatic Asylum.[14] Mordecai died there shortly afterwards, on 2 December, from what his death certificate states as exhaustion and General Paralysis, meaning syphilis.[15] Nobody in their extended family could have guessed that Hyam Hyams would be admitted to the same institution, twenty-nine years later.

In 1863, Hyam's tenth year, a double tragedy struck the family. In August, his three-year-old sister Priscilla died of inflammatory croup.[16] That October, his father died aged only forty of what his death certificate stated to be *Phthisis Pulmonitis*, a form of tuberculosis.[17] The loss of Isaac must have been a crisis point for Rebecca and her five surviving children. Now widowed, Rebecca had to take over his role as head of the household and wage earner. The children were forced to adapt to living without a father, which might have impacted on the boys, aged ten and younger, more heavily than the girls. Also without grandfathers, they needed to find male role models elsewhere, or go without. The family's erstwhile addresses of Love Court and Providence Place did not deliver on their names.

In the 1871 census, the widowed Rebecca Hyams and her family were living at 2 Eastmans Court, off Bell Lane.[18] Her occupation was listed as 'fruiterer', indicating that she continued her late husband's business. Her four eldest children were also working in the same trade, with only the youngest, nine-year-old Lewis, still at school. Hyam as the oldest child would have taken on more responsibility since his father's death, joining his mother as the family's main breadwinner and decision-maker. They probably had a modest shopfront, or maybe only an open window to show and sell their wares, while taking a barrow around the streets to attract a wider market.

On 30 October 1877, Hyam Hyams married Sarah Davis at the Whitechapel Register Office, following the British legal requirement for Jews to marry first at a register office and, later, at a synagogue. They both gave their address as 16 Wentworth Court, Spitalfields, and their ages as twenty-five and twenty-six years old respectively.[19] Five months later, on 3 April 1878, they were married by Chief Rabbi Nathan Adler at the Great Synagogue. Their new address was 8 Ebenezer Square, Gravel Lane, Houndsditch.[20]

Hyams recorded his job as a cigar maker. He later registered a change of occupation that was probably caused by his arm injury. On his first admission to Colney Hatch, Hyams was listed as a general dealer, meaning a shopkeeper or salesman. His extended family of uncles and cousins, who worked in cigar sales and manufacturing, could have offered him opportunities as a cigar salesman operating out of their own premises.

The newly married couple's residence at No. 8 Ebenezer Square was the Davis family home. It was situated east of Gravel Lane in Portsoken Ward of the City of London. Sarah's father was Henry Davis, a general dealer who was born in Holland. Her mother, Catherine née Jacobs, known as Kate, was a local woman, born in Whitechapel. Sarah's unmarried brothers George and Gabriel, a general dealer and butcher, also lived there. George was Sarah's twin. She was born an hour after him, on Monday 9 December 1850, at the stroke of midnight.

Ebenezer Square was demolished in the early 1880s to make way for the City of London's Artizans' Dwellings, which in 1888 provided a home for Hyams' brother Mark, close to the fourth canonical murder location of Mitre Square.[21] Mark Hyams was married to Leah Romain, the daughter of Dutch immigrants who lived in Spitalfields' White's Row.[22] White's Row hosted a lodging house at No. 8 called Spitalfields Chambers, which was used by the possible Ripper victim Frances Coles and another 'unfortunate', Annie Millwood, as discussed in Chapter 11.

Whether Sarah Davis met Hyam Hyams through the synagogue, family or social connections, she cannot have recognized him as a man who was on the edge of a mental and physical decline. Described by her as kind and industrious, he must have displayed those and other positive qualities during their engagement and early marriage. That said, his epilepsy must have affected his quality of life and ability to work, causing him and his relatives constant anxiety.

On 20 July 1884, their first child, Isaac, named after his late paternal grandfather and known as 'Ike', was born at 23 Heneage Street. The small family was living at 3 Wentworth Court on 22 January 1887, when Ike was admitted to the London Hospital suffering from bronchitis.[23] Four days earlier, on Tuesday 18 January 1887, seventeen members of the local Ashkenazi Jewish community died in what became known as the 'Spitalfields disaster'. Hyam Hyams and his extended family would have known most, if not all, of the dead, who included the parents-in-law of Abraham Levy, a neighbour at 18 Wentworth Court, and twenty-two-year-old Kate Silverman, a former neighbour at 27 Heneage Street.[24]

The seventeen victims were crushed to death during a Yiddish theatre performance by the Hebrew Dramatic Club at Prince's Street Hall, in today's Princelet Street. An attendee accidentally broke a gas pipe near his seat, someone else turned off the gas at the meter, and the theatre was plunged into darkness as the cry of 'Fire' was raised. The resulting stampede of audience members from the pit and the gallery met at a 'fatal point' at the bottom of the gallery stairs.

'The rush for the stairs'. The Spitalfields disaster was a tragic loss of Jewish life.

Two days later, Coroner Wynne Baxter, who would preside over the inquests of three of the canonical five Ripper victims, convened an inquest. On that Thursday, his aim was to establish the causes of the victims' deaths and have their bodies formally identified, to enable their burial as soon as possible, according to Jewish tradition. The Hyams' Rabbi, Nathan Adler, was a distant relative of the Hebrew Dramatic Club's actor-manager Jacob Adler and attended the inquest, as did in their official capacities H Division's Superintendent Arnold and Inspectors Frederick Abberline and John West. Coroner Wynne Baxter and the three policemen would all participate in the investigation into the Whitechapel Murders. Inspector West was a capable Essex man who covered for Arnold during his absences prior to the murder of Elisabeth Stride.

The themes of justice and its shadow side, injustice, recur in the Ripper case, and in the 'Spitalfields disaster', claims and counter-claims arguably impeded the course of justice. Rumours were spread that the cry of 'Fire' was malicious, causing the fatal stampede, with the supplementary questions of who broke the gas pipe, and who turned off the gas. The police investigation also looked into whether the building was licensed for entertainment purposes, whether its exits sufficed, and whether too many people were allowed in, many of whom were not members of what was a members-only club.

Its manager Abraham Smith claimed to have been threatened by rival club owner Marks Rubenstein. Rubenstein was alleged to have said that he would set fire to the place. His brother-in-law Philip Lipski attended court on his behalf, to deny the allegations, while Wynne Baxter ruled out the suggestion that a criminal gang was behind the incident.[25] Lipski would testify in court for a second time that year, when his brother Israel was tried for murder at the Old Bailey,[26] in a case that had a bearing on the third canonical Ripper murder, of Elisabeth Stride.

On Friday 11 February, Wynne Baxter summed up the evidence, stating tactfully that there was 'no evidence to show the cries of "Fire" were raised with a malignant object, or that the gas was not extinguished from motives of prudence. The question was whether the exits were adequate.' The jury returned a verdict of Accidental Death, with a long rider about the hall's safety and supervision.[27] Prince's Street synagogue, where Mark Hyams had married Leah Romain, was draped in black crepe in mourning for the victims.

Just over a year later, on 14 February 1888, Sarah Hyams gave birth to a daughter, Katey, at her mother-in-law's home, 3 Eastman's Court.[28] At the same time, Hyams incurred the injury to his left arm, which stopped him from working, while leaving him in a state of constant pain. It was recorded as 'caused by kicking when on the ground';[29] Hyams might have fallen in an epileptic fit, and may even have been kicked by another person when down. It was yet another source of frustration for this angry man, and possibly a triggering event for his desire to kill. Acutely aware of his own vulnerability when he lost mental and physical control during his fits, he might have carried a knife to defend himself against the attacks he felt sure were coming.

Hyam Hyams' life experiences and disabilities convincingly match the FBI profile of Jack the Ripper. In a dysfunctional childhood featuring the early death of his father, he became heavily reliant on his mother as his single parent. She might also have relied on him during their family's existential struggles to help her to earn money and nurture his younger siblings. As an adult, he developed severe epilepsy alongside other characteristics such as an unusual gait, dilated pupils and hesitant speech. Hyams would be well described as a man with a 'poor self-image ... some physical abnormality, scarring or speech problem that he perceived as psychologically crippling'. The physical and psychological burden of his epilepsy represented a lack of control that triggered a strong impulse to exert control where he could. In addition, the injuries to his left arm triggered physical and emotional pain, contributing to his paranoia, or what his medical staff called terror; fear that the police or his doctors were going kill him; fear of poisoning; and the delusion that his wife was unfaithful to him, including with his own brothers and the medical officers who treated him.

Hyams had an unspecified venereal disease, which he probably picked up from a local prostitute. Similar to the FBI's 'quiet, shy loner, slightly withdrawn, obedient and fairly neat and orderly in appearance', he was quoted in his medical records as being, 'quiet industrious civil and attentive to his personal appearance'.[30] An alcoholic, he frequented the local pubs. He both lived and worked in the Whitechapel area, although his arm injury either prevented him from working or caused him to sell cigars or other goods instead of making them.

In a minor divergence from the FBI profile of the Ripper, Hyams' marriage, although troubled, did last. Sarah, who as the FBI suggested, was older than her husband if only by two years, persisted with their relationship despite Hyams' violence towards her, which extended to the use of bladed weapons. Hyams' delusions frequently involved his wife, centring around her supposed infidelities with a range of men, which caused her to transmit venereal disease to him. He also repeated allegations that she wanted him dead, had admitted him into medical facilities in order to have him killed, and that she had induced a certain 'Doctor Long' to give him medicine that caused his epilepsy. His intense antipathy and bitterness towards his wife triggered his wish to emigrate to America.

As a possible extension of his deluded thinking, it is possible that Hyam Hyams regarded his victims as similar to his thirty-seven-year-old wife. They were his proxies for the one woman who loved him unconditionally and whom he was unable to kill. And they might also be blamed for the births of illegitimate children, for spreading infectious venereal diseases, and for alternately preying on men, and rejecting them.

His delusions often caused him to make 'entirely unfounded charges' against those around him, and led to physical assaults. He violently attacked at least two of his medical officers, and two other patients, one of whom he accused of being responsible for his detention. He asked for a knife to kill himself, and when excited, deliberately broke one of his own fingers, and accidentally re-fractured his left elbow.

Hyams did not have a trade that gratified his destructive fantasies, but as a cigar maker he did work with a sharp knife, which he may have continued to carry after his injury. The question of his social skills can only be answered by stressing comments made about his kindness and civility. When in reasonable health, Hyams seems to have been socially adept, as was the Ripper, whom witnesses saw and heard interacting pleasantly with his victims. In accosting her, he even made Mary Jane Kelly laugh, and gifted her a handkerchief.

Hyams' personal description and measurements of his height and weight, taken at the Infirmaries and Asylums where he was housed,[31] are a close fit to information provided to police by eyewitnesses at several of the Ripper crime scenes. In summary, they saw:

> A man of medium height and build, between 5 foot 5 in. and 5 foot 8 in. tall, stout and broad-shouldered.

Hyams was 5 foot 7½ inches, and weighed 10 stone 7 lbs, or 66.7 kilograms. Against the modern body mass index, he was towards the top end of a healthy weight. His photograph demonstrates that he was noticeably broad-shouldered.

> Aged between 30 and 40, he had dark hair, a moustache, and possibly a beard. The colour of his eyes was never noted.

In the summer of 1888, Hyams was aged thirty-five. His hair was dark brown, and he is likely to have had a moustache or beard. His eyes were brown.

> His clothing was shabby-genteel, or shabby chic, typically a dark jacket or coat and trousers, with a bowler hat or peaked cap.

Hyams' clothing in 1888 cannot be determined. He had relatives in the tailoring trade who might have helped him to source worn clothing that was formerly of good quality.

> He spoke colloquial English, with one witness referring to his mild voice.

Hyams would have spoken colloquial English, although it is impossible to determine whether he would have had an East End accent, or one influenced by the Yiddish language. He talked with 'a slight hesitancy of speech'.

> There was disagreement about whether his complexion was dark or fair, whether or not he was foreign, meaning Jewish, and whether he looked as rough as a sailor or respectable, like a clerk.

A Jewish man, Hyams was described as 'quiet … civil and attentive to his personal appearance'.[32]

> Some witnesses perceived the identifying characteristics of a stiff arm, and stiff knees, not bending as he walked or ran. One possible eyewitness referred to 'a fearful look about the eyes'; another said that his eyes were 'like two very luminous glow worms coming through the darkness'.[33]

In addition to his disabled left arm, which he could not fully bend or extend, and regular epileptic seizures, Hyams had further distinctive physical attributes that were also reported by eyewitnesses who believed they had seen the Ripper. It was reported in 1904 that Hyams had an irregular gait,[34] which presented as asymmetric foot dragging. He could not straighten his knees, and walked with them bent. It was a possible indication of brain damage. He had sluggish pupils, which reacted slowly to changes in light, and were probably abnormally dilated, accounting for any 'fearful look'. It was reported in 1905 that he had a harmless excess of choroidal pigment or melanin, causing refractive yellow or brown spots on the whites of his eyes.[35]

As evidenced by his signature on both of his marriage certificates, he was literate, as was the man, assumed to be the Ripper, who wrote the Goulston Street graffito.

Hyams' visible physical disabilities might have caused others to feel sorry for him. People might have treated him sympathetically, failing to perceive him as a threat. He may have been on the receiving end of mockery and physical violence from local thugs. Walter Dew reported that poor Polish Jews were the main target of robberies and blackmail by Whitechapel's organized gangs, adding, 'In most cases the attacks would be so sudden that the victim never saw the faces of his assailants, and even if he did he was more often than not too scared to give any assistance to the police.'[36]

As demonstrated in the double event, Jack the Ripper had a persecution complex, protesting in chalk writing on a wall about the Jews being *blamed for nothing*. This might refer to almost anything: social disruption resulting from the influx of Russian Jews after 1881;

or a repudiation of a petty accusation. It might also signal a perceived injustice in the law courts.

In the early 1880s, three criminal charges were made against Hyam Hyams' brother Mark for conducting an illegal street lottery. On Tuesday 25 October 1881, Mark Hyams, described as a 'cigar maker, of Tenter-street, Spitalfields',[37] was charged at Greenwich police court with carrying on a lottery at Greenwich Market. Hyams was selling tickets for one shilling, and when his box was seized, it contained 141 blank tickets and 12 for prizes of threepence. Hyams attempted to bribe the arresting officer two shillings to let him go, and said in open court that 'he did not know he was doing wrong, as he had seen policemen in Whitechapel looking on at lotteries without interfering'. Police Magistrate John Balguy fined him twenty shillings, calling it 'the worst form of gambling, and if caught at it again Prisoner would be imprisoned for three months'.[38]A minor scam, it demonstrates Mark Hyams' disregard for the law and his disrespect of the police, not to mention his lack of compassion for his impoverished dupes, which included a barefoot boy. Those sentiments arguably extended to his older brother.

In September 1882, Mark Hyams went before Magistrate Madan at Lichfield County Court in Staffordshire, again for running a bogus lottery, this time at Whittington Heath racecourse. As the Magistrate was unaware of Hyams' antecedents, he imposed a fine of one shilling with a further ten shillings in costs.[39] The latter case links Mark Hyams to the world of horse racing, which had possible relevance to his older brother's leisure activities in a theory further expounded in later chapters. Mark Hyams' brother Hyam either did not engage in bogus trades, or did not get caught, but in this proposition he was a gambling man. The Ripper murders coincided with significant horse-racing fixtures, explaining how he could afford to spend nights out drinking and persuade victims such as Mary Jane Kelly that he was flush with cash. Yet the women who went out on the East End streets soliciting clients to pay for their doss-money, or for a measure of gin and cloves, were engaging in a type of lottery, a game of chance or chicken with their own lives at stake.

Hyam Hyams' extended family had several brushes with the law, and their business premises as cigar manufacturers and tobacconists on the Whitechapel and Mile End Roads are significant to the Ripper case. They not only mark the killer's area of operation, but could also have provided him with hideouts on escape routes from the Ripper murders. One of his maternal uncles, cigar manufacturer Abraham Mordecai, ran a cigar factory at 230 Whitechapel Road.[40] That address is significant because, after the double event, a bloodied knife was found on a doorstep in the same block.[41] No. 230 Whitechapel Road could have been used by Hyams as a temporary stop after the murder of Elisabeth Stride, and it was also close to the site of Polly Nichols' murder.

Another of Hyams' maternal uncles, Joseph Mordecai, a clothes dealer with a shop east of Abraham's at 209 Whitechapel Road, was implicated in the Great Silk Robbery of 1877. One of the 'Big Three' on the Ripper investigation, Detective Inspector Walter Andrews was by coincidence the lead officer on the case. When it reached the Old Bailey, Mordecai was discharged due to lack of evidence.

By 1881, the rag trade perhaps getting too hot for him, Joseph Mordecai joined his brothers Abraham and Mark Mordecai as a cigar manufacturer. It was also a year when he testified before George Collier, Wynne Baxter's deputy coroner, who would sit on the inquests into the deaths of Martha Tabram and Annie Chapman. Mordecai had witnessed the accidental death of a passenger in a horse and cart outside his shop, and assured the court that the cause was not a slip on the tramlines but the 'disgraceful state' of Whitechapel Road, being 'full of holes and hills'. The jury agreed and included in their verdict a request that the road should be repaired.

Joseph Mordecai's two sons, Emanuel and Lazarus, each managed a tobacconist shop on the north side of Whitechapel Road, close to Whitechapel station, at numbers 130[42] and 175 respectively.[43] In 1886, Emanuel Mordecai successfully prosecuted a customer at his shop, for claiming that he was an Excise officer and had suspicions about the provenance of cigars kept at the shop.[44] Those two shops were well placed for Hyams to seek refuge in as he escaped from the scenes of, first, Polly Nichols' and, second, Annie Chapman's murders.

On two other occasions, the Mordecais placed themselves on the other side of the law, as prosecutors not defendants. In February 1888, Abraham Mordecai summonsed an apprentice at his cigar factory, Louis Phillips, for threatening to kill him with a cigar cutter, which was similar to a short-bladed penknife, 'whereby he went in fear of his life'.[45] Phillips had issued a counter-summons against Mordecai for punching and threatening to kill him. Although Mordecai had been bound over to keep the peace for a previous assault on another apprentice, the case was dismissed.[46]

The second case involved Mark Mordecai's son Lewis Mordecai, who had his business premises near the London Hospital at 6 Raven Row, and resided at Bancroft Road. In August 1878 Lewis Mordecai brought 'an unfounded charge of felony'[47] against one of his suppliers, that was heard by Magistrate Franklin Lushington at the Thames police court. Lushington would encounter Hyam Hyams at the same police court, after his first arrest in December 1888, and at the start of the official interventions that would place him in an asylum.

Lewis Mordecai's testimony stated that, on the morning of Wednesday 7 August, Abraham Calo, fifty-two, a cigar manufacturer, personally delivered a consignment of cigars to him. Mordecai placed a cheque for £28 12s 6d on the table and proceeded to examine the cigars, which he said were 'not so well made as usual'. Instead of engaging in debate, Calo 'snatched up the cheque and put it in his pocket. As he refused to give it up a constable was called, and the defendant given into custody.' Mordecai's brother was called in support of the case for the prosecution, but in vain. When dismissing Mordecai's case, Lushington called it 'perfectly absurd'.[48] In addition to losing a supplier, that branch of the Mordecais might have lost their faith in the workings of Gentile justice.

Lewis's brother and father Mark Mordecai also lost a court case brought against them in 1890, for selling cigars to which a false trade description had been applied.[49] Mark Mordecai's business premises at 108 Mile End Road were probably too far east to have any relevance to the Ripper case.

Both sides of Hyam Hyams' extended family, many of whom spent time in the United States, might have been name-checked by a key witness in the murder of Elisabeth Stride, fruiterer Matthew Packer. On the night of her murder, he had sold a bag of black grapes to a couple who might have been Jack the Ripper and Stride, the third of the canonical five Ripper victims. Packer later made the sensational claim to the press that he sold twelve shillings' worth of rabbits to two men, one of whom claimed that the Ripper was his own cousin, an Englishman by birth, who had spent a few years in America and returned threatening to 'turn a London Jack Ripper'.[50] The journalist copied his report to the Home Secretary and police, causing a Sergeant White to be sent to interview Packer at his shop at 44 Berner Street.[51]

It is pure speculation whether any of Hyams' relatives might be the 'American cousin' brought to the authorities' attention by Matthew Packer. Hyams himself was noted in Stone Asylum as saying that, 'He still dislikes his wife and says if discharged from here he will make his way to America and never see her again.'[52] It is fortunate for our American cousins that Hyams never managed to make his way to Liverpool in order to board a ship across the Atlantic. In October 1888, the police set up a ports watch, with a particular focus on Liverpool and its transatlantic routes, in case the Ripper tried to leave the country.[53]

Hyam Hyams' brothers Lazarus and Lewis both lived in the United States as young adults. In June 1884, both Lazarus and Lewis Hyams travelled steerage to New York.[54] Lazarus did not stay as long as his brother, having returned to London by 1887. That year's Electoral Register lists his place of residence as 259 Brunswick Buildings on Goulston Street, near other relatives living within that block. Close to the site of the infamous graffito, his brother's home provided Hyam

Hyams with a second reason for knowing Goulston Street well, beyond its proximity to his lodgings.[55]

On 30 September 1887, Lewis Hyams, a cigar maker, married Ellen Hambro, a regalia maker, in Boston, Massachusetts.[56] In the 1891 census, Lewis and Ellen were recorded as resident in London.[57] Their three children were all born in Whitechapel between 1895 and 1903. Lewis Hyams regularly transited between the US and the UK,[58] and at around 1901, he remained permanently in London.

There are also several Mordecai connections to the US. Hyams' maternal first cousin Emanuel Mordecai, the shopkeeper and publican, emigrated to Boston, Massachusetts, in 1892, returning in 1894 to collect his children.[59] But there are earlier links: other first cousins of Hyams, his uncle Abraham Mordecai's son Nathan and daughter Esther, were born there during his period of residence in Brooklyn, New York, *c.*1865–71.[60] Abraham's brother Mark also lived in Brooklyn *c.*1855.[61] His son Lazarus was born there in 1857,[62] and came to England as a baby.

Whatever the nationalities and residences of Hyam's cousins, further mentions in the press were clear that City of London Police Inspector James McWilliam, a principal detective in the Ripper case, dismissed Packer's claims. The conclusion was that, 'Rightly or wrongly, the police are stated to attach no importance to it.'[63] Although easier to discount than to prove, Packer's statement, which could potentially identify the Ripper, was made after the death of Mary Jane Kelly, at a time when the City of London Police developed a firm lead on the perpetrator.

What was life like for Hyam Hyams in 1888? Aged thirty-five, he had a wife and two children to support in their cramped rented housing. Their baby daughter would have disrupted Sarah and Hyams' sleeping patterns, their whole routine, and inevitably their sex life. He no longer had the manual dexterity to work as a cigar maker and was reduced to the lower status and pay of a cigar salesman or delivery man. His epilepsy and alcohol abuse were worsening, and his gambling habit, like his health, was a roller coaster that alternately intensified and alleviated his money problems. He was suffering from pain and debility from his broken arm, which, in addition to his two young children, was causing sleep deprivation. His deluded beliefs were expanding to take up his full mental capacity: his wife was having sexual relations with his brothers; she had infected him with a venereal disease; he might not be the father of the two demanding cuckoos in his nest.

Violence against his wife was not enough. As Hyams' pitch of distress increased, he turned outwards on to the streets to satisfy his rage. Despite the increasing police presence, as a true marauder, he never moved far from the comfort of home to commit his crimes. It explained how he evaded Inspector Reid's 'complete police cordon' intended to prevent the killer from escaping. He did not need to go far from his crime scenes to reach the safety of his own home. And he simply chose victims more defenceless than himself, within an arm's length of wherever he happened to be.

4

THE MURDER OF POLLY NICHOLS

The murder of Mary Ann 'Polly' Nichols on Friday 31 August 1888, between 3.15 and 3.45 a.m. on Buck's Row, Whitechapel.

The first of The Five was forty-two-year-old Mary Ann Nichols, known as 'Polly'. Petite, with brown eyes and hair, she was the daughter of a typeface engineer, and her mother, Caroline, had died when Polly was only seven years old. Although Polly did help around the house for her father and brothers, she was educated at school until the comparatively advanced age of fifteen.[1] She spent her early life in the Soho and St Bride's districts of central London before marrying Fleet Street printer William Nichols.[2] Some eight years before her death, she left her husband and their children, along with the security of a model dwelling, a Peabody flat in Southwark. It was a difficult time to go, shortly after the birth of their fifth child, pushed out by William's affair with a neighbour employed as their nursemaid.[3]

Polly Nichols took refuge at Lambeth Union Workhouse, leaving it periodically when she had an alternative: the home that her father shared with her brother's family, various lodging houses, the rented rooms of men she had relationships with, and a brief stint of live-in domestic service. She was atypical of the Ripper victims in having those options available to her; nor did she become destitute owing to widowhood. Alcohol was her problem, as was money, and she lived a hand-to-mouth existence entirely separate from that of her children.[4]

Nichols' murder, in the early hours of Friday 31 August on a quiet back street, provides little evidence of its perpetrator. Whoever he was, he was neither seen nor heard. But her murder does reveal early evidence of his *modus operandi*: a rapid blitz-style attack, cornering his victim and using his body weight to compensate for his weak arm, then rendering his victim unconscious from suffocation before cutting her throat. Several cuts to her abdomen, including one that ran deep into her tissues, indicated an intention to remove her internal organs. As in the later murder of Elisabeth Stride, while the killer was bending over her body planning to cut her further, he was interrupted by the approach of a local man and escaped without detection. Owing to the lack of evidence or any eyewitness, the police could not have solved the case at this point.

Although the murder earlier that month of a local woman similar to Nichols, Martha Tabram, had increased newspaper sales, and shocked the community, it was quickly forgotten. The attack on Nichols was reported to have reduced Whitechapel's residents to a state nearing abject terror, with them talking of it only in whispers.

Compared to the other victims, little is known about Polly Nichols' movements in the hours before her death. At 1.20 a.m., she was turned away from a common lodging house at 18 Thrawl Street as she lacked the necessary fourpence. Nichols left laughing, saying that her jolly bonnet would soon earn her doss money. She was last seen alive at 2.30 a.m. drunkenly staggering past a woman with whom she often shared her dosshouse bed, Ellen Holland, at the corner of Osborn Street and Whitechapel High Street. She refused Holland's offer to return to the lodging house with her, saying, 'I've had my lodging money three times today and I've spent it.'[5] Nichols' body was found shortly before 3.45 a.m. on Buck's Row, a quiet, narrow street running north of, and parallel to, Whitechapel Road, a short walk eastwards from that last sighting.

Two carmen or cart drivers, Charles Cross and Robert Paul, were making their separate ways to work. When walking westbound along

Buck's Row, Cross 'saw something lying in front of [a] gateway like a tarpaulin. I then saw it was a woman.' Cross called out to Paul as he came up behind him. Feeling one of the woman's hands and finding it cold, Cross concluded, 'I think she is dead.' Paul put his hand over her heart and, feeling some movement, said, 'I think she is breathing.' As her clothes were pushed up above her knees and it was too dark to notice any injuries or blood, he thought that she 'had been outraged [raped]'.[6]

They agreed to walk on to Baker's Row in search of a policeman. Quickly locating an H Division Constable at its crow's foot corner with Hanbury Street, Cross told him, 'You are wanted on Buck's Row,' adding that a woman had been found there 'lying down on the broad of her back', and believed to be dead.[7]

Buck's Row was marginally east of the H Division boundary, falling within the jurisdiction of Bethnal Green's J Division. At 3.45 a.m., while the two carters were on Baker's Row seeking help, Constable John Neil walked down Buck's Row on his regular beat and made a second discovery of the body. He saw a woman lying lengthways outside a stables gateway, her head towards the east, with her left hand touching the gate: 'With the aid of his lamp he examined the body and saw blood oozing from a wound in the throat. Deceased was lying upon her back with her clothes disarranged. Witness felt her arm, which was quite warm from the joints upwards, while her eyes were wide open. Her bonnet was off her head and was lying … close by the left hand.'[8]

Seeing his colleague Constable John Thain ahead on Brady Street, Neil signalled to him with his lamp and, at his approach, told him to run for the J Division police surgeon, Doctor Rees Llewellyn. It was established procedure for a police surgeon to examine the body for any signs of life, as soon as possible. Summoned by the carters, Constable Jonas Mizen ran up from Hanbury Street and was sent to fetch the wheeled handcart that served as an ambulance. Arriving quickly from his surgery 300 metres away at 152 Whitechapel Road, Llewellyn confirmed that the woman was dead and instructed her removal to Whitechapel mortuary.[9]

An officer of seventeen years' experience, distinguished by his iron-grey hair and beard, Inspector John Spratling was called out from Hackney Road police station. Having first visited the murder site, he arrived at the mortuary to find the body was still on the ambulance in the yard. While waiting for 'the keeper of the dead-house' to arrive, he took a description of the as yet unidentified body, entered as follows on a police descriptive form:

Age	45
Profession or calling	Prostitute
Hair	Dark (turning grey)
Eyes	Brown
Face	Discolouration of face
Complexion	Dark
Marks or peculiarities	On person a piece of looking glass, a comb, and white handkerchief
Dress	Brown ulster [an overcoat with a waist-length cape over long sleeves], seven large buttons, [with the pattern of a] horse & man standing by side thereon, linsey frock [made of a mixed cloth combining linen with wool], brown stays, blue ribbed woollen stockings, straw bonnet ...[10]

Her height was 5 foot 2 in. The only clue to the woman's identity were the words marked on her dress, 'Lambeth Workhouse P.R.', with the initials standing for Prince's Road, today's Black Prince Road in Vauxhall. While taking the description of her clothing, Spratling lifted the woman's skirts to discover that 'the lower part of her person had been completely ripped open'.[11] He immediately sent for Doctor Llewellyn to examine her. That done, at 10 a.m., Llewellyn conducted a full post-mortem examination.

The inquest into the death of Polly Nichols began on 1 September and was reconvened on the 3rd, 17th and 23rd of that month, straddling the murder and inquest of the next Ripper victim, Annie Chapman. Its coroner was Sussex-born Wynne Edwin Baxter. Thorough to a fault, he was often impatient and testy in his pursuit of the truth. One of the few coroners able to boast that none of 'his' bodies had ever been exhumed,[12] Wynne Baxter's legacy to the Ripper case is a meticulous record of his hearings, as relayed in the press; the official records being lost. Keen to assist the police investigation, in what could have been a career-limiting move, he would put forward his own theory about the killer's motivation, at Chapman's inquest.

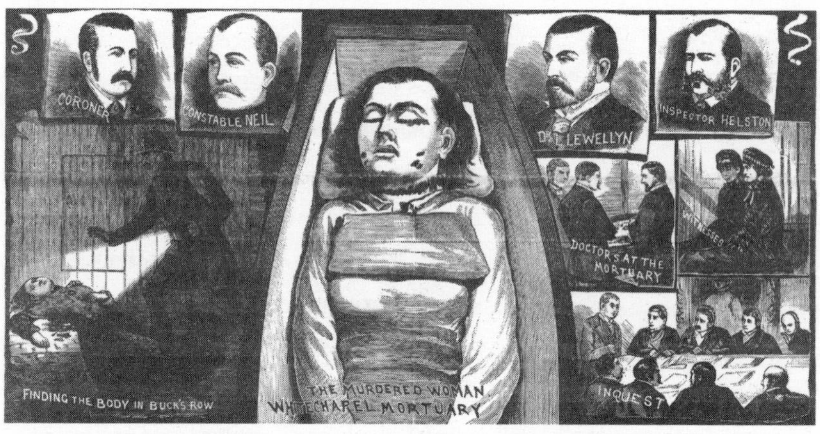

Part of an edition of the Illustrated Police News, *reporting the murder of the Ripper's first canonical victim, Polly Nichols, and highlighting the key figures at the inquest.*

For the first of his inquests into the death of a Ripper victim, Wynne Baxter was fresh from a holiday in Scandinavia. A man with a reputation for being well dressed, he appeared 'in a pair of black and white checked trousers, a dazzling white waistcoat, a crimson scarf, and a dark coat'.[13] The contrast of his dark brown hair and moustache against his pale face completed his striking look.

The inquest took place in the Alexandra Room at the Working Lads' Institute at 139 Whitechapel Road. The lecture room and library, named after the Princess of Wales and future Queen, was only nine doors east of Hyams' cousin Emanuel Mordecai's tobacconist shop. It was filled with jurymen, police, reporters and other interested parties. The senior officers who attended on behalf of the police were Inspector Abberline and the local CID Inspector, Joseph Helson. Experienced and astute, Helson would also work on the investigation into Annie Chapman's murder.

As soon as the jury were sworn in, they were taken by the coroner's officer to view the body, lying in a black shell coffin in the Whitechapel mortuary. They were presented with the 'sickening spectacle' of her throat and abdominal wounds. On their return to the Alexandra Room, Wynne Baxter took his seat at the head of the table and placed a roll of paper in front of him for his notes, while Polly Nichols' father Edward Walker was called as the first witness. An old man with grey hair and beard, he went slowly up to the stand with his head lowered.

Walker – a retired blacksmith living in Camberwell – testified that he had not seen his daughter for three years. He had wept to see her body, and said by way of identification, 'I recognise her by her general appearance and by a little mark she has had on her forehead since she was a child [caused by a fall]. She also had either one or two teeth out, the same as the woman I have just seen.'[14] The mortuary photograph of Nichols shows her lying in a shell coffin, covered to the chin with a white sheet, her eyes still open. The scar below her hairline on the left is clearly visible.

Walker confirmed that his daughter drank, 'and that was why we did not agree ... I never turned her out. She had no need to be like this while I had a home for her.' He explained that she had five children, 'the eldest being 21 years old and the youngest 8 or 9 years'. He had heard 'some three or four years ago' that she was living with a man named Drew, causing William Nichols to withdraw her small allowance. He did not think his daughter was 'fast' with men, and neither did she have any enemies, 'she was too good for that'.[15]

The coroner read out a letter that Walker had received from his daughter at Easter. She wrote that she was in a situation as a housemaid in Wandsworth, which she liked very much, adding, 'They are teetotallers and religious so I ought to get on.' Within three months, she had absconded, stealing some of her employers' clothes. Preferring a less conventional lifestyle, Nichols simply returned to her previous ways. Her father had not heard from her since.[16]

Constable Neil, tall and fresh-faced, with brown hair, a straw-coloured moustache and a small tufted beard called an imperial, testified that when he found the body, 'There was not a soul about. I had been round there half-an-hour previously [he later stated the specific time of 3.15 a.m.] and I saw no one then.'[17] He confirmed the coroner's assertion that Whitechapel Road was a busy thoroughfare in the early morning, saying, 'At that time any one could have got away.'[18] In response to a question from the jury about whether the woman could have been killed elsewhere and her body moved to where she was found, he stated, 'I examined the road, but did not see the mark of wheels.'[19]

Doctor Rees Llewellyn was the next witness, notable for his quiet professional manner. He was as much of a local as his patients, having been baptized at St Mary's Church and taken over the Whitechapel Road medical practice run by his Welsh father. He reported the details of his post-mortem examination:

> [The body] was that of a female of about 40 or 45 years. Five of the teeth were missing, and there was a slight laceration of the tongue. There was a bruise running along the lower part of the jaw on the right side of the face. That might have been caused by a blow from a fist or pressure from a thumb. There was a circular bruise on the left side of the face, which also might have been inflicted by the pressure of the fingers.
>
> On the left side of the neck, about 1in. below the jaw, there was an incision about 4in. in length, and ran from a point

> immediately below the ear. On the same side, but an inch below, and commencing about 1in. in front of it, was a circular incision, which terminated at a point about 3in. below the right jaw. That incision completely severed all the tissues down to the vertebrae. The large vessels of the neck on both sides were severed. The incision was about 8in. in length. The cuts must have been caused by a long-bladed knife, moderately sharp, and used with great violence. No blood was found on the breast, either of the body or clothes.
>
> There were no injuries about the body until just about the lower part of the abdomen. Two or three inches from the left side was a wound running in a jagged manner. The wound was a very deep one, and the tissues were cut through. There were several incisions running across the abdomen. There were also three or four similar cuts, running downwards, on the right side, all of which had been caused by a knife which had been used violently and downwards. The injuries were from left to right, and might have been done by a left-handed person. All the injuries had been caused by the same instrument …[20]

In response to questions from the jury, Doctor Llewellyn added:

> The murderer must have had some rough anatomical knowledge, for he seemed to have attacked all the vital parts. It was impossible to say whether the wounds were inflicted by a clasp-knife or a butcher's knife, but the instrument must have been a strong one. When he first saw the body, life had not been out of it more than half-an-hour. The murder might have occupied four or five minutes.[21]

In addition to the injuries related by Doctor Llewellyn, a special police report by Spratling referenced 'two small stabs on private parts …' Extreme violence was used in the attack. Nichols' head was nearly severed from her body, and in a belief later overturned by Llewellyn, Spratling thought that she had been disembowelled.[22]

Llewellyn's suggestion that the perpetrator might have been left-handed originated from the bruising on Nichols' face, caused by a man's right hand with his right thumbprint marked on her right cheek and other fingermarks on her left. The forcing of her jaw up and shut might have closed her teeth against the side of her tongue, making the slight laceration referred to. If her throat were cut at the same time, it must have been done left-handed. But the two acts of violence were probably consecutive, not concurrent, with her killer incapacitating her through partial strangulation before laying her down and cutting her throat. Donald Swanson, then a Detective Inspector, revisited this point in a report dated 19 October, commenting: 'At first the doctor [Llewellyn] was of opinion that the wounds were caused by a left-handed person but he is now doubtful.'[23]

Swanson's CID senior Melville Macnaghten later discounted the Ripper's possible sinistrality: 'The theory that the Whitechapel murderer was left-handed, or, at any rate, "ambi-dexter", had its origins in the remark made by a doctor who examined the corpse of one of the earliest victims; other doctors did not agree with him.'[24] While it is not possible to deduce which hand the perpetrator used, or the sequence of positions he adopted during his assaults, the police surgeon's reports did specify the entry points of the knife and the direction of the wounds. Running from left to right, they were most likely to have been inflicted by a right-handed man facing his victim. Although his injury had not fully debilitated his left arm, Hyam Hyams would have favoured the use of his right hand for knife work.

On the second day of the inquest, Inspector Spratling testified that he had first heard of the finding of the body at 'about half-past four in the morning … in the Hackney-road'.[25] By the time he reached Buck's Row, Nichols' body had been taken to the mortuary, and he went there to take a description of her body. He itemized her clothing, which had not been cut or torn by her assailant, including her stays, or corset, which he described as 'of the ordinary size, and … not injured'.[26]

Spratling said that he and Constable Thain had searched Buck's Row and its surrounding area for bloodstains or a weapon of any kind.[27] With Sergeant Godley, he examined the East London and District Railway lines and embankment as well as the Great Eastern Railway yard, 'but they were unable to find anything likely to throw any light on the affair … A constable [watchman of the Great Eastern Railway] on duty at the gate of the railway yard, which was about fifty yards [46 metres] from the spot where the body was found … had not heard anything.'[28]

Spratling made inquiries among local residents, 'none of whom heard any scream during the night, or anything to lead them to believe the murder was committed there'.[29] Among the inhabitants of the row of cottages that ran eastwards from the stables gateway who heard nothing was a Mrs Emma Green, 'whose window looked out upon the very spot where the body was discovered'. She testified that she slept well, and did not remember waking before the police knocked at the door.[30]

Henry Tomkins, one of three men working at a horse slaughter-house in the adjacent Winthrop Street, testified that he did not see or hear anything from one o'clock in the morning until a quarter past four, when Constable Thain passed by and told them that a murder had been committed. This prompted the men to take a walk to see the body, and they remained standing on Buck's Row until it was taken to the mortuary.[31]

Inspector Helson testified that he heard about the murder at a quarter to seven in the morning. He went to the mortuary, where the body was still fully clothed. He said that Nichols was wearing a long ulster with large buttons, five of which were fastened, and that the bodice of her dress was fastened, with the exception of two or three buttons at the neck. Her stays were fastened fairly tight, with clasps. Helson stated that Nichols' dress was saturated with blood at the back of her neck, and the hair at the back of her head was clotted with blood. There were no cuts in the clothes, and no indications of any struggle having taken place. He was of the opinion that the murder was committed on the spot.[32]

Helson was followed on the stand by Constable Mizen and carman Charles Cross, who explained their respective roles in the discovery of the body. The second carman, Robert Paul, testified on the next day of the proceedings. Like Cross, he appeared in court in his work clothes, a rough sacking apron, and recounted his uncertainty as to whether the woman was dead or alive, as he detected a slight movement as of breathing, but very faint. He had seen no one running away, nor did he notice anything whatever of a suspicious nature.[33]

The victim's estranged husband William Nichols, a printing machine operator living at Coburg Road, off the Old Kent Road, had identified her body before giving testimony. On recognizing her, he spoke directly to her: 'I forgive you, as you are, for what you have been to me.'[34] Quiet and gentlemanly, looking very pale, with a full light brown beard and moustache, he told the hearing that he and his wife had lived apart for eight years. She left him of her own accord, and 'had no occasion for so doing'. He blamed her 'drinking habits', not his alleged adultery, for their separation. He said that he last saw her alive about three years ago, and did not know what she had been doing in the meantime.[35]

Polly Nichols' former bed-mate, Ellen Holland, was an elderly woman in a brown dress with a loose coat and bonnet. She gave her evidence nervously, with frequent interruptions from Wynne Baxter asking her to speak up. She testified that she was a lodger at a common lodging house at 18 Thrawl Street, where Nichols had stayed in the recent past. In the early hours of 31 August, she had seen Nichols the worse for drink, making her way down Osborn Street towards Whitechapel Road. Holland tried to persuade her to come back with her, but Nichols was not to be persuaded. The two women were talking for seven or eight minutes, during which time the clock at St Mary's Church struck half past two.

Holland made some observations about Nichols' character: '[I] did not know in what way she obtained a living. She always seemed ... to be a quiet woman, and kept very much to herself ... [I] had never seen her quarrel with anybody. She gave the impression of being weighed down by some trouble ...' When asked by the foreman, Holland confirmed that she was the first to identify Nichols' body and that she was crying as she did so, adding: 'It was enough to make anybody shed a tear, sir.'[36]

Mary Ann Monk, a young woman with a flushed face and defensive air, was the final witness of the day. An inmate at Lambeth Workhouse, she had also been asked by police to identify the body. She said that she had last seen Nichols in that area seven weeks ago, in the Duke's Head pub on the Lower Kennington Road. Monk had no knowledge of her means of livelihood or of her acquaintances.[37]

The inquest was adjourned for a couple of weeks until Monday 17 September. In the interval, on the morning of 8 September, Annie Chapman was murdered. The intestines and uterus had been removed from Chapman's body, which prompted a re-examination of Nichols' corpse to detect similarities between the two murders.

Doctor Llewellyn was recalled as the first witness on the third day of the inquest into Nichols' death, to confirm that he had re-examined her body and that no part of her internal organs or viscera was missing.[38] It is possible that, if he had not been interrupted during his murderous attack on Nichols, her killer would have removed her uterus and taken it as a trophy. The fourth of the canonical five, Elisabeth Stride, was not mutilated, probably for the same reason. The remaining three victims in the canon, Annie Chapman, Kate Eddowes and Mary Jane Kelly, were all disembowelled and had internal organs removed.

After Doctor Llewellyn came the testimony of two inmates of Whitechapel Workhouse on Baker's Row, who worked in its mortuary. Neither acquitted himself well in the witness box. Robert Mann and James Hatfield had not been given instructions by the police to undress the deceased, but they went ahead so as to have the body ready for the doctor. Her clothes were intact before they cut for removal the bands of her petticoat and tore her undergarment, a chemise or light smock, down the front. Hatfield inexplicably claimed that the deceased did not have any stays on, before being challenged by a juror: 'Why, when we were in the yard [viewing the body] you showed me the stays. You even put them on to show me how small they were. (Laughter.)'[39] The coroner questioned the reliability of both mens' memories, before wearily concluding, 'We cannot do more.'[40] The mortuary workers would later attend Chapman's body with the same amateurish haste.

The foreman of the jury, a Mr Horey, boldly spoke up to propose that a reward should be offered by the government: 'It mattered little into whose hands the money went so long as they could find out the monster in their midst, who was terrorising everybody and making people ill.' Inspector Helson replied that rewards for information had been discontinued for years.[41] The official line from the Home Office was that it simply encouraged the offering of misinformation.[42] The inquest was then adjourned for the rest of the week.

It was not mentioned in court that, as well as Samuel Montagu – the Member of Parliament for Whitechapel – having offered £100 as a reward, the men of H Division had subscribed £50 from their own pockets to supplement it. Like his brother officers, Harry Garrett would have subscribed, as they did regularly for the Police Orphanage and other good causes. At Montagu's request, Superintendent Arnold had the reward notices posted up across Whitechapel. After Annie Chapman's murder came the 'double event' of two killings in one night, when City Police Chief Sir James Fraser and the Corporation of London offered a £500 reward for 'information as shall lead to the discovery and conviction of the Murderer or Murderers'.[43]

A week after Polly Nichols' murder, a resident of Buck's Row approached the press with new information. Harriet Lilley, who lived two doors away from the murder location, claimed to have heard noises in the night:

> I slept in the front of the house, and could hear everything that occurred in the street. On that Thursday night I was somehow very restless. Well, I heard something I mentioned to my husband in the morning. It was a painful moan – two or three faint gasps – and then it passed away. It was quite dark at the time, but a luggage train went by as I heard the sounds. There was, too, a sound as of whispers underneath the window. I distinctly heard voices, but cannot say what was said – it was too faint …[44]

The newspaper report continued: 'It has been ascertained that on the morning of the date of the murder a goods train passed on the East London railway at about half-past three – the 3.7 out from New-cross – which was probably the time when Mary Ann Nicolls [*sic*] was either killed or placed in Buck's-row.'[45] Although it is tempting to establish 3.30 a.m. as the exact time of the murder, Lilley was not called as a witness, and neither did Coroner Wynne Baxter made any reference to her claim during his summing-up. She may not have been a credible witness, and had perhaps been encouraged by a reporter to come up with something. The paucity of evidence led Inspector Abberline to file a report stating: 'Inquiries were made in every conceivable quarter with a view to trace the murderer but not the slightest clue can at present be obtained.'[46]

On Saturday 23 September, the inquest resumed for its final day, with Wynne Baxter's summing-up, which was reported verbatim in the press. After firmly making the point that a public mortuary was needed in Whitechapel in place of the current shed, he turned his attention to the facts of the case. He described Nichols' lifestyle as 'intemperate, irregular and vicious',[47] and related the discovery of her body by first the carters and then Constable Neil:

> The condition in which the body was found appears to prove conclusively that the deceased was killed on the exact spot in which she was found. There is not a trace of blood anywhere,

> except at the spot where her neck was lying. This appears to me sufficient to justify the assumption that the injuries to the throat were committed when the woman was on the ground, whilst the state of her clothing and the absence of any blood about her legs equally proves that the abdominal injuries were inflicted whilst she was still in the same position.
>
> Nor does there appear any ground for doubt that if deceased was killed where she was found that she met her death without a cry of any kind. Not a sound was heard, nor is there any evidence of any struggle …
>
> The deceased could not have been killed long before she was found. Police-constable Neil is positive that he was at the spot half an hour before, and then neither the body was there nor was anyone about.
>
> It seems astonishing at first thought that the culprit should have escaped detection, for there must surely have been marks of blood about his person. If, however, blood was principally on his hands, the presence of so many slaughter-houses in the neighbourhood would make the frequenters of this spot familiar with blood-stained clothes and hands, and his appearance might in that way have failed to attract attention while he passed from Buck's Row in the twilight into Whitechapel Road, and was lost sight of in the morning's market traffic.[48]

He went on to observe that Polly Nichols and Annie Chapman were killed by similar instruments, and had similar injuries:

> There are bruises about the face in both cases: the head is nearly severed from the body in both cases; there are other dreadful injuries in both cases; and those injuries again have in each case been performed with anatomical knowledge. [In the case of Polly Nichols] Dr. Llewellyn seems to incline to the opinion that the abdominal injuries were inflicted first, and caused instantaneous

> death; but, if so, it seems difficult to understand the object of such desperate injuries to the throat, or how it comes about that there was so little bleeding from the several arteries that the clothing on the upper surface was not stained, and, indeed, very much less bleeding from the abdomen than from the neck. Surely it may well be that, as in the case of Chapman, the dreadful wounds to the throat were inflicted first, and the others afterwards.
>
> This is a matter of some importance when we come to consider what possible motive there can be for all this ferocity. Robbery is out of the question, and there is nothing to suggest jealousy; there could not have been any quarrel, or it would have been heard.
>
> I suggest to you [the jury] as a possibility that these two women may have been murdered by the same man with the same object, and that in the case of Nicholls [*sic*] the wretch was disturbed before he had accomplished his object, and having failed in the open street he tries again, within a week of his failure, in a more secluded place. If this should be correct, the audacity and daring is equal to its maniacal fanaticism and abhorrent wickedness …[49]

At the end of Wynne Baxter's speech, the jury returned a verdict that would become all too familiar: Wilful murder by a person or persons unknown.

Wynne Baxter came close to understanding the killer's mindset and his intent, if not his actual motivation. The murderer was sufficiently clever to learn from his experience, developing his techniques with each killing. His savage attacks, with suffocation followed by throat-cutting, succeeded in preventing the women from defending themselves, or even crying out. But what provided him with sexual gratification was the posing of their bodies, mutilating them, and removing their uteri as trophies.

How the Ripper acquired his anatomical knowledge has often been the subject of debate. The occupations of butcher, slaughterman or Jewish *shochet*, and doctor occur as the most common suggestions.

Ordinary people in Victorian England would have had a far greater knowledge of domestic butchery than we do, as many kept their own livestock or chickens, or purchased meat in large cuts.

An alternative suggestion is inspired by the Victorian fascination with the macabre. Anatomical shows, both fixed and itinerant, were familiar to the visiting public from the time of Charles Dickens. A fascinating example of its type was Doctor Joseph Kahn's Anatomical and Pathological Museum, which opened in 1851 at the top of Piccadilly's Haymarket. Its advertising declared it as 'Open daily for gentlemen only, from 12 to 5, and from 7 to 10. Admission: One Shilling.'[50] Far more sophisticated than waxworks displays at a penny a look, it was consulted by medical students learning human anatomy, as well as by gentlemen with an interest in the human form.

One of its three full-length figures was called Venus, which separated into eighty-five pieces. 'Intentionally reminiscent of classical sculpture', a beautiful young woman lies naked, except for a fig leaf, resting her head on her bent right arm, her left ankle crossed over her right. Her inviting pose emits an erotic charge. The surface layer of her 'Chest and Abdomen' from collarbone to pubis has been removed, revealing her lungs, heart, diaphragm, liver, stomach, spleen, transversal intestine, small intestine and bladder. Further pieces were removable; taking out her intestines exposed her uterus, vagina and kidneys.[51] For all the museum's claims to serve the medical establishment, its visitors came for titillation. In 1873, when Hyams was aged eighteen and might already have acquired his anatomical knowledge there, the police closed it down on charges of obscenity.[52]

A further speculation involves whether Hyams was already familiar with his victims before he attacked them. It is possible that he knew many of them by sight, not only from the local streets and pubs but from Shuttleworth's,[53] a chop house popular with the down-and-outs. Based in Ann's Place, the courtyard next door to his home in Wentworth Court, it was the place to eat if you were staying in any of the local lodging houses; cheap, and not over-particular about its clientele. Yet Shuttleworth's was too far west to be a good place to pick up Polly Nichols on that particular night. Hyams probably accosted her on Whitechapel Road, close to Buck's Row, where he took her to her death.

Of his escape route, Wynne Baxter had suggested in court that, after the murder, the killer went on to Whitechapel Road and merged with the bustle of its market. Hyam Hyams knew that area well enough to devise at least one effective escape route. It was a fifteen-minute walk west from his home to Buck's Row. In addition, the daughters of his first cousin Emanuel Mordecai attended Buck's Row school from 7 May 1886. They were Esther and Pauline Mordecai, aged nine and seven respectively, who in 1891 moved to Settles Street Board School.[54] That road featured in the third murder in the canon, when Elisabeth Stride transited a pub on Settles Street on her night out with an unidentified male.

Emanuel Mordecai, the tobacconist who had once been visited by a fraudulent Excise officer, occupied 130 Whitechapel Road, a shop with his family's living quarters above it. On the north side of the road between Court Street and Whitechapel Station, it backed on to Winthrop Street, which forked off Buck's Row. A Victorian-era four-storey building, it still stands today, its yellow London-brick facing recently restored. Notable features are its orange decorative brickwork and, on the third storey, an oriel window.

A cut-through called Wood's Buildings then ran from Winthrop Street to Whitechapel Road.[55] Called 'piss alley' decades later, not least owing to the urinal it housed, the arched passageway still exists. The old route through to Winthrop Street is blocked by a modern store-yard, but in 1888 it would have taken the Ripper away from the scene of his crime quickly and invisibly. It would also take Hyams six doors away from his cousin's tobacconist shop. Polly Nichols' murder, and those of the other Ripper victims, is reconstructed here from known facts, and with Hyams as the killer.

CRIME RECONSTRUCTION FOR THE MURDER OF POLLY NICHOLS

It is half past three in the morning and, despite the early hour and the rain, the number of people on Whitechapel Road is perceptibly increasing. Many need to get to work, a few of them stopping at a coffee stand on the way. Some have spent the night on the streets, and are moving from one place of shelter to the next. Hyam Hyams is looking for a woman and a drink. Wherever he meets Polly, whether on the road itself or in one of its many pubs, that spot lies close to Buck's Row. Polly has no idea that her customer's wicked intent overreaches the sex act negotiated for a fee that is never paid.

Seeking privacy, the couple walk up Baker's Row on to Buck's Row and past the Board School, stopping short of the row of cottages. The road becomes narrower here, where the stable gates are. The spot is perfect, dark and deserted, and the woman easy prey. Hyams brings his physical weight to bear on Polly as he leans her against the gates. He throttles her with both hands, bruising her face and lower jaw. It takes two or three minutes for her to lose consciousness, then he manoeuvres her to the ground with a hand on the neck of her dress. Crouching over her, he takes his knife from his pocket. He cuts her throat deeply, twice, in the same direction from below her left ear.

He shuffles back, raises her skirts and cuts her belly from her pubes to her sternum. He makes a couple of downward cuts on her left side and two stabs to her pubic mound. Five minutes after he started, he is about to remove her intestines when he hears something, and looks up. An indistinct figure is approaching from the Brady Street end of Buck's Row. He cannot be caught like this, red-handed, with a copper nearby on his beat.

He pulls down Polly's skirts and backs away, leaving her bleeding and exposed. Concealing his knife, he doubles back around the Board School and cuts down Wood's Buildings alleyway on to Whitechapel Road. In his haste, he executes a clumsy left-hand turn to reach his cousin's tobacconist shop at No. 130. It is only a quarter to four, and he is safe to wait downstairs until the family above him stirs.

5

THE MURDER OF ANNIE CHAPMAN

The murder of Annie Chapman on Saturday 8 September 1888, between 5.30 and 6 a.m., at 29 Hanbury Street.

In contrast to the ubiquitous post-mortem depictions of the Ripper victims, a photograph taken shortly after Annie Smith's marriage in May 1869, in upmarket Knightsbridge of all places, depicts her in life.[1] She is portrayed with her new husband John Chapman, a coachman, in the classic pose of a seated wife flanked by her standing spouse. John is dapper in a long coat with matching waistcoat decorated with a watch chain, and smart light trousers. His wife looks trim and fresh in a light wide-skirted frock, striped blue to match her eyes, with her dark braids pinned back. She has a book on her lap, most likely the Bible in accordance with her Sunday best. It is almost inconceivable that, within twenty years, her death would be recorded as the murder of a destitute prostitute in Whitechapel.

Both heavy drinkers, their marriage lasted fifteen years. Subsequently, Annie's mother and sisters took in their two surviving children, while John Chapman drank himself to death within two years and Annie took up with a sieve-maker in Whitechapel. That relationship finished eighteen months before her death, when her husband's allowance stopped coming.[2] Aged forty-seven, she was a chronic alcoholic who made a living from hawking her own crochet work, and, when out of funds, selling her body for casual sex.

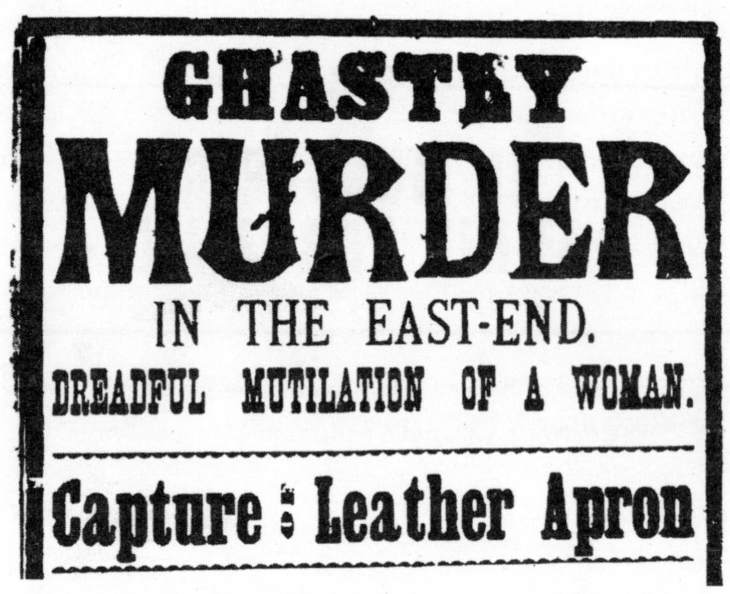
GHASTLY

MURDER

IN THE EAST-END.

DREADFUL MUTILATION OF A WOMAN.

Capture : Leather Apron

A newspaper broadsheet published immediately after the murder of Annie Chapman. The following article noted the 'even more diabolical' nature of the murder as the Ripper's violence increased.

Annie Chapman's was the first of the Ripper murders where a man with a distinctive gait, his knees not bending as he ran, was witnessed hurrying away from the scene of the crime. And it was not the only one, as a man with an unusual gait was seen with Mary Jane Kelly. Those sightings provide evidence that places an identifiable suspect at a Ripper crime location. That suspect is Hyam Hyams, the first man ever to be linked to the crimes through his physical attributes.

Shortly before 2 a.m. on Saturday 8 September, Annie Chapman left Crossingham's lodging house at 35 Dorset Street, like Polly Nichols, to earn money to pay for her bed for the night. The lodging house keeper, or deputy, Tim Donovan, who would later identify her body, had declined her request to let her stay on trust, observing 'that she could find money for her beer but not for her bed'. Chapman retorted that she had 'only been to the top of the street', meaning the Britannia public house. Her plea that she was weak and ill, and had been in the infirmary, carried no weight. Chapman left, adding: 'I have not any money now, but don't let the bed; *I will be back soon.*' She repeated that final phrase to the nightwatchman, John Evans, and he watched as she entered Paternoster Row heading northbound for Brushfield Street.[3]

Chapman's movements over the next three and a half hours are not recorded. She might have found a punter, and drunk the proceeds if she found a pub that was open. The Ten Bells public house near Spitalfields market was one that opened early to accommodate market traders. Or, as she was known to, she might have rested on a bench in 'Itchy Park', the graveyard of Christ Church, where vagrants collected, or in a sheltered doorway on a quiet back street.

At 5.30 a.m., local woman Elizabeth Long saw a woman believed to be Chapman on Hanbury Street talking to 'a foreigner … close against the shutters of No. 29'. No. 29 Hanbury Street was almost half a mile west of the junction with Baker's Row, where Charles Cross had alerted a Constable to Polly Nichols' murder. Long testified at the inquest into Chapman's death about what she saw and heard:

> I never saw the deceased till Saturday morning, the 8th … when I was passing along Hanbury-street to the Spitalfields market. A public clock had just struck half-past five when I passed No. 29, Hanbury-street, and I there saw a gentleman and lady standing on the pavement talking together …
>
> I have seen the face of the deceased in the mortuary, and I recognise it as the same. I am sure it is the same person. I did not see the man's face. I only saw he had a brown hat on and he was dark. I cannot tell you what kind of clothes he had on; but I think he had a dark coat on. He was a man of over 40 years by the look of him. He appeared to be a little taller than the woman. In my opinion he looked like a foreigner – very dark. He looked, I think, like what is called shabby genteel.
>
> They were talking loudly; and I heard him say, 'Will you?' The woman said, 'Yes.' That is all I heard. I passed on. I did not see where they went. I went to my work.[4]

The couple seen by Long were presumed to have opened the front door of No. 29, walked down a passage and through the back door into its yard.

The accuracy of the 'public clock' of the Eagle brewery of Messrs Truman, Hanbury and Co., on Brick Lane, heard striking by Long, came into question with the testimony of the next eyewitness, or rather ear-witness. Next door to the murder scene, at No. 27, lived Albert Cadosch, a carpenter in his late twenties, who worked in Shoe Lane, off Fleet Street. He was recovering from an unspecified operation that caused him to make frequent visits to the lavatory.

He overheard a conversation that seemed of little importance at the time. Having paid a visit to the privy in his own back yard at about 5.25 a.m., as he was stepping back into his house he heard an exchange between people in the neighbouring yard. The only word he could catch through the fence of about 5 foot 6 in. high that divided the two properties was 'No', spoken in a woman's voice. Cadosch then heard 'a kind of scuffle going on' and a noise as if someone had fallen heavily against the bordering fence, concluding: 'As I thought it was some of the people belonging to the house, I passed into my own room, and took no further notice.'[5] He walked straight out of the house to work, seeing nobody on Hanbury Street. When he passed Spitalfields Church, it was about thirty-two minutes past five.[6]

At 5.45 a.m., one of the residents of 29 Hanbury Street, middle-aged market worker John Davis, got up to the chime of Christ Church bell, had a cup of tea and, on the hour chime of six o'clock, walked through the house, presumably on his way to the outside privy. He testified that, when he opened the back door, he saw 'a female lying down, her clothing up to her knees, and her face covered with blood. What was lying beside her I cannot describe – it was part of her body.'[7] Annie Chapman had been killed in the yard, with her intestines and the contents of her pockets laid out around her body.

The inquest into Chapman's murder was, like Polly Nichols', held at the Whitechapel Working Lads' Institute.[8] On this occasion, Wynne

Baxter was assisted by George Collier, who, a month previously, had conducted the inquest into the Ripper-style murder of Martha Tabram. Collier was a generation older than his colleague and able to offer a highly experienced second opinion on what appeared to be linked murders. Inspectors Abberline and Helson attended on behalf of the police in what was now a packed room, with crowds standing outside the building, held off by Constables. With the crime occurring only eight days after the murder of Polly Nichols, not only had the police realized they were dealing with a serial killer but the neighbourhood entered a state of wild excitement bordering on panic.

Once sworn in, the jury were taken to view Chapman's body at Whitechapel mortuary, covered to the neck with a white sheet. On their return to the library that served as a courtroom, the first witness was John Davis. Although he was in his mid-fifties, Davis was described as an elderly man with a stoop. He worked as a carman at Leadenhall Market and had only lived at No. 29 for a fortnight. He testified about his discovery of the body outside the back door and explained that anyone could get through the front and back doors to the yard, and that he was aware that 'immoral women' used it. When he went into the yard on that Saturday morning the back door was shut but the front door was wide open. It was frequently left open all night.[9]

In shock, Davis ran through the front of the house and out into the street. He called out to two men outside No. 23A, James Kent and James Green, who worked for a packing-case maker, 'Here's a sight; a woman must have been murdered.'[10] Kent and Green went to have a look in No. 29's back yard, joined by a passer-by, Henry Holland. Holland later said that the time was eight minutes past six.

While Holland tried to get help from a constable on fixed point duty at Spitalfields market, who, following police procedure, would not budge, Davis himself went to H Division's Commercial Street police station to report what he had seen. Kent and Green, after necking a much-needed brandy, returned to the yard with some canvas sacking to cover the body.[11] Having found it harder than might be imagined to fetch a policeman, Holland went on to Commercial Street police station to complain.[12]

Amelia Palmer, who was like Chapman an unfortunate, related to the court her friend's history as far as she knew it. A pale, dark-haired woman described as 'poorly clad', Palmer testified that she had known Chapman for 'quite five years', during which time she 'never … had a settled home'. Chapman's estranged husband had died about eighteen months earlier, when his allowance to her of ten shillings a week stopped. Palmer said that Chapman was generally industrious, and clever. She had been in a casual relationship with a labourer called Edward (or Ted) Stanley, who was also known as 'the Pensioner' as he reportedly received an Army pension. Palmer called him 'a very respectable man'.[13]

Palmer stated that Chapman made a living by selling crocheted antimacassars (protective furniture covers), and flowers. She was not very particular what she did to earn a living and at times used to stay out very late at night. She often complained of feeling unwell. On one occasion, meeting by chance by the side of Christ Church in Spitalfields, Chapman said that she was so ill that she would go into the workhouse casual ward for a day or two to seek temporary shelter. She mentioned that she had had nothing to eat or drink that day, not even a cup of tea. Palmer handed her twopence, saying, 'Have a cup of tea, but don't have rum.'[14]

Palmer had last seen Chapman at five o'clock in the evening of Friday 7 September. When asked if she was going to Stratford, 4 miles north-east of Spitalfields, where she used to go to sell her wares, Chapman had said that she felt too ill to do anything. She later said, 'It's no use my giving way. I must pull myself together and go out and get some money, or I shall have no lodgings.'[15]

Tim Donovan was called to describe Chapman's departure from his lodging house and what he knew of 'the Pensioner'. He testified that the Pensioner would typically stay there with Chapman on a Saturday night. Donovan had been asked by him not to let Chapman a bed if she came with any other man. As she left Crossingham's a few hours before her death, he saw that Chapman had 'a slight touch of a black eye', but she did not say how she got it.[16]

In addition to describing Chapman's direction of travel as she left the lodging house for the last time, nightwatchman John Evans added: 'I never heard any man threaten the deceased at any time. I have never heard her express any fear of any one.'[17] The inquest was adjourned for two days.

At the second hearing of the inquest into Annie Chapman's death, her brother Fountain Smith, a printing warehouseman with the same thick brown hair that she had, testified in low and reluctant tones that he had identified Chapman's body at the mortuary. He had bumped into her by chance a fortnight earlier, in Commercial Street, and given her two shillings. He did not know where she was living or anything about her associates.[18]

No. 29's landlady Amelia Richardson, small and neatly dressed, replied clearly and directly to the questions of the coroner, accurately rattling off the names and businesses of all of the lodgers in the house. She explained that houses such as No. 29 were all let out as separate rooms. This meant that, although each room had its own key, the communal areas were left unlocked, and the front door was on the latch. She said that people did go through to the back yard who 'had no business' to do so. She had heard no noise on the night of the murder.[19]

The next witness, John Richardson, was the son of Amelia Richardson, the house's landlady. In contrast to his mother, he was tall and shabbily dressed. He lived on nearby John Street and often checked the cellar door padlock of 29 Hanbury Street on his way to work as a porter at Spitalfields market. Between 4.45 and 4.50 a.m., he went through the house into the back yard and sat on the second of its back steps to trim a piece of leather from his boot. He used a knife, about 5 inches long, that he kept in his pocket. Although it was 'not quite light', he testified that he was sure that there was no body in the yard at that time, adding, 'I could not have failed to notice the deceased if she had been lying there.'[20] The coroner asked him severely why he was carrying a knife and, to his discomfort, asked him to return to produce what turned out to be a 'rusty little table knife without a handle'.[21]

Mrs Richardson was recalled to provide information about the leather apron that had been hanging in the yard. She confirmed that her son wore a leather apron when he worked in the cellar and that, finding it mildewed, she had put it under the tap in the yard and hung it out to dry. The coroner posed the question of whether it was a rather dangerous thing to wear, referring to the local miscreant known only as 'Leather Apron'. Replying in the affirmative, Mrs Richardson's testimony averted her son from being identified as that anonymous figure. The day's proceedings closed with the appearance of potential suspect John Pizer, who was allowed to exonerate himself as being neither 'Leather Apron' nor Jack the Ripper. Stating his alibi, he was publicly discounted from the police investigation.[22]

On the next day, the inquest resumed with testimony from the first police officer to enter the crime scene, H Division's Inspector Joseph Chandler. Despite the difficulties experienced by Hanbury Street residents in securing police attention, Chandler – who happened to be on duty in Commercial Street at about two minutes past six on the morning of the murder – quickly took charge of the situation. Hearing from a passing man that yet another woman had been murdered, he followed him to 29 Hanbury Street and saw Chapman's body lying in the back yard.

An officer of unremarkable appearance except for a scar behind his left ear, where he had been stabbed with a chisel during his first year in the Force,[23] Chandler testified about the position of the body and the arrival of the local police surgeon:

> Her head was towards the back wall of the house, but it was some 2 ft. from the wall, and the body was not more than 6 inches or 9 inches from the steps. The face was turned on the right side, and the left hand rested on the left breast. The right hand was lying

> down by the … side, and the legs were drawn up. The body was lying parallel with the fencing …
>
> [He] … sent for the divisional surgeon, Dr. Phillips, and also to the station for the ambulance and further assistance. When the constables arrived he removed all persons from the passage, and saw that no one touched the body until the doctor arrived. He obtained some sacking from one of the neighbours [James Kent] to cover the body pending the arrival of the doctor. Dr. Phillips arrived about half-past 6 and examined the body. He then directed the body to be removed to the mortuary, which was done on the police ambulance …
>
> He could not detect any appearance of a struggle having taken place … The palings near the body were stained with blood … There were also a few spots of blood on the back wall at the head of the body and some 2 ft. or 3ft. from the ground. The largest spot was about the size of a sixpenny piece [approximately today's five-pence piece]. They were all within a small compass.[24]

Not stated in court, Chandler had taken down the as yet unidentified woman's description for the police record: 'Age 45, length 5ft, complexion fair, hair (wavy) dark brown, eyes blue, two teeth deficient in lower jaw, large thick nose; dress black figured [patterned] jacket, brown bodice, black skirt, lace boots, all old and dirty.'[25] Her possessions, neatly laid out around her feet, were itemized as a piece of coarse muslin, a small tooth comb, a pocket hair comb in a case, and a portion of an envelope, which contained two pills. Visible abrasion marks on her left hand showed where she had worn at least two brass rings, the last a 'keeper', an extra ring worn to keep others from slipping off, believed to have been taken by her killer.[26]

In response to a question from the jury foreman, Inspector Chandler stated that the police had not as yet been able to find Chapman's partner Edward Stanley. The coroner commented acerbically: 'The pensioner knows his own business, but I should have thought he would come forward himself.'[27] Stanley finally appeared in court on the penultimate day of the inquest, to confirm that he last saw Chapman on the afternoon of Sunday 2 September.[28]

Sergeant Edward Badham was called to state whether he had taken away every portion of the body when removing Chapman to the mortuary. Badham said that he had, indirectly confirming that the killer had taken his victim's missing organs away with him.[29] In two months' time, he would escort Mary Jane Kelly's coffin to Shoreditch mortuary.

The next witness of note was Doctor George Bagster Phillips. A significant figure in the Whitechapel Murders investigation, he was described by Walter Dew as 'An elderly man, he was ultra-old-fashioned both in his personal appearance and his dress. He used to look for all the world as though he had stepped out of a century-old painting. His manners were charming; he was immensely popular with both the police and the public, and he was highly skilled.'[30] A serious-looking man with a prominent nose and grey chinstrap beard, he testified as follows about Chapman's injuries and her cause of death:

> On Saturday last I was called by the police at 6.20 a.m. to go to 29, Hanbury-street. I arrived there at half-past six. I found the dead body of a female in the possession of the police, lying in the back yard on her back, on the left hand of the steps that lead from the passage … The head was about 6 inches in front of the level of the bottom step, and her feet were towards a shed … at the bottom of the yard. The left arm was placed across the left breast, the legs were drawn up, the feet resting on the ground, and the knees turned outwards. The face was swollen and turned on the right side. The tongue protruded between the front teeth, but not beyond the lips … [it was] evidently much swollen …
>
> A portion of the small intestines and of the abdomen was lying on the ground over the right shoulder, but still attached to the body. Two other parts of the wall of the belly were lying in a

pool of blood above the left shoulder. There was still warmth in parts of the body, but *rigor mortis* was setting in. The throat was severed by a jagged cut extending all round the neck …

Having received your instructions … soon after two [o'clock] on Saturday afternoon I went to the labour yard of Whitechapel Union for the purpose of further examining the body and making the usual examination. I was surprised to find that it had been stripped and was lying ready on the table for my examination … The body had evidently been attended to since its removal to the mortuary – probably partially washed.

I noticed the same protrusion of the tongue, a bruise over the right malar bone [cheekbone], and reaching over the temple and the upper eyelid. There was a bruise under the clavicle, and two distinct bruises, each the size of the top of a man's thumb, on the forepart of the chest.

The stiffness of the limbs was now well marked. There was a bruise over the middle carpal bone of the first finger of the right hand. The finger nails were turgid [distended]; the lips also. There was an old scar of long standing on the left of the frontal bone. The stiffness was more noticeable on the left side, and especially in the fingers, which were partly closed. There was an abrasion over the bend of the first joint of the ring finger. There were distinct markings of a ring or rings – probably the latter – and there were small sores on the fingers.

The head being opened showed that the membranes of the brain were opaque, and the veins and tissues coated with blood of a dark character. The front [of the neck] had been severed, and the entire structures from the bony portion of the vertebral or spinal column had been entirely separated. The incisions of the skin indicated that they had been made from the left side of the neck on a line with the angle of the jaw, carried entirely round, and again in front of the neck, and ending at a point about midway between the jaw and the sternal or breast bone on the right side.

> There were two distinct cuts on the body of the vertebrae on the left side of the spine. They were parallel to each other, and separated [by] about half an inch. There were appearances as if an attempt had been made to separate the bones of the neck. There are various other mutilations of the body, but I am of opinion that they occurred subsequently to the death of the woman, and subsequently to the large escape of blood from the neck.[31]

Here, Doctor Phillips paused to ask the coroner if it was necessary to describe the further mutilations. Wynne Baxter replied that he would postpone making a decision on whether or not to hear the details, and asked for the cause of death, which was given as 'syncope, or failure of the heart's action, in consequence from the loss of blood [caused by the severance of the throat]'.[32]

In response to a question from Wynne Baxter about the type of weapon that might have been used, Doctor Phillips provided specific details. After confirming the probability that the same instrument was used for cutting the throat as for the later mutilations, he stated:

> It must have been a very sharp knife, probably with a thin, narrow blade, and must have been at least six to eight inches in length, and perhaps longer …
>
> [The knife might have been one such as a slaughterer uses], well ground down. I think the blade of the knives used in … [the cobbler and leather] trades would not be long enough in the blade.[33]

Doctor Phillips confirmed that there were 'indications of … anatomical knowledge [which] were only less displayed or indicated in consequence of haste … [and] the mode in which the [absent portions of the abdomen] … were extracted did show some anatomical knowledge.'[34] When asked about the size of the missing parts, he said, 'It would all go into a breakfast cup.'[35]

Doctor Phillips provided a view about the timing of the murder, which did not tally with eyewitness accounts. He timed the moment of death to at least two hours before he first saw the body at 6.30 a.m., making it at least an hour too early at 4.30 a.m. *Rigor mortis*, or as he put it, 'stiffness of the limbs [after death]', was starting and the body was cold apart from 'a certain remaining heat, under the intestines, in the body'. He did qualify his opinion to introduce the possibility of a later time: 'it is right to say that it was a fairly cold morning, and that the body would be more apt to cool rapidly from its having lost the greater portion of its blood'.[36] According to modern scientific studies, people like Chapman in 'more feeble or exhausted muscular conditions', have a more rapid onset of *rigor mortis*.[37] Given those circumstances, her body could have been colder and stiffer than Phillips would have expected, within less than an hour of her death.

He added a distressing commentary about the state of Chapman's health: 'Disease of the lungs was of long standing, and there was disease of the membranes of the brain. The stomach contained a little food … There were probably signs of great privation. I am convinced she had not taken any strong alcohol for some hours before her death …'[38] When asked whether the bruising on her head and chest was recent, Doctor Phillips said:

> The marks on the face were recent, especially about the chin and sides of the jaw. The bruise upon the temple and the bruises in front of the chest were of longer standing, probably of days. I am of opinion that the person who cut the deceased's throat took hold of her by the chin, and then commenced the incision from left to right … By pressure on the throat no doubt it would be possible [that a person could not cry out] … My impression is that she was partially strangled … the handkerchief [around her neck] was … saturated with blood.[39]

After an adjournment until Wednesday 19 September 1888, Doctor

Phillips was recalled. Wynne Baxter asked 'several ladies and boys' to leave the room before stating that 'in the interests of justice' all the evidence from the post-mortem examination should be on the records of the court. Although not reported in any newspaper for reasons of delicacy, the gist of it was included in *The Lancet* on 29 September:

> The abdomen had been entirely laid open: the intestines, severed from their mesenteric [membrane] attachments, had been lifted out of the body and placed on the shoulder of the corpse; whilst from the pelvis, the uterus and its appendages with the upper portion of the vagina and the posterior two thirds of the bladder, had been entirely removed. No trace of these parts could be found and the incisions were cleanly cut, avoiding the rectum, and dividing the vagina low enough to avoid injury to the *cervix uteri*. Obviously the work was that of an expert – of one, at least, who had such knowledge of anatomical or pathological examinations as to be enabled to secure the pelvic organs with one sweep of the knife ...[40]

Doctor Phillips in his testimony estimated the time taken to inflict those injuries as at least a quarter of an hour, adding: 'If I had done it in the deliberate manner usual with a surgeon, it would probably have taken me the best part of an hour ... The conclusion I came to was that the whole object of the operation was to obtain possession of a certain portion of the body.'[41] That statement led Wynne Baxter to put forward a related theory about the killer's motive to remove his victims' uteri and sell them for medical use.

In response to a question from the foreman of the jury, Doctor Phillips confirmed that the police had considered and rejected ideas to photograph the eyes of the deceased 'in case they should retain any impression of the murderer', or to use a bloodhound to track him. He thought that the employment of bloodhounds would be useless, and the blood of the murdered woman would be more likely to be traced than that of her killer. Those questions were submitted to him by the authorities within twenty-four hours of the crime.[42]

Before Doctor Phillips, a fellow lodger of Chapman's at Crossingham's called Eliza Cooper took the stand. She said that they had argued on the Tuesday before her death about a piece of soap that she lent Chapman for her partner 'Ted' Stanley to wash himself with. On the next day, the quarrel continued at the Britannia pub, called 'Ringer's' after its landlord. It turned into a fight when Chapman slapped Cooper in the face, whereby Cooper hit her in return on the left eye and chest. She had not seen Chapman since.[43]

Recorded for posterity owing to its Ripper connection, another reason for the altercation was unofficially put forward. While at the Britannia's bar, 'Harry the Hawker', perhaps better pronounced without any aspiration, drunkenly put down a florin, worth two shillings, to pay for some beer. Cooper stole his florin and replaced it with a penny. Chapman observed this, and words were spoken and blows struck.[44]

Chapman's casual partner, the 'Pensioner' Edward Stanley, who was the beneficiary of Cooper's soap, contacted the police on the day of Chapman's funeral. Her burial had taken place in the utmost secrecy, to avoid public attention, on the morning of Friday 14 September. Chapman's brother and other relatives chose not to have a funeral procession, meeting her coffin inside Manor Park Cemetery at Forest Gate. That evening, Stanley walked into Commercial Street police station and made a statement to Inspector Helson. Although forty-seven years old, he was described as a tall, elderly working man,[45] and 'superior to the ordinary run of those who frequent the lodging houses'.[46] Although he felt 'considerable diffidence' in coming forward, given the nature of his relationship with Chapman, he had responded to the coroner's appeal.

Stanley confirmed that he had known Chapman for two years and had last seen her on the Sunday before her murder. He was not aware of any man on bad terms with her, or who might seek to kill her. Picking up on what was probably an unofficial remark made by the police, the press reported that Stanley's explanation was regarded as perfectly satisfactory, and there were no grounds for linking him with her murder.[47]

The eye- and ear-witnesses, Elizabeth Long and Albert Cadosch, appeared respectively before and after Stanley. Their timings remained out of step with each other. Lastly, the testimony of William Stevens, Chapman's fellow lodger at Crossingham's, explained away the piece of torn envelope found by Chapman's body, which the police had been investigating as a clue to a possible military perpetrator. Stevens told the court that the envelope was a piece of litter that Chapman had picked up from the kitchen floor to wrap her pills in. The day's proceedings closed with a juror asking, in tune with public opinion but without success, whether the Home Secretary might offer a reward for information leading to the arrest of the murderer.[48]

The final hearing of the inquest resumed a week later, in the absence of any additional police evidence, with the coroner's summing-up. Controversially, Wynne Baxter stated his opinion that the killer's motive was to harvest the women's organs for commercial purposes, in what became known as 'the American theory':[49]

> I ... was informed by the sub-curator of the [unnamed] Pathological Museum that some months ago an American had called on him, and asked him to procure a number of specimens of the part that was missing in the deceased. He stated his willingness to give £20 apiece for each specimen ... his object was to issue an actual specimen with each copy of a publication on which he was then engaged.
>
> He was told that his request was impossible to be complied with, but he still urged his request; he wished them preserved not in spirits of wine (the usual medium), but in glycerine in order to preserve them in a flaccid condition, and he wished them sent to America direct. It is known that this request was repeated to another institution of a similar character.

> Now, is it not possible that a knowledge of this demand may have incited some abandoned wretch to possess himself of a specimen? ... I at once conveyed my information to the Detective Department at Scotland Yard ... I believe that publicity may possibly further elucidate this fact ...
>
> We are confronted with a murderer [*sic*] of no ordinary character, committed, not for jealousy, revenge, or robbery, but from a motive less adequate than many ...[50]

The jury having returned the requisite verdict of murder by some person or persons unknown, the inquest was over. Wynne Baxter's theory was not well received by the press or by the medical experts, who wrote letters to editors debunking it as 'ridiculous'. It attributed a logical motive to 'wanton' mutilations.[51]

A witness had observed a man behaving strangely in the hours after Annie Chapman's murder. Thomas Eade, a twenty-two-year-old 'signalman in the employ of the East London Railway company' informed police about a man he saw near the East London railway line. Although the inquest into Chapman's death was still open, Eade was called to give evidence at one of the hearings into Polly Nichols' death. Reluctant to take testimony for the wrong inquiry, Coroner Wynne Baxter prevaricated that 8 September was the morning of the other murder before letting Eade take the stand with his extraordinary story:

> On Saturday morning, the 8th ... at noon, I was coming down the Cambridge-heath-road [going towards Whitechapel Road], and when near the Foresters' Arms I saw a man on the other side of the street. His peculiar appearance made me take notice of him. He seemed to have a wooden arm.
>
> I watched him until level with the Foresters' Arms, and then he put his hand to his trousers pocket, and I saw about four inches of a knife. I followed him, but he quickened his pace, and I lost sight of him.

> He was about 5 feet 8 inches high, about 35 years of age, with a dark moustache and whiskers. He wore a double peak cap [with a peak front and back], a short dark brown jacket, and a pair of clean white overalls over dark trousers. The man walked as though he had a stiff knee, and had a fearful look about the eyes.[52]

When questioned by the coroner, Eade said that the man looked like a mechanic. He was not a muscular man. Eade could not see what kind of a knife it was. Inspector Helson stated that, to date, the police had been unable to trace the man.[53]

No official record of Eade's testimony is extant, making it impossible to verify an alternative version stating that the suspect was carrying a long knife concealed up his sleeve, not in his pocket.[54] With a knife up his sleeve, his arm would look completely stiff and wooden. Another version of his testimony reported Eade as saying that the man's wooden arm was 'hanging by his side'.[55]

Disregarding the man's arm, Eade's suspect is consistent with Hyams' disability, age, height, appearance and even his style of walking with 'a stiff knee'. The description of a moustache and whiskers could have referred to either a moustache and beard, or a moustache and sideburns. Other sightings of a man who might have been the Ripper suggested that he wore a moustache. Hyams might well, in his younger years, have had a moustache with no beard.

Hyams arguably had some reason to be in the area. His cousin Lazarus Mordecai's tobacconist shop at 175 Whitechapel Road was on the corner with Cambridge Heath Road, two doors away from the Blind Beggar pub. Hyams' uncle Mark Mordecai, who had been involved in the trademark fraud court case, operated as a cigar manufacturer at 108 Mile End Road, a ten-minute walk from Northampton Row. It is possible that Hyams, unable to make cigars with his broken arm, picked up boxes of cigars from his uncles Mark and Abraham, who manufactured them, and delivered them to his cousins' tobacco shops for sale. A double peaked cap would keep the weather off, rain or shine.

The first individual linked by police to the sighting by Thomas Eade was a vagrant hawker called Edward McKenna, who was arrested on Friday 14 September, answering the description of a man who acted in a suspicious manner in Heath Street. He held a knife behind his back, and was chased by some boys. On the day after his detention, McKenna 'was confronted by several witnesses, who failed to recognise him, and he was in consequence liberated'.[56]

Police found a second suspect, whom Eade was taken to view. As a result, Eade was recalled to court on the last day of Polly Nichols' inquest, to testify that he had identified John James of 'Clara-street [Clare Street], Bethnal Green' as the man whom he had seen with the knife, 'and that he did not possess a wooden arm'. Wynne Baxter dismissed James as 'a well-known harmless lunatic', adding brusquely, 'from enquiries made by the police they were satisfied that he was innocent of any complicity in this case ... He has, however, on various occasions exhibited a knife in a menacing manner, but as to why he is allowed to go at large with it there was no explanation.'[57]

Another reported sighting was of a man running away from Hanbury Street, at 6 a.m. on the morning of Annie Chapman's murder. Although not called as a witness at the inquest, forty-eight-year-old John Thimbleby, a coppersmith at the nearby Eagle brewery, reported what he had seen to the police:

> [He] went to the Commercial-street station at one o'clock [in the afternoon, on the day of the murder] to say that at six o'clock that morning a man attracted his particular attention before he heard of the murder. He was hurrying from Hanbury-street, below where the murder took place, into Brick-lane. He was walking, almost running, and had a peculiar gait, his knees not bending when he walked. (This is a peculiarity of Leather Apron's gait.)
>
> He was dressed in a dark stiff hat and cutaway coat [cut diagonally from the front waist to the back], reaching to his knees.

> His face was clean shaven, and he seemed about 30 years old. Thimbleby says he can identify him.[58]

This is the first time that a named suspect can be placed at the scene of a crime in an identifiable manner. According to the article, the man's unusual gait was considered to be characteristic of the mysterious 'Leather Apron', but it was also a distinctive feature of Hyam Hyams, which might also have been witnessed by Thomas Eade. It is worth noting that Thimbleby described the man as clean-shaven, presumably meaning entirely without facial hair, while most of the later sightings gave him a moustache.

Thimbleby suggested that the perpetrator's escape route out of what might have been 29 Hanbury Street was a right turn, across or 'below' the road and then southbound into Brick Lane. If this man were Hyams, and he was heading straight home, a route down Brick Lane would keep him away from Commercial Street police station. A possible cut-through via Flower and Dean, then George and Wentworth Streets, would quickly take him to Wentworth Court.

Thimbleby's attention was caught by the perpetrator's gait and his speed of movement rather than by any knife or bloodstains. If he had been walking normally and at average speed he might never have made it into the newspapers. Thimbleby's description is similar to that of Elizabeth Long, who also saw a man wearing a dark coat and what in some versions of her testimony was called a 'brown deerstalker hat',[59] although she thought the man was over forty years of age. His timing is not precisely stated and implies that the murder occurred later than previously thought. But that would either make Long's timing ten minutes too early, or mean Thimbleby's sighting was ten minutes earlier than stated.

If Long were right, the killer accosted Chapman at around 5.30 a.m. and went with her through to the back yard within minutes. At or after 5.35 a.m., Albert Cadosch heard people speaking followed by a thump on the fence. Allowing between five and ten minutes for the duration of the knife attack, as similar wounds were inflicted on the later victim Kate Eddowes within that time frame, the time of the killer's departure would have been around 5.45 a.m. If these assumptions hold good, Thimbleby would have seen Hyams escaping closer to a quarter or ten to six than on the hour.

Hyams narrowly escaped detection by John Davis, by no more than ten minutes. If only Davis had gone into the yard earlier, Hyams would have had to retreat through No. 29's passageway, where the local workmen outside No. 23A, James Kent and James Green, would have been strong and quick enough to catch him and forestall the legend of Jack the Ripper. In an alternative scenario, Hyams kills Davis, and another resident of No. 29 discovers two bodies in its back yard.

CRIME RECONSTRUCTION FOR THE MURDER OF ANNIE CHAPMAN

Shortly before 5.30 a.m., Hyams accosts Annie in Itchy Park, the street-walkers' hangout in the grounds of Christ Church, Spitalfields. She agrees to go with him to a quiet spot, and the couple cut down Church Street and left up Wood Street to hit Hanbury Street, with its open doors leading to their secluded back yards. They arrange terms, unaware of Elizabeth Long looking on, as they stand outside the front of No. 29. It is a question simply put: *Will you?*, and answered: *Yes.* Hyams follows Annie through the house's unlocked front door, down its side passage and out of the back door into the yard.

Coming up behind her, Hyams corners Annie behind the back door, between the rear wall of the house and the side fence, and quickly takes her by the throat. Perceiving danger, Annie cries out: *No!* He uses both hands to strangle her as she is pinioned in position against the wall and held there by his body weight. In Annie's struggle to free her neck, it is scratched on both sides. After a brief pause, Annie loses consciousness and drops to the ground, hitting the fence with a thud.

Thinking nothing of the cry or the thump against one side of his fence, Albert Cadosch crosses his back yard from the privy to his room. It has gone quiet next door, and in any case, he does not understand the significance of what he has heard. He sees nobody on Hanbury Street as he departs for work.

Hyams crouches at Annie's right side and removes a knife from his pocket. He works silently, in a state of high excitement, holding her by the chin to cut her throat twice from below her left ear. He takes his knife back to its starting point and tries and fails to slide it between two vertebrae and separate her head from her body.

He moves downwards and lifts her skirts. He pushes her legs back and open and cuts her abdomen open with three strokes to make a flap. He reaches inside the cut to pull out her intestines and places them, still partly attached to her body, above her right shoulder. A flap of skin is deposited there too, while two other portions of skin, including Annie's pubic hair, are placed above her left shoulder. The next cuts remove her uterus along with the upper portion of her vagina and the posterior two-thirds of her bladder. These are his trophies, to take home.

He moves Annie's left hand across her breast and wipes his knife against her hand and face. A 'wiper' not a 'washer', he does not use a bowl of standing water in the yard beneath a tap to wash himself. He uses his knife finally to cut open her pockets, laying their contents out on the stones of the yard. He takes any small change away with him, and two rings that he pulls roughly from her hand.

Knowing he is undiscovered, he stashes his knife in his pocket and retraces his steps through the side passage. Almost running, he turns left on to Hanbury Street. A man on his way to work, John Thimbleby, takes notice of him in passing, hurrying away with his stiff knees.

Hyams crosses the street and turns right into Brick Lane. A few minutes later, another right turn into the insalubrious Flower and Dean Street will deter any pursuers, but there are none. A left turn into George Street and a right turn on to Wentworth Street take him up to Wentworth Court. Safely home, he can stash his trophies, wash, and calm himself down.

6

THE MURDER OF ELISABETH STRIDE

The murder of Elisabeth 'Liz' Stride, Sunday 30 September 1888 between 12.45 and 1 a.m., at Dutfield's Yard, 40 Berner Street.

On 7 February 1866, twenty-five-year-old Elisabeth Gustafsdotter left her native Sweden for London.[1] A licensed sex worker in Gothenburg, treatment for venereal disease had caused her to miscarry a baby daughter. The windfall of a small inheritance from her mother funded her ticket to a new life, as a servant in Bloomsbury's Gower Street. Within three years, her reinvention was complete, as she married ship's carpenter John Stride.[2] Together, the couple ran a coffee shop in East London's Poplar and remained childless.

By late 1881, their marriage was over, and three years later, John died of heart disease. Elisabeth Stride's situation worsened as she moved from Poplar Workhouse to the dosshouses of Whitechapel. She was charged several times in the local police courts for being drunk, disorderly, and also for soliciting.[3] In addition to cleaning and sewing, she was known to char for Jewish families, who hired Gentile help to perform certain types of work prohibited to them on their Sabbath. Similarities between the Swedish language and German, from which the Yiddish language spoken by Ashkenazi Jews was derived, helped her to learn a bit of Yiddish by ear. In 1885, she struck up a casual relationship with dock labourer Michael Kidney, which continued intermittently until her death.

Shortly after arriving in London, Stride registered at the Swedish Church in Prince's Square, where she was treated kindly and received gifts of a hymn book and money. She prized the book, although, being illiterate, she was unable to read it. The clerk at her church was one of several witnesses at the inquest into Stride's death who recounted the story she had told them, of having escaped from the wreck of the *Princess Alice* steamship. In a disastrous collision with a collier on the Thames, over six hundred of the steamer's passengers lost their lives. Stride claimed that her husband and 'children' were among those drowned. It was a tale that guaranteed her sympathy and the occasional payout, exposed as a lie by Coroner Wynne Baxter. No one by the name of Stride had applied for relief from the Lord Mayor's Fund for the families of the dead and missing.[4]

By coincidence, four months before her murder, someone known to Stride died at sea. In 1871, she and her husband had a young visitor named Charles Thew, aged fifteen, staying with them in Poplar.[5] In the 1880s, Thew took a job as a leading cable hand on the *Scotia*, a twin-screw cable-layer commissioned to lay a transatlantic telegraph cable. On 23 May 1888, halfway across the Atlantic on a voyage to New York, he fell overboard during a heavy lurch and drowned.[6] Stride might not have known of Thew's passing, although, combined with the deaths of her husband and baby daughter, it makes her invented story about multiple losses more poignant.

Stride's death was the first of two on the same night, within a scant thirty-five minutes of each other, known as the double event. Minutes before her murder, she was seen socializing with a man. Her killer took a risk with its location, a yard in front of a busy working men's club. Although he was interrupted in the act, his *modus operandi* – the blow to the head, partial asphyxiation, a deep cut to the throat, and then wiping of the knife on the victim – are consistent with other Ripper murders.

On the evening of Saturday 29 November 1888, Elisabeth Stride's preparations for a night out on the town were completely different from those of Polly Nichols and Annie Chapman. She had just been paid sixpence for cleaning at her lodging house, 32 Flower and Dean Street, which she intended to spend in the local pubs. Her money might stretch further if a kind stranger were to stand her a drink or two. But she was out for enjoyment, not trade.

She owned just one set of clothes – their age less discernible in the dark – a long, 'rusty' or faded, black jacket with a fur trim, a long black skirt and her everyday black ankle boots. She finished her outfit with a checked silk neckerchief, tied with a bow, and a black crepe bonnet, lined with a copy of *The Star* newspaper, to make it fit. Aged forty-four with a long oval face, regular features and clear unlined skin, she looked younger, and rather attractive, when she scrubbed up. Walter Dew observed after viewing her dead body: 'Traces of prettiness remained in her face, and there must have been a time when she had been exceedingly proud of her curly dark hair.'[7] The contrast of her brown hair against her fair skin and light-grey eyes was stunning.

Stride was described by her fellow lodgers as being of a calm temperament, rarely quarrelling; in fact, she was so good-natured that she would do a good turn for anyone. Then, as now, people would not speak ill of the dead, and the times when she had appeared before the Magistrate for being drunk and disorderly, and using obscene language, were forgotten.

Two of her fellow lodgers featured briefly in Stride's preparations for her departure. She showed Catherine Lane the sixpence she had to spend and entrusted a piece of velvet to her to look after. She asked barber Charles Preston if she could borrow his clothes brush, but he had mislaid it. It was Charles Preston and another lodger, John Arundel, who were to identify her body at St George's mortuary. Between 6 and 7 p.m., she left, looking cheerful, saying that she was not going to meet anyone in particular. She would soon find herself on a date, whether planned or not, with a man whom she might already have known from the highways and byways of Whitechapel.

Nothing is known of Stride's movements in the three or four hours after she left her lodgings. However, the two hours preceding her murder are the most witnessed of any of the Ripper victims. The first sighting of her occurred shortly before 11 p.m., when two labourers named as J. Best and John Gardner went into the Bricklayer's Arms pub on Settles Street. As it was raining very hard, a man and woman had stopped in the pub doorway, as if unwilling to go outside.

A newspaper interview with Best continues:

> He was hugging her and kissing her, and as he seemed a respectably dressed man, we were rather astonished at the way he was going on with the woman, who was poorly dressed. We 'chipped' [teased] him, but he paid no attention. As he stood in the doorway he always threw sidelong glances into the bar, but would look nobody in the face. I said to him 'Why don't you bring the woman in and treat her?' but he made no answer. If he had been a straight fellow he would have told us to mind our own business, or he would have gone away. I was so certain that there was something up that I would have charged him if I could have seen a policeman. When the man could not stand the chaffing any longer he and the woman went off like a shot soon after eleven.
>
> I have been to the mortuary, and am almost certain the woman there is the one we saw at the Bricklayers' [*sic*] Arms. She is the same slight woman, and seems the same height. The face looks the same, but a little paler, and the bridge of the nose does not look so prominent …
>
> The man was about 5ft. 5in. in height. He was well dressed in a black morning suit with a morning coat. He had rather weak eyes. I mean he had sore eyes without any eyelashes. I should know the man again amongst a hundred. He had a thick black moustache and no beard. He wore a black billycock hat, rather tall, and had on a collar. I don't know the colour of his tie. I said

> to the woman, 'that's Leather Apron getting round you.' The man was no foreigner; he was an Englishman right enough.[8]

Best's description was so detailed that it specified the taller height of the billycock or bowler hat the man was wearing. His 'Englishman' is a good match for Hyams, setting to one side the question of whether, as an Anglo-Jew, the latter was deemed to be a foreigner or an Englishman. As to his sore eyes, a generalized tonic seizure could have caused postictal, or post-seizure, red eye. Its symptoms are red, bloodshot eyes and a petechial periorbital rash, presenting as red spots from broken capillary blood vessels in the skin around them. That condition might have caused Hyams to rub them, snagging his eyelashes as he did.

After that sighting, the couple turned out of the pub in the direction of Commercial Road. Three eyewitnesses saw them standing at varying locations in Berner Street, until around half past midnight, when they were outside the International Working Men's and Educational Club, a Jewish club affiliated to the Socialist League. The debate that evening was entitled 'Is it necessary that a Jew should be a Socialist?' It was attended by nearly a hundred people, mainly German Jews. The debate was followed by a concert with 'considerable singing' by the thirty people who had stayed on at the club in Dutfield's Yard. It was observed that the noise would have drowned out any outcry in the yard, which was not known to be used 'for immoral purposes'.[9]

At approximately one o'clock in the morning, Lewis Diemshitz, a jewellery salesman who was also the club's steward, was returning from a day's work at Westow Hill market in Sydenham, 8 miles south of Whitechapel. He described his discovery of the body on the dark, right-hand side of the yard:

> I drove up to the gate of the clubhouse in my little cart drawn by a pony, after being all day at the market. The pony is inclined to shy a bit, and it struck me when I was passing through the double

> gates into the yard [that] he wanted to keep too much to the left side against the wall. I could not make out what was the matter, so bent my head to see if there was anything to frighten him.
>
> Then I noticed that there was something unusual about the ground … there was something there like a little heap, but I thought it was only mud or something of that kind, and did not take much notice of it. However, I touched it with my whip handle, and then I was able to tell that it was not mud. I wanted to see what it was. So I jumped out of the trap and struck a match. Then I saw that there was a woman lying there. At that time I took no further notice, and didn't know whether she was drunk or dead.
>
> All I did was to run indoors and ask where my missis [wife] was, because she is of weak constitution, and I did not want to frighten her … I then told some of the members in the club that something had happened in the yard … One of the members, who is known as Isaacs, went out with me. We struck a match, and saw blood running from the gate all the way down to the side door of the club. We had the police sent for at once …[10]

Chief Inspector John West was the senior officer at Leman Street police station, and was called to the scene while covering for Superintendent Arnold's absence on leave.

The inquest into Elisabeth Stride's death began on Monday 1 October under Coroner Wynne Baxter at the Vestry Hall in Cable Street, St George-in-the-East. Inspector Reid attended on behalf of the CID. The jury viewed her body at the mortuary at St George's Church, but it remained officially unidentified until the last day of the inquest. Stride's identification was hindered by a Mrs Mary Malcolm, a fantasist and time waster, who claimed that the dead woman was her sister, Elizabeth Watts. It took until the fifth and final day of the inquest for her testimony to be discredited.[11]

The first three witnesses were club members, called to describe its physical layout in Dutfield's Yard, its membership, and the discovery of the body inside its gateway. Printer William West confirmed that 'there was no thoroughfare through the yard, and anybody entering would have to go out the same way'. He had left for home at about quarter past midnight, and if there were any object lying on the ground, he might have missed seeing it in the dark.[12] After the body had been found, commercial traveller Morris Eagle ran towards Commercial Street to fetch a policeman, while Lewis Diemshitz ran in the opposite direction down Fairclough Street.

On the second day of the inquest, Constable Henry Lamb testified that at about 1 a.m., two men ran to fetch him from Commercial Road to the scene of the murder. On discovering 'a woman lying in Berner-street with her throat cut, and apparently dead', he sent Constable Gunner, who had followed him there, to fetch the nearest doctor, and 'a young man' to Leman Street police station to fetch the Inspector. He said that there were about twenty or thirty people in the yard, and others followed him in.

Lamb continued:

> As I was examining the body some crowded round. I begged them to keep back, and told them they might get some of the blood on their clothing, and by that means get themselves into trouble. I then blew my whistle. I put my hand on the face and found it slightly warm. I then felt the wrist, but could not feel the pulse …
>
> Deceased was lying on her side, and her left arm was lying under her … her right arm was across the breast … her face was about five or six inches away [from the wall] …[13]

Lamb said that her clothes were not disturbed, and added:

> I could hardly see her boots. She looked as if she had been laid quietly down. Her clothes were not in the least rumpled … Some [of the blood was in a liquid state] … [and] the part nearest to her throat was congealed …

> [Her feet] went just behind [the gate], and I was able to close the gates without disturbing the body. I put a constable at the gate and told him not to let any one in or out. I then entered the club and, starting from the front door, examined the place. I turned my light on and had a look at the different persons there, and examined a number of their hands and also their clothing to see if I could detect any marks of blood. I did not take up each one's hand. I should say there were from 15 to 20 persons in the club-room on the ground floor. I then went into every room, including the one in which there was a stage, and I went behind it …
>
> When further assistance came a constable was put in charge of the front door. I did not see any one leave by that entrance, and could not say if it was locked. After I examined the club, I went into the yard and examined the cottages. I also went into the water-closets. The occupiers of the cottages were all in bed when I knocked. A man came down partly dressed to let me in. Every one I saw, except this one, was undressed … The people seemed very much frightened and wanted to know what was the matter. I told them nothing much, as I did not want to frighten them.[14]

In response to questions from the coroner, Lamb said that the killer might have escaped while he was examining the corpse, as 'there was a lot of confusion, and every one was looking towards the body'.[15] He had passed the top of Berner Street about six or seven minutes before he was called to the scene of the crime and had seen nothing suspicious.[16]

Police surgeon Doctor Frederick Blackwell, a Birmingham-born man in his late thirties, whose practice was at 100 Commercial Road, gave the first medical evidence, stating that he arrived at the scene of the crime at ten past one in the morning:

> The deceased was lying on her left side completely across the yard. Her legs were drawn up, her feet against the wall of the right side

of the yard passage. Her head was resting almost in the line of the carriage way, and her feet were about three yards from the gateway. The feet almost touched the wall, and the face was completely towards the wall.

The neck and chest were quite warm; also the legs and face were slightly warm. The hands were cold. The right hand was lying on the chest, and was smeared inside and out with blood … The left hand was lying on the ground and was partially closed, and contained a small packet of cachous [sweets or candies] wrapped in tissue paper … The appearance of the face was quite placid, and the mouth was slightly open.

There was a check silk scarf round the neck, the bow of which was turned to the left side and pulled tightly. There was a long incision in the neck, which exactly corresponded with the lower border of the scarf. The lower edge of the scarf was slightly frayed, as if by a sharp knife. The incision in the neck commenced on the left side, 2½ in. below the angle of the jaw, and almost in a direct line with it. It nearly severed the vessels on the left side, cut the windpipe completely in two, and terminated on the opposite side 1½ in. below the angle of the right jaw, but without severing the vessels on that side …

The blood was running down the gutter into the drain. It was running in an opposite direction to the feet. There was a quantity of clotted blood just under the body …

The dress was undone at the top … [She had been dead] from 20 minutes to half an hour when I arrived. It was a very mild night and was not raining at the time. There was no wet on deceased's clothing …

I formed the opinion that the murderer first took hold of the silk scarf, at the back of it, and then pulled the deceased backwards, but I cannot say whether the throat was cut while the woman was standing or after she was pulled backwards. Deceased would take about a minute and a half to bleed to death.[17]

On that sobering thought, the inquest was adjourned until the following day.

The third day, Wednesday 3 October, opened with three witnesses from the Flower and Dean Street lodging house – Elizabeth Tanner, Catherine Lane and Charles Preston – who all testified that they had identified the body in the mortuary as a Swedish woman who went by the name of 'Long Liz'.[18] That nickname might have been coined from her surname, as a stride means a long step. It was also a little ironic, as she was only 5 foot 2 in. tall. They were followed by Michael Kidney, a pained-looking man with a large walrus moustache, who worked as a waterside labourer. Having lived with Stride for the best part of three years, he stated that he had seen her body in the mortuary and 'had no doubt whatever' about it being her. Theirs was an on-and-off relationship, and he had not seen her since 'Tuesday week ... she was subject to go away when she thought she liked to'.[19]

When questioned by the coroner and Inspector Reid about 'anyone that was likely to have run foul of her', he was forced to admit that he had no relevant information to pass on. Kidney then began to rant, claiming that two days earlier, he went to Leman Street police station to solicit a 'young detective to act on his information', while believing that he himself 'could place 100 constables in such positions in the neighbourhood that the murderer must be caught'. Wynne Baxter turned the discussion by noting, to the amusement of the court, the difficulties that would arise if every person with a theory sought to command the police.[20]

Owing to his familiarity with the series of murders, at 1.20 a.m. on the morning of 30 September, Doctor Phillips had been called to Leman Street police station, and sent on to Berner Street. He testified:

> I found Chief-Inspector West ... in possession of a body, which had already been seen by Dr. Blackwell, who arrived some time before me [according to Blackwell, this was 20–30 minutes] ... The throat was deeply gashed, and there was an abrasion of the skin

about 1¼. in. in diameter, apparently stained with blood, under her right brow.

At 3 p.m. on Monday, at St George's mortuary, in the presence of Dr. Rygate and Mr. Johnston, Dr. Blackwell and I made a post mortem examination. Dr. Blackwell kindly consented to make the dissection. *Rigor Mortis* was still thoroughly marked. There was mud on the left side of the face and it was matted in the head. We then removed the clothes. The body was fairly nourished. Over both shoulders, especially the right, and under the collar-bone and in front of the chest there was a blueish discolouration, which I have watched and have seen on two occasions since.

There was a clean-cut incision on the neck. It was 6 in. in length and commenced 2½ in. in a straight line below the angle of the jaw, ¾ in. over an undivided muscle, and then, becoming deeper, dividing the sheath, the cut was very clean, and deviated a little downwards. The artery and other vessels contained in the sheath were all cut through. The cut through the tissues on the right side was more superficial, and tailed off to about 2 in. below the right angle of the jaw. The deep vessels on that side were uninjured. From this it was evident that the haemorrhage was caused through the partial severance of the left carotid artery … There was no recent external injury save to the neck …

On removing the scalp there was no sign of bruising or extravasation of blood …

[Cause of death] is undoubtedly from the loss of blood from the left carotid artery and the division of the wind-pipe …

The blood had run down the waterway [gutter] to within a few inches of the side entrance of the club … Roughly estimating it I should say there was an unusual flow of blood considering the stature and the nourishment of the body.[21]

The inquest was adjourned and, when it resumed on Friday 5 October, Doctor Phillips was recalled. He gave his opinion that Stride had been alive within an hour of his arrival and the injury to her 'might be done in two seconds'. Wynne Baxter sought clarification on specific points. He asked whether the presence of the cachous in Stride's hands indicated a sudden attack. Phillips said that he could not answer the question, but that some of the cachous were found in the gutter. Later commentators in the press saw her grasp of the sweets as evidence that she did not defend herself.

Wynne Baxter then homed in on similarities with the other cases. Phillips identified one similarity as an apparent knowledge of where to cut the throat. But there was 'great dissimilarity' between this and the case of Annie Chapman: 'In Chapman's case the neck was severed all round down to the vertebral column, the vertical bone being marked, and there had been an evident attempt to separate the bones.'[22] He did not think the murderer was necessarily bloodstained. By standing on her right side and cutting the left side of her throat, the stream of blood was directed away from him.

Phillips stated that there was no perceptible sign that any anaesthetic had been used, and that it was possible that Stride had called out and not been heard. He concluded by stating that there was no trace of malt liquor in the stomach. He had previously testified that Stride's stomach contained 'partly-digested food, apparently consisting of cheese, potato, and farinaceous edibles'[23] – a cheese and potato pie.

Doctor Blackwell, who was also recalled, confirmed Doctor Phillips' statement, adding:

> There were what we call pressure marks on the shoulders, which became better defined some time after death. They were not what are ordinarily called bruises, neither is there any abrasure of the skin. There is a mark on each shoulder, and they would be caused by the pressure of hands on the shoulders. It is rather difficult to say how long before death they were caused.[24]

The three eyewitnesses who had seen a man and a woman at various stations on Berner Street gave their respective testimonies. William Marshall, a labourer who was resident at 64 Berner Street, had viewed Stride's body at the mortuary and recognized her 'by her face and her dress'. He testified that, at 11.45 p.m., he saw a couple talking quietly on the pavement opposite No. 58. He said that he was standing at his front door, and that his attention was 'first attracted by their standing there for some time, and he was kissing and cuddling her'.[25]

The man's arms were around the woman's neck, and he was facing Marshall. Marshall did not see the face of the man distinctly, as the nearest lamp was some yards away outside No. 70. He admitted that he did not pay much attention to what the man looked like. He wore 'a black small coat and dark trousers … [and] a round cap with a small peak to it, somewhat like what a sailor would wear … He was about 5 ft. 5 in … rather stoutish … decently dressed … a middle-aged man.'[26]

Keen to elicit as much detail as possible, Wynne Baxter had the following exchange with Marshall:

> **Coroner:** What class of man did he look?
> **Marshall:** He looked as if he worked at some respectable business.
> **Coroner:** Everybody works at a respectable business (laughter).
> **Marshall:** He did not look like a dock labourer nor a sailor. He had more the appearance of a clerk than anything I can suggest. I do not think he had any whiskers. He was not wearing gloves. He had no stick or umbrella in his hand. He had a cutaway coat.
> **Coroner:** Are you sure it was not me? (Laughter).
> **Marshall:** No, sir.[27]

It was a rare moment of levity. Marshall went on to say that he heard the man say to the woman, in a mild voice like an educated man: 'You would say anything but your prayers.'[28] The woman laughed as they moved away. The phrase means 'You're fibbing; you're having me on.' It was a colloquialism that only a local native speaker would have used.

The pair went past Marshall, walking in the middle of the road towards Ellen Street, which would take them away from, not towards, the club at 40 Berner Street, where Stride's body was later found. Neither of them appeared to be the worse for drink and they were not hurrying, as it was not raining. It is a matter of conjecture where they spent the following ten minutes. Perhaps they simply took a slow turn down to the bottom of Berner Street, crossing from No. 82 to 81, and went back up its eastern side. They might conceivably have visited the George IV pub at No. 68, or the Nelson at No. 46.

The next eyewitness, H Division Constable William Smith, passed a man and woman on his beat, at 12.30 a.m. He said that the couple were 'standing a few yards up [Berner] Street, on the opposite side to where she was found'. He was the only witness to state that the man talking to the deceased 'had a parcel, covered with a newspaper, in his hand'. It was about 18 inches long, and 5 or 6 inches wide. Smith described the man as 'about 5ft 7in. in height, and [he] wore a hard felt dark deerstalker hat, with dark clothes. He had on a kind of "cutaway" coat. He looked about 28 years of age … [and of] respectable appearance.'[29]

Dock labourer James Brown testified that he saw the couple several minutes later at 12.45 a.m., standing by the Board School. Brown, who lived on Fairclough Street, was on his way home having bought his supper at a shop at the corner of Fairclough Street and Berner Street. Brown heard the woman say, 'No, not tonight, some other night.' Brown then turned round and looked at them.[30]

Brown said that he was 'almost certain deceased was that woman … The man had his arm up against the wall, and the woman had her back to the wall facing him.' He described the man as 'about five feet 7 inches in height … stoutish built … [wearing] a long coat … which came very nearly down to his heels … I could not say what kind of cap he had on. The place where they were standing was rather dark. I saw nothing light in colour about either of them. I then went on and went indoors.'[31]

Inspector Reid testified that he was first alerted to the murder by receiving a telegram at 1.25 a.m. at Commercial Street police station. After he had taken part in the search of the club and examination of everyone there, at 4.30 a.m. the body was moved to the mortuary. Reid himself proceeded to the mortuary and noted a description of the body and clothing. Part of that description read: 'There was a small bunch of flowers on the right side [of her jacket] (maidenhair fern and a red rose).' He closed the day's proceedings with a sentence that was intended to be reassuring: 'Every endeavour is being made to arrest the assassin, but up to the present without success.'[32] No comment was made about the extraordinary fact that Stride was wearing a proper corsage, assembled by a florist. It was the type of arrangement worn to a wedding or event, not on a night out in Whitechapel. The origins of her corsage were never established, although a likely option is that her companion was dressed for a day at the horse races and gave Stride his buttonhole.

The inquest was adjourned until Tuesday 23 October. At the final day of the hearing, Constable Walter Stride of Clapham's W Division testified that he recognized the deceased by her photograph, presumably one taken in the mortuary, as the person who had married his uncle John. Elizabeth Watts, also known as Stokes, appeared to say that she was the missing sister of Mrs Malcolm, whose claim that Watts was the murdered woman was 'an infamous lie'.[33]

Coroner Wynne Baxter summed up the case, calling the difficulty of identification a 'Comedy of Errors'. He related Elisabeth Stride's history up to the night in question, when three witnesses saw the deceased 'with more or less certainty, and at times within an hour and a-quarter of the period when, and at places within 100 yards of the spot where she was ultimately found'.[34] Those witnesses were William Marshall, Constable William Smith and James Brown. Wynne Baxter observed that there were 'many points of similarity, but some of dissimilarity'[35] in their descriptions of the man seen with her:

> Brown, who saw least in consequence of the darkness of the spot at which the two were standing, agreed with Smith that his clothes were dark and that his height was about 5 ft. 7 in., but he appeared to him to be wearing an overcoat nearly down to his heels; while the description of Marshall accorded with that of Smith in every respect but two. They agreed that he was respectably dressed in a black cut away coat and dark trousers, and that he was of middle age and without whiskers.
>
> On the other hand, they differed with regard to what he was wearing on his head. Smith stated he wore a hard felt deer stalker of dark colour; Marshall that he was wearing a round cap with a small peak, like a sailor's. They also differed as to whether he had anything in his hand. Marshall stated that he observed nothing. Smith was very precise, and stated that he was carrying a parcel, done up in a newspaper, about 18 in. in length and 6 in. to 8 in. in width.
>
> These differences suggested either that the woman was, during the evening, in the company of more than one man – a not very improbable supposition – or that the witness had been mistaken in detail. If they were correct in assuming that the man seen in the company of deceased by the three was one and the same person it followed that he must have spent much time and trouble to induce her to place herself in his diabolical clutches ...[36]

A different interpretation of the coroner's commentary is that the couple were on a Saturday night date, whether pre-planned or not, and that they were already comfortably acquainted.

Wynne Baxter defined the timing of the murder as between forty minutes past midnight, when club member Morris Eagle passed through the front gateway to the club's back door, and 1 a.m., when Diemshitz rode his pony and 'two-wheeled barrow' into the yard and discovered the body. Having described her injuries, and the lack of motive for her murder, he highlighted the similarities between this and the cases of Polly Nichols and Annie Chapman. Despite the lack of 'skilful mutilation … there had been the same skill exhibited in the way in which the victim had been entrapped, and the injuries inflicted, so as to cause instant death and prevent blood from soiling the operator, and the same daring defiance of immediate detection …'[37] Wynne Baxter thanked the jury for their kind assistance and the police for their great attention, at which point the jury returned their verdict of 'Wilful murder by some person or persons unknown'.[38]

Two men who were not called to testify at the inquest, Matthew Packer and Israel Schwartz, were questioned by police about what they saw on Berner Street that night. In the hours following the discovery of the body, Sergeant Stephen White questioned all of the residents of Berner Street, including Packer, an elderly fruiterer whose shop at No. 44 was two doors down from the club. Packer, who would later tell police that the Ripper was a local man's 'American cousin',[39] said that he had shut up his shop early due to the rain, and seen nothing suspicious.

When later approached by two private detectives employed by a local Vigilance Committee to help them find the murderer, Packer told them that he had sold some grapes to a young man accompanied by a woman, and insisted that he had never been approached by the police. The detectives took Packer to the mortuary where he identified Elisabeth Stride as the woman he had seen, and bundled him into a cab to see the Police Commissioner at Scotland Yard.

Although he did not meet Sir Charles Warren, Packer was interviewed by Assistant Commissioner Alexander Carmichael Bruce, who made an abbreviated semi-verbatim report in Packer's own words:

> On Sat night about 11 p.m., a young man from 25–30 – about 5[foot] 7[in.] with long black coat buttoned up – soft felt hat, kind of Yankee hat rather broad shoulders – rather quick in speaking, rough voice. I sold him ½ pound black grapes 3d.
>
> A woman came up with him from … the lower end of the street … She was dressed in black frock & jacket, fur round

> bottom of jacket a black crape [*sic*] bonnet, she was playing with a flower like a geranium white outside & red inside. I identify the woman at the St George's mortuary as the one I saw that night.
>
> They passed by as though they were going up Com- Road [Commercial Road], but – instead of going up they crossed to the other side of the road to the Board School, & were there for about ½ an hour until I shd. [should] say 11.30, talking to one another. I then shut up my shutters.
>
> Before they passed over opposite to my shop, they wait[ed] near to the club for a few minutes apparently listening to the music.
>
> I saw no more of them after I shut up my shutters.
>
> I put the man down as a young clerk.
>
> He had a frock coat on – no gloves.
>
> He was about 1½ or 2 or 3 inches – a little higher than she was.[40]

Matthew Packer's assessment of the time was one hour too early to fit with other witnesses such as James Brown, who saw the couple standing outside the Board School.

A sketch of the man described by Packer was published widely in the press on 6 October 1888, the police rebutting any allegation that they were official drawings. It featured the head and shoulders of an unremarkable-looking clean-shaven man of average weight, wearing a trilby, collar and tie and, not delineated below the middle of his lapels, what looks like a short jacket or waistcoat under another jacket or coat.[41] Packer later said that the sketch was practically useless for identification as it bore no resemblance whatever to his description. He called it 'the portrait … of a mere boy with no expression whatever … [while] the man he saw was about thirty years of age'.[42] Both Packer and the sketch excluded a moustache.

Donald Swanson's official conclusion was that Packer 'has unfortunately made different statements so that apart from the fact of the hour at which he saw the woman … any statement he made would be rendered almost valueless as evidence'.[43] Packer's contribution is tantalizing, as Lewis Diemshitz claimed that Stride was clutching grapes in her right hand, and Walter Dew that police found spat-out grape skins and pips in the yard. It is plausible that Matthew Packer did see Stride and her killer that night, but needed his memory jogging, or his palm greased by eager private eyes, to retrieve flawed fragments of information.

Perhaps courting press attention, at the end of October 1888, Packer claimed to have seen the man again, while selling from his barrow on Greenfield Street, which was extremely close to Berner Street. Believing that the man, who had 'a most vicious look on his face', also recognized him, Packer was slow to take action: 'Too frightened and staggered to know what I was about … I sent a young chap for a policeman, and the man seeing there was something up jumped into a tram that was going to Blackwall [east of Poplar].'[44] Walter Dew commented, 'If the shopkeeper was right in his second identification it was about the worst piece of luck the police could possibly have had.'[45]

The second possible witness to events prior to Stride's murder was a passer-by called Israel Schwartz, a Hungarian Jew who did not speak English. Through an interpreter, he told police that, when he walked south down Berner Street on his way home to 22 Ellen Street, he saw a couple in the club's gateway at 12.45 a.m. If correct, Schwartz arguably saw the couple's actions within a few minutes of the murder. And if he had reacted differently, fetching a Constable, the Ripper might have been caught in the act.

When Schwartz spotted the couple, he was on the same side of the street. Swanson's record of his statement reads as follows:

> He saw a man stop & speak to a woman, who was standing in the [club] gateway. The man tried to pull the woman into the street, but he turned her round and threw her down on the footway & the woman screamed three times, but not very loudly. On crossing

> to the opposite side of the street, he saw a second man standing lighting his pipe. The man who threw the woman down called out apparently to the man on the opposite side of the road 'Lipski' & then Schwartz walked away, but finding that he was followed by the second man he ran as far as the railway arch but the man did not follow so far.
>
> Schwartz cannot say whether the two men were together or known to each other. Upon being taken to the mortuary Schwartz identified the body as that of the woman he had seen & he thus describes the first man who threw the woman down:- age about 30, ht. 5 ft. 5 in., comp. fair, hair dark, small brown moustache, full face, broad shouldered, dress: dark jacket & trousers, black cap with peak, had nothing in his hands.
>
> Second man age 35, ht. 5 ft 11 in. Comp.fresh, hair light brown, moustache brown, dress: dark overcoat, old black hard felt hat wide brim, had a clay pipe in his hand …[46]

Schwartz's description of the first man is a good likeness to Hyam Hyams. Swanson commented that it was doubtful whether Schwartz and Constable Smith were describing the same man, owing to what he called serious differences in the descriptions of their dress. Smith reported a black diagonal coat, meaning one made of a twilled fabric woven with distinctly diagonal lines, and a hard felt hat, while Schwartz reported a dark jacket and a black cap with a peak. That disparity of clothing would continue in eyewitness accounts of a man seen with the next victim, Kate Eddowes.

Swanson also suggested that Stride 'being a prostitute she accosted or was accosted by another man and there was enough time for this to take place and for this other man to murder her before 1:00 a.m.'. He added the marginal note to his report: 'The use of "Lipski" increases my belief that the murderer was a Jew.'[47] Israel Lipski was a Polish Jew who was hanged for murder on 21 August 1887.[48] The house at 16 Batty Street, where he poisoned Miriam Angel in what he claimed was a failed robbery, was on a road adjacent to Berner Street. The case had a high profile owing to a campaign claiming there was insufficient evidence to hang Lipski, which was swiftly terminated by his confession.

The shout of 'Lipski' has been variously interpreted as simply the name of someone living in the neighbourhood, an insult aimed at Schwartz or the other man as Jews, or as 'I'm doing a Lipski' (killing a woman). The latter resonates, as Miriam Angel was six months pregnant at the time of her death, fitting the Ripper's seeming mission to stop the reproduction of illegitimate children. A further interpretation could be 'I'm doing this for Lipski', as an act of revenge for the man's execution. Lipski was the second Jew hanged for murder since Oliver Cromwell's resettlement of the Jews.

The Ripper's escape route from Dutfield's Yard did not take him home. Interrupted, and with an unsatisfied appetite for mutilation, he walked fifteen minutes west towards Whitechapel High Street. Somewhere in the busyness of that thoroughfare, he encountered his next victim, Kate Eddowes.

CRIME RECONSTRUCTION FOR THE MURDER OF ELISABETH 'LIZ' STRIDE

It is a quarter to one in the morning, towards the end of a convivial night out. Liz is enjoying herself with this young man, who has made a killing on the races. A few gins never harmed anyone, and he has also treated her to a pie from a stall, and grapes for afters. In a real gesture of gallantry, he has given her his buttonhole to wear, a red rose with maidenhair fern, now pinned to her lapel. Several men have chaffed them, as if they were a courting couple, but she only wants a night out, with some innocent fun, before the weather turns.

While chatting outside the Board School, Liz unthinkingly rejects Hyams' sexual advances. She wants to be escorted home like a lady, savouring her memories of these last carefree hours, not to be pushed up against a wall. With her words, *No, not tonight, some other night*, the atmosphere between them changes from one of enjoyment to something darker.

They walk on, stopping outside the Working Men's Club gates to listen to the singing. Brooding on his thoughts, Hyams pulls at Liz to walk on. As she resists, he turns her around and throws her down on the pavement. She cries out three times in shock and pain, drawing attention from two passers-by. Hyams is quick to react to the threat. Noticing Israel Schwartz looking over, Hyams shouts, *Lipski!* and succeeds in frightening him and a second man away.

Liz manages to stand up, and, with his arm around her, Hyams steers her inside the club gates. Safe in the darkness, he grasps her neckerchief at the back and forces her down to the ground. He tears the front of her bodice as he grabs it to force her flat on her back. She is lying close to the gutter that runs along the base of a side wall. Sensing his presence, she rolls away from her attacker to face the wall, pulling up her legs as a defence against rape. Whether from instinct or experience, she knows what to do. Her mind is only focused on the here and now: will he hurt her, or can she make him go away?

Hyams kneels heavily on the front of her shoulders, his weight marking the skin on her chest with red welts that will bruise. Tucking his weaker left hand into her neckerchief, he draws it tight to restrict her breath. Pulling out his knife with his right hand, he shifts his weight off her and on to the ground to her right. He cuts her throat deeply along the kerchief's bottom edge, and once again. Preparing for further work, he folds her right arm across her chest, out of his way. By now, he hears the oncoming pony and cart before he sees it. The sound of hooves is getting too close; he must move. He wipes his knife against Liz's prone right hand, covering it with blood interspersed with 'small oblong clots',[49] and stands up.

As Lewis Diemshitz drives his pony and cart in on the left side of the entrance, Hyams slips out against the opposite wall, leaving Liz bleeding out behind him. He runs up Berner Street northwards, crosses Commercial Road, where he is lucky not to be seen by Constable Lamb, and slows his pace up Plumbers Row. Busy Whitechapel Road lies ahead, where he can merge with everyone else who is out and about on a Saturday night. He is ahead of the authorities, who are starting to move towards Berner Street. Doctor Phillips and Inspector Reid each cross Whitechapel Road southbound, forty-five minutes after him.

Plumbers Row leads close to his uncle Abraham Mordecai's business premises at 230 Whitechapel Road. Hyams stops there to hide away and clean himself up, perhaps discarding his bloodied coat, before moving on. Not ready to go home yet, he turns left along Whitechapel Road and heads towards the City.

He is on the hunt for a drink and a woman. Although the pubs closed at 1 a.m., the area around St James's Place, known as the Orange Market after its fruiterers' stalls, features several private clubs and pubs that also serve as illicit gambling houses with late closing hours and lock-ins. One such is the Sir John Falstaff Tavern at 45 & 46 Houndsditch, on the corner with Goring Street, part of the beat of Constable Edward Watkins of the City of London Police. It is still open, its gaming tables busy with players of cards and dice. Hyams joins in a game of faro, marking the edge of a green baize table cover with chalk to count which cards are played. Despite this permitted tactic, he soon loses most of the coins he possesses.

As he exits on to Houndsditch, St Botolph's Church appears ahead, its grounds populated by prostitutes. He steps into its churchyard to see who is there. Within half an hour of leaving Berner Street, he has hooked up with Kate Eddowes and escorted her to a place that is dark and secluded: Mitre Square.

7

THE MURDER OF KATE EDDOWES

The murder of Catherine 'Kate' Eddowes on Sunday 30 September 1888 between 1.32 and 1.44 a.m. in the City of London's Mitre Square.

Three days before her murder, forty-six-year-old Kate Eddowes and her common-law partner, market labourer John Kelly, returned to London from a stint of hop-picking in Kent, curtailed by bad weather and a poor harvest. Their lack of earnings caused them to split up for several nights: one of them could use the few pennies they had from pawning their scant possessions to sleep in a dosshouse, while the other, often Eddowes, queued for temporary accommodation at a workhouse casual ward, to exchange a day's labour for two nights' shelter.

The former street singer's optimism and resilience masked a history of deprivation and domestic violence. Orphaned at the age of fifteen, she left Bermondsey to live with an uncle and aunt in her native Wolverhampton. Six of her siblings, including her older brother Alfred, who had a 'weak mind from birth'[1] and suffered from epileptic fits,[2] were admitted to Bermondsey Union Workhouse. Unlike Hyam Hyams, whose epilepsy developed as late as 1880, Alfred Eddowes had a lifelong dependency on his family and public institutions. Kate Eddowes would have learned from a young age how to manage her brother's seizures. As an adult, however, her erratic lifestyle prevented her from actively helping him.

Within a year of the 1861 census, which recorded Eddowes' residence with relatives at Wolverhampton and her job as a scourer, cleaning and polishing plates in a tin plate factory,[3] she had given up her job and home. Aged approximately twenty, Eddowes took up with ex-soldier Thomas Conway, of whom her family disapproved, and went on the road with him, selling pamphlets with popular appeal that were known as chapbooks. Eddowes was always quick to refer to her 'marriage lines', insisting she had married Conway,[4] but she was the only person to believe in them.

Eddowes and Conway had three surviving children, born in workhouses on their peripatetic route; the first, Annie, in early 1863. Theirs was a volatile relationship, and Eddowes often sported bruises and black eyes. In 1879, their younger children, Thomas, eleven, and George, six, were found on the street by a policeman and taken to Greenwich Union Workhouse, their mother having deserted them, and not for the first time.[5] As adults, Eddowes' children distanced themselves, holding the precariousness of their formative years against her.

In late 1881, Eddowes and Conway split up, preventing him from fulfilling his prophecy that he would 'hang for her one day'. Seven years later, it was his initials, 'T.C.', tattooed on her left arm that led to the identification of her body. The savagery of the murderous assault on Eddowes had disfigured her face. Her killer cut slits through her eyes, sliced off the tip of her nose and one earlobe, and traced his knife down her right cheek for the sheer fun of it. The horror that was inflicted on her would only be surpassed in the final Ripper murder of Mary Jane Kelly. The removal of organs from both women verified a theory proposed by Coroner Wynne Baxter that the killer's deranged intention was to take away their wombs, or uteri.

Eddowes' was the only murder in the series committed within the City of London's Square Mile, with its investigation directed by the City of London Police. It was also the only Ripper crime where the perpetrator left evidence behind him: a piece cut from her apron and some scrawled words in chalk, on his route home from the crime scene, Mitre Square. It was also the occasion when he was closest to being caught red-handed, pursued from the scene by City detectives, and hiding out at a safe location before it felt safe enough to move on. Despite the heavy police presence, he made it home undetected.

On the eve of her death, Eddowes and her partner John Kelly were staying at a common lodging house in the notorious Flower and Dean Street: No. 55. At two o'clock in the afternoon, she slipped him the excuse that she was going to Bermondsey to visit, meaning to scrounge money from, her now-married daughter Annie Phillips. Whatever Eddowes did that afternoon, she cannot have visited Annie, who had changed address without telling her.

Eddowes did not dress up for the occasion, as she had no finery to put on. Her clothes were very old, and she was wearing everything she owned. Three skirts and a petticoat were removed from her body at the mortuary alongside a man's white vest worn back to front, a chemise and a brown linsey, or linen-and-wool, dress bodice. She wore no drawers or stays. The toes of her brown stockings were darned with white thread.

Her outer layer featured a dark green chintz skirt with a Michaelmas daisy and lily pattern, perhaps chosen to set off her auburn hair and hazel eyes. Her skirt was covered by an apron that had once been white, but was now black with dirt. She also wore a black cloth jacket edged with imitation fur, a black straw bonnet and a pair of men's lace-up boots. Like some of the other Ripper victims, who wore neckerchiefs, she wore at her neck, for warmth or ornament, a piece of red gauze silk.[6] Aged forty-six, her still-dark hair, skin tanned from hop-picking, and slim, undernourished figure gave the illusion of a younger woman. She was just five feet tall.[7]

At about half past eight in the evening, Eddowes was taken into police custody on Aldgate High Street for causing a drunken disturbance. Two City of London Police Constables pulled her up from a reclining position on the pavement outside 29 Aldgate High Street, close to the Hoop and Grapes pub, and escorted her on foot to

Bishopsgate police station. On arrival, smelling very strongly of drink, she refused to give her name to the Sergeant in the charge room and, following standard police procedure, was taken through to one of its six cells to recover. She spent the time alternately snoozing and singing.

Eddowes was released at her own request at 'just gone' 1 a.m. Sergeant Byfield insisted that she provide her name and address, so Eddowes improvised: 'Mary Ann Kelly, 6 Fashion Street'. In reply to a question about what she had been doing, and presumably aimed at whether or not she was soliciting, she said that she had been out hawking, or selling goods. Since she appeared to be sober, her white lies led Eddowes to be let out on to the streets instead of being kept safely in the station.

As Constable Hutt was letting her out, Eddowes asked what time it was. The answer came: 'Too late for you to get any more drink.' Eddowes confided in him: 'I shall get a damn fine hiding when I get home', a consideration that might lead her to stay out until Kelly had left for work. Hutt replied: 'Serves you right, for you have no business to go getting drunk.' He asked her to close the main door behind her when she left, and her last recorded words were: 'All right. Good night, old cock.' That phrase caused a ripple of laughter in court, when read out at the inquest into her death.[8]

According to Constable Hutt, Eddowes turned left out of the police station towards Houndsditch instead of right to cut back to her lodgings. The pubs having already closed, she was in the reckless hope of encountering a half-drunk punter on the streets, and trusting that he was not the Ripper. It would take her 'eight minutes ordinary walking'[9] to reach Mitre Square, if that were her destination. She was known to hang around the Aldgate Pump, a prominent feature at a busy three-way junction where she could attract trade. St Botolph's churchyard was a similar venue, as was along Houndsditch, with several late-opening bars on its side streets. The next sighting of her was over half an hour after leaving Bishopsgate police station, close to the scene of her murder.

An illustrated front-page feature captures the moment when Kate Eddowes' body was discovered by Constable Edward Watkins. He must have missed the Ripper by minutes.

Just after 1.30 a.m., three men were leaving the Imperial Club on Duke Street, which was exclusively for Jews, and close to the Great Synagogue. A rain shower had delayed their departure. Joseph Hyam Levy and Henry 'Harry' Harris were walking as a pair, with Joseph Lawende slightly apart from them. Across the road, they saw a man and a woman talking quietly on the corner of the entrance to Church Passage – a covered entry leading to Mitre Square. The woman had her back to them, and she had her hand on the man's chest. The man might have been partly or even fully facing them. The three men quickened their steps to pass the shabby-looking couple, their homes awaiting them. No further thought would trouble them until several hours later, when questioned by policemen making house-to-house inquiries after the murder.

On the night in question, two City Constables, with thirty years' police experience between them, were on duty in the Houndsditch area, each on one of the two proscribed beats. Constable Edward Watkins' beat, which took twelve to fifteen minutes to complete, was patrolled 'left-handed' that night, meaning in reverse. That procedure was intended to prevent criminals from predicting police movements. His beat included a full circuit of Mitre Square from Mitre Street. He was tasked to check with his lantern, but not patrol, one of the other entrances to the square: Church Passage. At 1.30 a.m., Watkins walked a circuit of Mitre Square, when 'nothing excited my attention ... I did not see anybody about'.[10]

Constable James Harvey was on the same shift as Watkins. His neighbouring beat stopped short of Mitre Square at the bottom of Church Passage, returning to Duke Street. Harvey walked through Church Passage and looked into the square at about 1.41 or 1.42 a.m. and neither saw nor heard anything untoward. Eddowes must then have been lying on the ground, dead, in the darkest corner of Mitre Square.

Watkins re-entered the square at 1.44 a.m. from Mitre Street and turned to his right, where he 'saw the body of a woman lying on the ground ... on her back, with her feet towards the square. Her clothes were above her waist ... she was laying in a great pool of blood.' He did not hear the footsteps of a man running away and to the best of his belief he was the only living person there.[11] He ran across to knock on the door of the Kearley and Tonge tea warehouse, where former Metropolitan policeman George Morris worked as its watchman.[12]

Morris vividly described their exchange:

> Watkins exclaimed, 'For God's sake, mate, come to my assistance.'
> I said, 'Stop till I get my lamp,' which was close at hand. I took it outside, and asked him what was the matter.
> He answered, 'Oh dear, there's another woman cut up to pieces.'[13]

Morris asked where she was, to which Watkins replied, 'In the corner.'

> [Morris] went over to the spot indicated and turned his lamp on the body. He immediately ran up Mitre-street into Aldgate, blowing his whistle. He saw no suspicious person about at the time. He was soon

> joined by two police-constables, and he told them to go to Mitre-square, where there had been another terrible murder. He followed the constables there, and took charge of his premises again. He had heard no noise in the square before he was called by Watkins. Had there been any cry of distress he would have heard it.[14]

It was Harvey who responded to Morris's whistle, having paced up and down Church Passage, turned right into Duke Street and right again into Aldgate High Street. He hailed Constable Frederick Holland from the other side of the street, and the two policemen followed Morris into Mitre Square. Watkins had remained by Eddowes' body in the south corner of the square, where her head lay close to the gate of a storage yard. He must have felt a sense of relief at the arrival of Morris with Constables Harvey and Holland.

Watkins sent Holland to fetch the nearest police surgeon, Doctor George Sequeira, from his premises at 34 Jewry Street. Senior officers were called from their beds at nearby police stations: Acting Superintendent Major Henry Smith from Cloak Lane; Detective Superintendent Alfred Foster from City Police headquarters at Old Jewry; and Inspector Edward Collard from Bishopsgate. Collard arrived at the scene of the crime at two or three minutes past 2 a.m., having telegraphed the fact of the murder to headquarters, and called out divisional police surgeon Doctor Frederick Gordon Brown from Finsbury Circus.

The inquest opened on Thursday 4 October before City Coroner Samuel Langham, at Golden Lane in the room above the mortuary. Like the Metropolitan Police, the City Force had put their best men on the job. In addition to City policemen Major Henry Smith and Inspectors James McWilliam and Alfred Foster, City Solicitor Henry Homewood Crawford attended as their representative. Coroner Langham gave Crawford his explicit permission to examine the witnesses, which he did thoroughly with particular regard to the reputation of the City Police.

The first three witnesses had all identified Eddowes' body in the downstairs mortuary, noting the tattoo in blue ink on her left forearm, with the initials T.C. for Thomas Conway. One of Eddowes' sisters, Eliza Gold, was the first called, to testify that she had identified her sister's body. She lived on Thrawl Street, near Flower and Dean Street, where her sister often lodged. Gold reported that she had last seen Eddowes with her partner John Kelly 'three or four weeks ago … They were on good terms.'[15]

A good-looking man with a black quiff, full moustache and imperial beard, John Kelly testified that he had last seen Eddowes on Saturday morning at Houndsditch:

> She promised me before we parted that she would be back by four o'clock and no later. She did not return. I heard she had been locked up at Bishopsgate-street … She had had a drop of drink. I never knew she went out for any immoral purpose. She was occasionally in the habit of slightly drinking to excess. When I left her she had no money about her … I do not know that she was at variance with anyone.[16]

The next witness was the impoverished couple's lodging house keeper Frederick Wilkinson, who stated: 'He had known [the deceased] and Kelly for the six or seven years. They passed as a man and wife, and were always on very good terms. They quarrelled now and again, but not violently, when the deceased was in drink … She got her living by hawking about the streets and cleaning amongst the Jews.'[17]

Wilkinson said that he had last seen Eddowes on the Saturday morning before her death, along with Kelly, between ten and eleven o'clock. He provided an alibi for Kelly by stating, 'When Kelly came in between seven and eight [on the night of the murder, I] asked him, 'Where's Kate?' and he replied that he had heard she was locked up …'[18] Kelly had taken a single bed.

Constable Edward Watkins testified that when he found the body, he sent watchman Morris for help, but saw no one about. Inspector Edward Collard testified that he arrived at the crime scene at about two or three minutes past two o'clock in the morning. Nothing was touched until the arrival of the doctors, and after their appraisal the body was moved to the mortuary. He produced a 'list of articles found on her', which covered all her clothing and possessions, adding that she had 'no money whatever'.[19]

He continued:

> I took immediate steps to have the neighbourhood searched for the person who committed the murder. Mr M'Williams [*sic*], Chief of the Detective Department, on arriving shortly afterwards, sent men to search in all directions in Spitalfields, both in streets and lodging-houses. Several men were stopped and searched in the streets, without any good result.
>
> I have had a house to house inquiry made in the vicinity of Mitre-square ... but I have not been able to find any beyond the witnesses who saw a man and woman talking together ...
>
> I endeavoured to trace footsteps [footprints] but could find no trace whatever. The backs of the empty houses adjoining were searched.[20]

The next witness was Doctor Gordon Brown, who had conducted the post-mortem examination at Golden Lane mortuary. At his request, H Division's Doctor Phillips had attended it. Not only had Phillips examined Annie Chapman's body, but on the following day, he was due to conduct the post-mortem examination on Elisabeth Stride. Gordon Brown had arrived at 2.18 a.m. at the crime scene, and described the position of Eddowes' body and his initial assessment of her injuries:

> The body was on its back – the head turned to left shoulder – the arms by the side of the body, as if they had fallen there, both palms upwards – the fingers slightly bent, a thimble was lying

> off the finger on the right side. The clothes drawn up above the abdomen, the thighs exposed, right leg bent at the thigh and knee.
>
> The bonnet was at the back of the head – great disfigurement of face, the throat cut across, and below the cut was a neckerchief. The upper part of the dress was pulled open a little way. The abdomen was all exposed.
>
> The intestines were drawn out to a large extent and placed over the right shoulder – they were smeared with some feculent matter [faeces]. A piece of about two foot was quite detached from the body and placed between the body and the left arm, apparently by design.[21]

Brown unwittingly caused a sensation in court, as his description of Eddowes' abdominal injuries tallied with those of Annie Chapman. He added the detail of a further mutilation and his estimate of the time of death: 'The lobe of the right ear was cut obliquely through; there was a quantity of clotted blood on the pavement, on the left side of the neck and upper part of the arm. The body was quite warm, and … had been there only a few minutes [certainly within thirty or forty minutes] …'[22]

Brown next described the findings of the post-mortem examination:

> The throat was cut across to the extent of about 6 in. or 7 in. The sterno cleido mastoid [*sic*] muscle [a pair of muscles in the sides of the neck supporting the head] was divided [on the left side]; the cricoid cartilage [a ring of cartilage around the windpipe] below the vocal cords was severed through the middle; the large vessels on the left side of the neck were severed to the bone, the knife marking the intervertebral cartilage [the disc between adjacent vertebrae] …
>
> All the injuries were caused by some very sharp instrument like a knife, and pointed. The cause of death was haemorrhage from the left common carotid artery [in the neck]. The death was immediate. The mutilations were inflicted after death.[23]

He next examined the injuries to the abdomen:

> The walls of the abdomen were laid open, from the breast downwards. The incision went upwards, not penetrating the skin that was over the sternum [breastbone]; it then divided the ensiform cartilage [of the lower breastbone], and being gristle they could tell how the knife had made the cut. It was held so that the point was towards the left side and the handle towards the right. The cut was made obliquely.[24]

The upwards cut took a line from her groin around the left side of Eddowes' umbilicus or belly button. It took three separate cuts to travel that length of her body from groin to below the umbilicus, then to the right away from it, and finally upwards to the bottom of the breastbone.[25] Those cuts were made in the opposite direction to that preferred by the medical profession, who made a single downward midline incision.

Doctor Gordon Brown's account continued:

> The incision went down the right side of the vagina and rectum for half an inch behind the rectum – There was a stab of about an inch on the left groin, this was done by a pointed instrument, below this was a cut of three inches going through all tissues making a wound of the peritoneum [the membrane lining the cavity of the abdomen and covering the abdominal organs] about the same extent.
>
> An inch below the crease of the thigh was a cut extending from the … [hip bone] obliquely down the inner side of the left thigh and separating the left labium forming a flap of skin up to the groin … There was a flap of skin formed from the right thigh attaching the right labium and extending up to the … [hip bone]. The muscles on the right side inserted into the poupart's ligament [groin ligament] were cut through.

ABOVE Hyam Hyams, photographed here at Colney Hatch Lunatic Asylum in 1899. While his image shows a man who looks deceptively harmless, his files state that 'his conduct was that of an insane person'.

LEFT CID Chief and Secret Service officer Robert Anderson claimed in his memoir that the Jack the Ripper case had been solved with 'no doubt whatever as to the identity of the criminal'. Wily and with great skills in agent handling and surveillance, his experience served him well in the hunt for the Whitechapel Murderer.

BELOW Melville Macnaghten served as Anderson's deputy from June 1889. Known to all as 'Mac', he was 'a man of action', and although he missed the peak of the Ripper investigation he made several astute observations about the case in confidential Scotland Yard reports.

ABOVE Author of the famous Swanson Marginalia, Donald Sutherland Swanson served as CID Detective Inspector. 'A very capable officer,' it was his writings that named one 'Kosminski' as a Ripper suspect.

LEFT Commissioner Sir Charles Warren was heavily influenced by the Army and led from the front. Determined to defend the reputation of the police, he maintained: 'Every single idea was investigated … people talk as if nothing had been done.' Unfortunately, his strong will and lack of finesse caused friction with the Home Secretary, leading to Warren's resignation within three years.

LEFT H Division Detective Constable Walter Dew (*left*) was ultimately promoted to Chief Inspector and used his memoir to guard the police's reputation against their failure to secure an arrest: 'Failure it was, but I have never regarded it other than an honourable failure.'

BELOW Published at the height of the Ripper killings, this *Punch* cartoon alluded to a phantom floating on 'the slum's foul air … 'tis murderous crime, the nemesis of neglect'.

ABOVE Frederick Abberline, CID Detective Inspector, was described as 'portly and gentle speaking. The type of police officer … who might easily have been mistaken for the manager of a bank or a solicitor.' In spite of the perceived failure of the police in the Ripper case, his colleagues said there was 'no question at all of Inspector Abberline's abilities as a criminal hunter'.

PUNCH, OR THE LONDON CHARIVARI.—SEPTEMBER 29, 1888.

THE NEMESIS OF NEGLECT.

"THERE FLOATS A PHANTOM ON THE SLUM'S FOUL AIR,
SHAPING, TO EYES WHICH HAVE THE GIFT OF SEEING,
INTO THE SPECTRE OF THAT LOATHLY LAIR.
FACE IT—FOR VAIN IS FLEEING!
RED-HANDED, RUTHLESS, FURTIVE, UNERECT,
'TIS MURDEROUS CRIME—THE NEMESIS OF NEGLECT!"

ABOVE A view of Wentworth Street *c.*1900. Located close to where Hyams lived, this was the epicentre of the Ripper killings, providing an ideal escape route as it was in walking distance of all the murders.

LEFT Buck's Row, where Polly Nichols, the first canonical five victim, was killed. Nichols was found just outside the stables gateway with her left hand touching the gate and 'the lower part of her person … completely ripped open'.

RIGHT Annie Chapman pictured with her husband, John Chapman, *c.*1869. Photographed in their Sunday best in upmarket Knightsbridge, this was the beginning of a fifteen-year marriage plagued with alcoholism. Few would have guessed the end Annie would eventually come to twenty years later.

ABOVE Coroner Wynne Edwin Baxter, pictured here at the 1888 inquest into Annie Chapman's death. Dr George Bagster Phillips is also featured, a significant person to the Ripper investigation as he conducted or attended autopsies on four of the canonical five victims.

LEFT The entrance to Dutfield's Yard, where the Ripper was apparently interrupted in his murder of Elisabeth Stride, is marked with a cartwheel. Leaving the killer in a frenzy and lusting for blood, this was the first of two murders on the night of 29 November 1888.

RIGHT A drawing of Catherine 'Kate' Eddowes in 1888. Her murder saw a marked escalation in the Ripper's violence as he spent valuable escape time disfiguring her face and removing her organs.

RIGHT The ground-floor room at Miller's Court where Mary Jane Kelly was killed. Given the relative safety of an indoor location to commit his crime, the Ripper took his time to mutilate Mary Jane beyond all recognition. The youngest of the victims, her cry of 'Murder!' was ignored by those who heard it.

LEFT A Victorian race day. Notably, the Ripper murders all coincided with significant horse-racing fixtures, explaining how he was able to afford nights out drinking with his victims and persuading them he was flush with cash.

BOTTOM RIGHT George Yard Buildings, where Martha Tabram was killed. Tabram's body was found in the dark stairwell, with the various testimonies of her neighbours placing her death many hours after she was last seen with a soldier client.

ABOVE Friern Hospital, formerly known as Colney Hatch Lunatic Asylum, photographed here in 1975. After various incarcerations elsewhere, Hyams was first admitted to Colney Hatch in April 1889, following an attack on his wife and mother.

RIGHT Harry William Garrett, H Division Sergeant from 1888 to 1896, and the author's great-great-grandfather.

> The skin was retracted through the whole of the cut in the abdomen but vessels were not clotted – nor had there been any appreciable bleeding from the vessel. I draw the conclusion that the cut was made after death and there would not be much blood on the murderer. The cut was made by some one on the right side of body kneeling below the middle of the body … There were no indications of connexion [*sic*: sexual intercourse].[26]

Repeated stabs were made to the liver 'as if by the point of a sharp instrument … shewn [*sic*: shown] by a jagging [uneven edge] of the skin'.[27] The pancreas and spleen were also cut.

In addition to the disembowelling, the killer had removed two organs from the body; the left kidney and the uterus: 'The womb was cut through horizontally leaving a stump ¾ of an inch, the rest of the womb had been taken away with some of the ligaments.'[28]

Eddowes' face 'was very much mutilated', the first victim to be so disfigured. Her eyelids were cut through with the tip of a knife, and part of her right ear removed. The tip of her nose was cut off 'by an oblique cut from the bottom of the nasal bone to where the wings of the nose join on to the face'. Her right cheek was cut through to the bone in a deep cut from the side of her nose in an arc across the cheek ending near the angle of her jaw. Three deep oblique cuts went through her upper lip into the gum of her right upper lateral incisor tooth, across the bridge of her nose, around the corner of her mouth and extending parallel with her lower lip. Additionally, 'There was on each side of cheek a cut which peeled up the skin forming a triangular flap about an inch and a half.'[29]

Dr Brown also testified to 'a great discolouration on the shoulder'[30] and 'a bruise the size of a sixpence, recent and red, was discovered on the back of the left hand between the thumb and first finger'.[31] He noted that there were no bruises on the scalp, meaning that she had not been hit on the head by her killer, or in falling. Her stomach contained 'very little … but from the cut end partly digested farinaceous [starchy] food escaped …'[32]

Brown concluded by stating his professional opinion about the act of murder, in response to a series of questions from Crawford:

> I believe the wound in the throat was first inflicted.
> I believe she must have been lying on the ground …
>
> [The] wounds on the face and abdomen prove that they were inflicted by a sharp pointed knife, and that in the abdomen by one six inches long.
>
> I believe the perpetrator of the act must have had considerable knowledge of the positions of the organs in the abdominal cavity and the way of removing them. The part removed would be of no use for any professional purpose.
>
> It required a great deal of knowledge to have removed the kidney and to know where it was placed, such a knowledge might be possessed by some one in the habit of cutting up animals.
>
> I think the perpetrator of this act had sufficient time or he would not have nicked the lower eyelids. It would take at least 5 minutes.
>
> I cannot assign any reason for these [body] parts being taken away.
>
> I feel sure there was no struggle.
>
> I believe it was the act of one person – the throat had been so instantly severed that no noise could have been emitted. I should not expect much blood to have been found on the person who had inflicted these wounds. The wounds could not have been self-inflicted.
>
> My attention was called to the apron – It was the corner of the apron with a string attached. The blood spots were of recent origin – I have seen a portion of an apron produced by Dr. Phillips and stated to have been found in Goulstone [*sic*] Street. It is impossible to say it is human blood.
>
> I fitted the piece of apron which had a new piece of material on it which had evidently been sewn on to the piece I have. The

> seams of the borders of the two actually corresponding – some blood and apparently faecal matter was found on the portion found in Goulstone [*sic*] Street.
>
> I believe the wounds on the face to have been done to disfigure the corpse.[33]

On that sombre note, the inquest was adjourned for a week, until Thursday 11 October. Doctor Sequeira was the first witness to testify at the second hearing, stating that he was the first medical man to arrive on the scene, at five minutes to 2 a.m. He said that, 'Life had not been extinct more than ¼ of an hour,' adding: 'I quite agree with the Doctor [Gordon Brown] in every particular … I formed the opinion that the perpetrator of the deed had no particular design on any particular organ. I do not think he was possessed of any great anatomical skill,' meaning his skill level resembled a butcher's.[34]

Doctor William Sedgwick Saunders, the Medical Officer of Health for the City and a forensic expert who had also attended the post-mortem examination, said that he had examined the stomach and its contents 'for poisons of the narcotic class with negative results'.[35] He too considered that the perpetrator had no particular design on any particular organ. Despite the removal of body parts, the City's medical professionals had publicly refuted Coroner Wynne Baxter's theory.

The next witness was Eddowes' daughter Annie Phillips, who attested that she had not seen her mother for two years and one month, since she had helped with her confinement. A month after that, Phillips had moved from Bermondsey and did not give her mother a forwarding address. Eddowes' two sons also did not let her know where they lived in London, 'that was purposely kept from her to prevent … being applied to for money'.[36] Phillips was not on good terms with her father Thomas Conway and was not able to assist the police in finding him and her two brothers, who lived with him.

Detective Sergeant John Mitchell gave evidence that he had been unable to find Conway and his sons. Detective Conway Baxter Hunt had found a man called Conway who was a pensioner belonging to the 18th Royal Irish, but he was not recognized by two of Eddowes' sisters. After the inquest concluded, having heard that the City Police were looking for him, Conway and his two sons went to their headquarters in Old Jewry. He reported that he had kept out of his former partner's way as far as possible, 'as he did not wish to have any further communication with her'.[37]

The next witnesses were the three City policemen who had dealt with Eddowes after her semi-collapse on Aldgate High Street. They were followed on the stand by watchman George Morris, himself a retired Metropolitan policeman, whom Constable Watkins had called for assistance, having found a woman 'cut up to pieces' in the corner of Mitre Square. He had not left the warehouse between 11 p.m. and 1 a.m.[38]

George Clapp was the caretaker of No. 5 Mitre Street, the back gate of which opened into Mitre Square at the spot where Eddowes' body lay. He said that he had heard no sound or any noise of any kind. The only tenant resident in the square itself was, ironically, City policeman Richard Pearce at No. 3. He had heard no noise or disturbance, and at twenty past two he first heard of the murder when he was called by a Constable. He commented: 'From my window I could see the spot where the deceased was found.'[39]

The next testimony came from two of the three eyewitnesses who, on leaving the Imperial Club, had seen a man and a woman talking in Church Passage. The third, furniture dealer Harry Harris, was not called to testify at the inquest. The press reported him as being 'the more communicative [of the three witnesses]. He is of opinion that neither Mr. Levander [*sic*] nor Mr. Levy saw anything more than he did, and that was only the back of the man.'[40]

Cigarette salesman Joseph Lawende was the nearest of the three to the couple, and facing the man as he and his companions walked past them. At the inquest, he testified:

> We noticed a man and woman together in Church Passage. The woman was standing with her face towards the man, so that I only saw her back. I noticed that her hand was on his chest. I could not see the woman's face, but the man was taller than she was. The woman wore a black jacket and a black bonnet …
>
> I cannot tell you the height of the woman; but she was about five feet high … [The man] had on a peaked cloth cap, the peak of the same material apparently as the cap … I doubt [that I would remember the man again] …
>
> Neither the man nor the woman appeared to be in an angry mood. There was nothing in their movements which attracted my attention, except that the man was a rough-looking fellow. The woman had her hand on the man's chest, but she did not seem as if she was pushing him away. They were standing together conversing quietly, and I was not curious enough to look back and see where they went.[41]

Henry Crawford prevented any further description of the man, presumably to avoid disrupting the police investigation. Lawende confirmed that the police had shown him the dead woman's clothing, 'and, as far as his belief went, he thought they were the same clothes which the deceased wore on the night in question'.[42]

According to a press report, the police were carefully guarding Lawende as a key witness:

> The fact [that the Duke Street trio sighted the murderer] is borne out by the police having taken exclusive care of Mr Joseph Levander [*sic*], to a certain extent having sequestrated him and having imposed a pledge on him of secrecy. They are paying all his expenses, and one if not two detectives are taking him about. One of the two detectives is Foster …
>
> The police, in imposing their idiotic secrecy, have allowed a certain time to elapse before making the partial description these

> three witnesses have been able to give public, and thus prevent others from acting upon the information in the event of the murderer coming under their notice.[43]

Butcher Joseph Hyam Levy of 1 Hutchinson Street, Aldgate, was the second and last of the Duke Street trio to give evidence:

> I was at the Imperial Club on the night in question with the last witness. We left about three or four minutes past the half hour (half past one). I saw a man and woman standing at the corner of Church-passage, but I passed on, and did not take any further notice of them. I walked along as fast as I could.
>
> I cannot give any description of either the man or the woman; all I can say is that the man was about three inches taller than the woman. I walked along home, which I reached, I should think, by twenty minutes to two. I fix the time by the clock in the club.[44]

In response to a question from a juror, he added:

> When I came out of the club I said to Mr. Harris, 'Here, I'm off. I don't like the look of those people over there (alluding to the man and woman he saw). I don't like going home by myself at this hour of the morning. I don't like passing this class of persons.'
>
> The spot is better lighted now than it was prior to the morning of the murder. There is a better light at the club now than there used to be, and with the aid of the lamp a few yards off I could distinguish almost anybody. On the night in question, however, there was not sufficient light to enable me to distinguish the colour of the dress which the woman was wearing …
>
> There was nothing in what I saw to suggest that the man was doing anything that was dangerous to the woman. Being a little deaf, I could not possibly have heard anything that was said.[45]

The next witness was Metropolitan Police Constable Alfred Long, seconded from A Division to increase H Division's manpower, and who had been on duty in Goulston Street, five minutes' walk to the east of Mitre Square. Inside an entrance to a block of flats, he had found a piece of fabric cut from Eddowes' apron that was wet with blood. Chalked above it on the doorway's black fascia was a sentence, split across several lines. Long described his discoveries as follows:

> About 2.55 a.m ... I found a portion of a woman's apron which I produce. There appeared blood stains on it, one portion was wet, lying in the passage leading to the staircases of 108 to 119, Model Dwelling House. Above it on the wall was written in Chalk – The Jews [*sic*: reported verbatim] are the men that will not be blamed for nothing.
>
> I at once searched the staircases and areas of the Building, but found nothing else.
>
> I at once took the apron to Commercial Road [*sic*: Commercial Street] Police Station and reported it to the Inspector on Duty. I passed that spot where the apron was found about 2.20 the apron was not there when I passed then.[46]

In response to questions from Crawford, Long repeated the chalked sentence and clarified his spelling of the word 'Jews': 'I copied the words from the wall into my report – I could not say whether they were recently written. I wrote down into my book and the Inspector noticed that Jews was spelled Juews – There was a difference between the spelling ...'[47]

The significance of that mis-spelling was not debated in court. While press reporting suggested that the variation meant the writer was Jewish, prominent Jews publicly rejected that idea:

> The word for Jews in 'Yiddish' [a language spoken by Ashkenazi Jews] is ... 'yidden', which is a corruption of the German Jüden ...

> I am far from saying that it is not possible one of my compatriots, suffering from brain trouble, committed the atrocious crimes, but had he written any word to denote his fellow Jews, except the English word, it would most assuredly have been 'yidden' ...[48]

The exact spelling of the word was quoted differently by a City of London Police witness, as was the sentence's phrasing.

Constable Long added that he had not made any inquiries in any of the flats, but he had searched six or seven staircases and 'found no traces of blood or recent footmarks'.[49] Before proceeding to the police station he had heard of the Mitre Square murder and he left a colleague in charge 'to take an observation as to any one who entered the building or left it'.[50]

A juror complained that the police did not make inquiries in the building, having found a piece of apron belonged to the victim. He observed, 'There was a clue at that point, but now it is completely lost.'[51] Crawford replied that, 'The find was not made known to the City Police for an hour or two afterwards, and the City Police immediately searched the buildings. The apron was found by a member of the Metropolitan Police.'[52]

Detective Constable Daniel Halse was one of three members of the City of London Police CID who were on plain-clothes duty in the area, as part of a strategy to flood the streets with officers. He was an early arrival at Mitre Square, alerted either by Morris's whistle or by colleagues making their way there from Old Jewry. He testified that he had visited Eddowes' body at the mortuary, and observed that a corner was cut from her apron.

By 5 a.m., Halse was at Goulston Street in a stand-off with H Division's Superintendent Arnold, Inspector Swanson and the Metropolitan Police Commissioner himself, Sir Charles Warren. Arnold was keen to erase the chalked-up sentence in order to avoid 'a riot or an outbreak against the Jews',[53] who were about to set up for Petticoat Lane's Sunday morning market. Halse suggested the few words that referred to the Jews should be removed, and the rest preserved until his superior Major Henry Smith and a photographer arrived. Despite his protests, a bucket and sponge was brought, and the writing washed off. Halse reported a different spelling and phrasing of the graffito: 'The Juwes [*sic*] are not the men that will be blamed for nothing.'[54] Further versions of the spelling of the word 'Jews' exist in the official records.

In summing up, the coroner commented that, 'The assassin had not only murdered the woman, defenceless as she was, but had so mangled the corpse as to render it almost impossible for the body to be identified.'[55] On its timing, he said: 'The murder must have been committed between 1.30 and 1.44, and, allowing five minutes for the crime to be committed, only nine minutes were left to be accounted for.'[56] Referring to Doctor Gordon Brown's belief that only one person was implicated in the murder, he advised the jury to return the verdict of 'Wilful murder by some person unknown', which they did.

On the first day of the inquest, Frederick William Foster, the son of Detective Superintendent Alfred Foster, an architect and surveyor, had produced two hand-drawn plans of the area. The first demonstrated that the distance from Berner Street, where Elisabeth Stride was killed, to Mitre Square was three-quarters of a mile, and a walk of twelve to fifteen minutes. Foster also proposed two possible routes from Mitre Square to Goulston Street, where the apron and graffito were found. He suggested that the perpetrator's end destination might have been a lodging house on Flower and Dean Street.[57] There was a difference of only 10 feet between Foster's two routes.

Both ran from Church Passage through Duke Street, across Houndsditch and on to Gravel Lane. The first ran closer to the Artizans' Dwellings than the second, which took a more direct route to the same end point: across Petticoat Lane to Goulston Street. Foster's plans were based on the 1873 Ordnance Survey map, which made them fifteen years out of date. Whether by accident or design, they failed to include the Artizans' Dwellings, completed in 1885. In 1888, Hyams' brother Mark and his family were living at 49 North Block, Artizans' Dwellings.[58] Mark Hyams' apartment and its common areas could have provided a hiding place for a killer when chased from Mitre Square, as was claimed by a senior City of London Police detective.

On his retirement in 1905, City Detective Inspector Robert Sagar was clear that the murderer was known to the police, having been pursued from the only Ripper crime scene in the City of London, Mitre Square. His account contained striking similarities to Robert Anderson's, citing what must have been the reluctant witness, and the cessation of crimes after the perpetrator's admission to an asylum:

> The police realised, as also did the public, that the crimes were those of a madman and suspicion fell on a man who, without a doubt, was the murderer. Identification being impossible, he could not be charged. He was, however, placed in a lunatic asylum and the series of atrocities came to an end.[59]

Observing that the case was indeed the most 'sensational' he had ever worked on, Sagar went on to state that the City Police pursued the perpetrator immediately after the event:

> As you know, the perpetrator of these outrages was never brought to justice, but I believe he came the nearest to being captured after the murder of the woman Kelly in Mitre-square. A police officer met a well-known man of Jewish appearance coming out of the court near the square, and a few moments after fell over the body.
>
> He blew his whistle, and other officers running up, they set off in pursuit of the man who had just left. The officers were wearing indiarubber boots, and the retreating footsteps of a man could be clearly heard. The sounds were followed to King's-block in the model dwellings [Artizans' Dwellings] in Stoney-lane, but we did not see the man again that night.[60]

Sagar's suspect, a 'well-known man of Jewish appearance', sounds like Hyams, who could have come to police attention by living and working locally, and attending the Great Synagogue on Duke Street. He might also have been noticed by the police owing to his epileptic seizures, strange behaviour and any misdemeanour committed by him or his extended family.

In an often-overlooked snippet, Anderson's CID deputy Melville Macnaghten also revealed a little-known police witness to the Eddowes murder: 'On this occasion it is probable that the police officer on duty in the vicinity [of Mitre Square] saw the murderer with his victim a few minutes before, but no satisfactory description was forthcoming.'[61] If that unnamed City of London policeman had identified the Ripper immediately after the double event, it might have been possible to save Mary Jane Kelly's life.

Sagar's 'court near the square' is presumably Church Passage, fitting a supposition that the Ripper tended to use the same route to arrive and depart from the scenes of his crimes. The presence of three firemen on overnight duty at a temporary fire station in the centre of St James's Place suggests that the perpetrator did not escape via St James's Passage in that direction.[62] It rules out any theory that Hyam Hyams might have used the shop at 8 St James's Place occupied by the Emanuel family, to whom he was related by marriage,[63] as an alternative hiding place on his escape from Mitre Square.

If the Ripper escaped via Church Passage, then Constable James Harvey was the only police officer on that beat. It is possible that Harvey narrowly missed the killer on exiting Church Passage at around 1.42 a.m., when he turned right on to Duke Street after the killer might have turned left. As the City Police had flooded the area with plain-clothes detectives, any one of them could have spotted the killer and raised the alarm. The officers wearing silent indiarubber boots, who ran up to follow him, must have been part of that contingent.

Sagar's reference to the Artizans' Dwellings provides a fascinating connection to Hyams. Completed in 1885, the five blocks of flats replaced Hyams' home at the date of his marriage, Ebenezer Square. From 1887, his brother Mark and his family lived in Flat 49, North Block. The blocks in the Artizans' Dwellings ran from north to south in a regular sequence. North Block was followed by Prince's, Queen's and King's Block. Stoney Lane divided the first four blocks from the last, South Block.

A man escaping from Church Passage heading north-east would have to transit Duke Street and Little Duke Street to pass quickly on to Houndsditch. If heading for the northern blocks of Artizans' Dwellings, the most direct path was via Stoney Lane. A man taking that route would first encounter King's Block, as referenced by Sagar, and that path would be equally consistent with a destination of North Block, the third block behind it, accessed from Artizans Street. One or more of the City Detectives could conceivably have followed Hyams as far as King's Block, where his trail was lost.

Hyams must have spent thirty to forty minutes hiding out. According to Constable Long, the piece of apron and graffito were not there when he patrolled Goulston Street at 2.20 a.m. At some time between 2.20 and 2.55 a.m., perhaps fearing that the police search would intensify, Hyams moved on from his hiding place. The doorway of Wentworth Dwellings, where he dumped the torn corner of bloodied cloth, and chalked up his protest, was on his direct route home to Wentworth Court.

CRIME RECONSTRUCTION FOR THE MURDER OF KATE EDDOWES

Excruciatingly poor timing leads Kate to leave Bishopsgate police station at about one o'clock in the morning – almost exactly the same time that Hyams slips from Dutfield's Yard. She has no intention of going back to her lodging, turning left towards Houndsditch to look for a punter making his way home.

Her path crosses Hyams' outside St Botolph's and it is all too easy for him, as a paying customer, to hook up with her. He walks her along Duke Street to the seclusion of Church Passage, where they stand negotiating terms. Three men leaving the Imperial Club quicken their steps to pass a woman and a man, up to something. Hyams pays them scant attention: he is just talking to his companion, and that isn't a crime.

Who knows what Kate is thinking as she faces her killer with her hand on his chest? She may already know this man, a few years younger than her, from one of her pick-up spots, the pump at Aldgate or its local pubs. She may even feel sympathy for him as a struggling epileptic, with his shambling walk like her brother Alfred's. As a punter, he seems nice enough, with a bit of banter and money in his pocket.

The couple walk down the narrow passage to the darkest corner of Mitre Square. Populated by the Horner & Co. warehouse, a locked yard behind a house, several empty houses and Mr Taylor's shop, that unlit spot could not be quieter. Gas lamps stationed at the square's two top corners, and at the junction with Mitre Street, throw no light on the scene.

Hyams boxes Kate against the corner of a gatepost and hits her to the ground with his right fist. Once she is down, he grabs the front of her bodice and pulls her to lie flat on her back. In the struggle, pushing her hand against her attacker's torso, Kate's left hand is crushed against one of the brown metal buttons on her bodice.

Hyams takes out his knife and cuts her throat deeply from under her left ear. As with Liz, he follows the edge of her neckerchief with his knife. Having been interrupted before, he intends this time fully to complete his mission. Squatting between Kate's legs, and using his left hand and knee to move her right knee upwards to a right angle, he pushes her skirts up above her waist.

He opens up her abdomen from the pubic bone to the breastbone and, almost surgically, disembowels her. He pulls out most of her intestines and places them, still attached to her body, over her right shoulder. Then, he cuts away another two feet of intestines and places that piece beneath her left arm. He removes her uterus and left kidney. Next, he makes a few downward cuts between the top of her thighs and her labia, on both sides, and a few upwards between her legs.

He uses his knife quickly on Kate's face, nicking cuts in her eyelids, taking off the tip of her nose and her right earlobe, and tracing a long deep cut down the side of her nose into her cheek. He cuts through her vest and chemise as well as the waistbands and top parts of her skirts, severing the tape strings that attach her three pockets to her waist. He shakes her pockets' contents out on to the ground to her left, but is disappointed if he thinks to find anything of value among her old tins and rags.

Finally, he cuts off a corner segment of her apron and wraps his trophies in it. He has worked fast, doing what he wanted to do in under nine minutes. He runs back the way he came, up Church Passage to Duke Street. Fearing or hearing pursuit, he hurries up Little Duke Street to Stoney Lane to gain access to the Artizans' Dwellings. He hides inside North Block, on the stairwell outside his brother's flat, for forty minutes. To avoid being cornered by the police, he decides to make for home.

He devises a zig-zag route that takes him eastwards. He crosses Petticoat Lane at speed – owing to its direct line of sight down to Aldgate – and goes on to New Goulston Street. Turning left on to Goulston Street, the doorway of 110–118 Wentworth Dwellings is on the opposite side of the street, near its far corner with Wentworth Street. Certain he is not being followed, he crosses over and, in a spirit of protest, chalks up his message with gaming chalk, removes his trophies from the piece of Kate's apron and, after wiping his knife on it, dumps it. He hits Wentworth Street, continuing east to enter Wentworth Court, where his wife and two children are sleeping.

Having committed two murders within thirty-five minutes, he is home by 2.50 a.m., as Constable Long notices the piece of apron on the ground and, looking up, the writing on the wall.

8

THE POLICE INVESTIGATION AFTER THE 'DOUBLE EVENT'

'The arc of the moral universe is long, but it bends towards justice.'

DR MARTIN LUTHER KING JUNIOR

By killing within the Square Mile of the City of London, Hyam Hyams had unwittingly introduced a second Police Force to the Whitechapel Murders investigation and 'brought upon his tracks some 900 additional officers'.[1] The Metropolitan and City of London Police Forces found themselves both cooperating and competing in an attempt to make the long-awaited arrest. On 9 October 1888, Sir Charles Warren wrote to his City counterpart Sir James Fraser proposing daily conferences between Metropolitan and City detectives to avoid 'our working doubly over the ground'.[2] They might also need to deconflict over ongoing liaison with witnesses.

The two detective chiefs, Swanson and McWilliam, set up a regular liaison, while the latter's junior, Robert Sagar, attended nightly meetings at Leman Street police station. At the beginning of November, Swanson noted that the inquiries 'of the City Police are merged into those of the Metropolitan Police, each force cordially communicating to the other daily the nature and subject of their enquiries'.[3]

But according to a contemporary American newspaper article, the City Police, called 'a far more intellectual class of men than their brethren of Scotland Yard',[4] had a different interpretation of the double event. The City Police disagreed with what they put forward as a Metropolitan Police theory that the killer had made appointments with each woman, to meet them at a certain place at a certain time. If he had not been interrupted when killing Elisabeth Stride, it is arguable that the Ripper would have spent far longer with her body, and could not have attended a meeting with a second victim within thirty-five minutes, at a location twelve minutes' walk away.

Crucially, the City Police did not believe that Eddowes was part of the Ripper series of killings. In this, they were guided by the renowned criminal lawyer George Lewis, who was later knighted and made a Baronet. Tasked to draw up his own profile of the killer, Lewis's assessment was very different to that of forensic expert Thomas Bond, and presumed that the murders of Stride and Eddowes were perpetrated by more than one man working in collaboration and motivated by a religious mission against prostitutes:

> From a careful and exhaustive consideration of the facts laid before him by the city detectives, Mr. Lewis is understood to have deduced the following conclusions [listed order of probability]:
>
> Positive – First. That the murders of Elizabeth Stride and Catharine Beddowes [*sic*] were not committed by one and the same person.
>
> Second. That the two or more murderers were acting in collusion and by pre-arrangement.
>
> Probable – First. That the series of murders have been committed by two or more men whose motive is the checking of prostitution. The unprecedented barbarities practiced [*sic*] on the bodies are perpetuated with the view of terrifying the women of the district into abandoning their mode of life.

Second. That the murderers are religious monomaniacs.[5]

Although the City and Metropolitan Forces were collaborating on the investigation, they had identified two wholly different targets. The City Police were looking for two or more men with a malignant hatred of prostitutes, who were committing murders as planned operations, while the Metropolitan Police focused on a single killer, an opportunistic marauder. However, H Division Superintendent Arnold disagreed with the concept that one man had killed all of the Ripper victims. He later professed to a journalist that he, like the City Police, discounted Eddowes from that series. Frustratingly, Arnold called his reasons 'convincing, but ... too long to detail now'.[6]

It was not only the police who resorted to criminal profiling. The day after the double event, a representative of the Central News Agency interviewed 'two eminent London physicians for the purpose of ascertaining whether they could throw any scientific light on the East End murders'.[7] Both previously quoted in Chapter 2, the most eminent of the two, Sir James Risdon Bennett, debunked the theory that a medical man was collecting female body parts as 'not only ridiculous ... but absolutely impossible of realisation'.[8]

He went on to give his professional opinion of the perpetrator's motivation:

> My impression is that the miscreant is a homicidal maniac. He has a specific delusion, and that delusion is erotic. Of course, we have at this moment very little evidence indeed; in fact, I may say no evidence at all as to the state of the man's mind, except so far as it is suggested by the character of the injuries which he has inflicted upon his victims.
>
> I repeat that my impression is that he is suffering under an erotic delusion, but it may be that he is a religious fanatic. It is possible that he is labouring under the delusion that he has a mandate from the Almighty to purge the world of prostitutes, and

> in the prosecution of his mad theory he has determined upon a crusade against the unfortunates of London, whom he seeks to mutilate by deprivation of the uterus …
>
> It is a matter of common knowledge … amongst 'mad doctors' that lunatics display a wonderful intelligence, if it may be called so, in their criminal operations; and I have little doubt that if the murderer were other than a madman, he would ere this have been captured by the police. In many instances a madman's delusion is directed to only one subject, and he is mad upon that subject alone.[9]

Bennett was the expert who considered that the perpetrator's 'acute mania', particularly demonstrated in the last two murders of Eddowes and Kelly, would be obvious to almost anyone he met, and that he was 'a man to whom the ordinary rules of motive and procedure do not apply'.[10] He argued against attributing any rational motivation to the killer, resolving the conundrum of the sane trying to comprehend the insane.

The second medical professional to put his views on the record was Doctor Forbes Winslow, regularly described in the press as 'the eminent specialist in lunacy cases'. Forbes Winslow called the Ripper 'a homicidal lunatic … and I see no reason why he should not, excepting at the periods when the fit is upon him, exhibit a cool and rational exterior'.[11] He outlined his theory as follows:

> I have here in my book – a work on physiology – a case in which a man had a lust for blood as in this case, and he was generally a person of bland and pleasant exterior.
>
> In all probability the whole of the murders have been committed by the same hand; but I may point out that the imitative faculty is very strong in persons of unsound mind …
>
> The murderer is a homicidal monomaniac … and I fear he will not be captured, unless discovered in the actual commission of crime.[12]

In his memoir, Forbes Winslow expanded on his thinking with specific mention of epilepsy, calling the Ripper 'an epileptic maniac … [having] seizures … frequently accompanied by a form of erotic frenzy'.[13] It was a theory that he held briefly, although an unnamed colleague, 'perhaps the most eminent specialist in mental diseases in England', took it further:

> 'Jack the Ripper' is an epileptic patient, one suffering from a peculiar form of epilepsy … the person so afflicted is liable to the attacks after excitation of the passions …
>
> [In cases of] 'masked epilepsy', that is epilepsy in which the convulsive symptoms are absent … persons suffering from this form of the disorder may, during a seizure, perform the most extraordinary, and at times the most diabolical actions, and upon their return to consciousness be in perfect ignorance of what has transpired.[14]

If Hyam Hyams were Jack the Ripper, then the specialist's identification of a violent epileptic was uncannily accurate. Although Hyams did not suffer from 'masked epilepsy', characterized by headaches or vomiting rather than convulsions, the concept of a man who does not remember what he has done is extraordinary because it removes the possibility of a confession and brings into question his criminal intent. If his post-fit episodes of violence led Hyams to kill, then his state of excitement after fitting, also described as 'delirium', implied diminished responsibility. Neither a religious fanatic nor operating in a gang, he was sexually motivated with a focus on removing his victims' uteri.

It is difficult to assess what knowledge or suspicion his immediate family might have had. His wife, awake herself with a young baby and toddler, would certainly have known of his nocturnal absences. But if Hyams went out every night, his movements could not easily be matched to the Ripper killings, unless he were followed or caught in the act. The police distribution of handbills, and their house-to-house inquiries and searches, would have included Wentworth Court and the family business premises frequented by Hyams. It is impossible to judge whether, as observed in other criminals, he avoided direct contact with the authorities, or encouraged it to boost a sense of superiority.

The chances of catching the perpetrator *in medias res* were increased after the murder of Annie Chapman, by the formation of the Whitechapel Vigilance Committee. Its chairman, local builder and Freemason George Lusk, notoriously received an anonymous letter in a parcel containing half a kidney purporting to be that of Kate Eddowes. The motivation of the Committee – a collection of public-spirited businessmen – was a healthy mix of the altruistic and selfish: to prevent further murders and restore order to the streets of Whitechapel, so that business could get back to normal.

Following the murder of Annie Chapman, the Whitechapel Vigilance Committee attempted to take matters into their own hands, protecting the people of the East End with their team of 'citizen detectives'.

Within twenty-four hours of their first meeting at The Crown pub at 74 Mile End Road on the evening of Monday 10 September, they had offered a substantial reward 'to anyone, citizens or otherwise, who shall give such information as will be the means of bringing the murderer or murderers to justice'.[15] They also set up their own brigade of what were called 'amateur policemen' or 'citizen detectives', who mustered at The Crown each night before midnight, when they would go out on to the streets. Armed with a stick and a whistle, they would man their 'beats', and visit 'the most sequestered and ill-lighted spots'.[16] It was a huge commitment by local men, who, like the police, were putting their lives on the line.

The Committee entered into correspondence with the Home Secretary about offering an official reward. Having met with a refusal, the double murder on 30 September led George Lusk to petition Her Majesty The Queen, stating with some foresight that 'without such reward the murderer or murderers of the above four victims will not only remain undetected, but will sooner or later commit other crimes of a like nature'.[17] On 6 October, Home Secretary Henry Matthews replied that he had laid the petition before the Queen without being able to advise Her Majesty that a reward would promote the cause of justice. Despite the negative response, he assured the Committee that 'no effort or expense should be spared in endeavouring to discover the person guilty of the murders'.[18]

Perhaps as a result of press reporting about his correspondence with the Palace, on the afternoon of Thursday 4 October, a strange visitor called at Lusk's home, and, on being informed that Lusk was at a local pub, followed him there. Described as 'a man, apparently from thirty to forty years of age, 5 foot 9 in. in height, florid complexion, with bushy, brown beard, whiskers and moustache … after asking all sorts of questions relative to the beats taken by members of the committee [he] attempted to induce Mr Lusk to enter a private room with him'.[19]

If the stranger is considered a Ripper suspect, that description generates a problem that Doctor Watson might have called 'The Case of the Vanishing Beard'. With only a moustache on the night of the double event, the Ripper cannot have grown a bushy beard between 30 September and 6 October. It is more likely that Lusk's visitor was a journalist, a detective or even a burglar.

On Tuesday 11 October, at three o'clock in the afternoon, Lusk received a small package containing a letter that became known as the 'From Hell' letter, and a chunk of offal. Written in scrawled handwriting with red ink, and blotted with the obligatory red smears, the letter looks and reads convincingly as a communication from a serial killer:

> From hell
>
> Mr Lusk
> Sor
> I send you half the Kidne I took from one woman prasarved it for you tother piece I fried and ate it was very nise I may send you the bloody knif that took it out if you only wate a whil longer
> signed
> Catch me when you can
> Mishter Lusk[20]

Convinced that this was a practical joke, Lusk took the letter and parcel to the Vigilance Committee meeting that was scheduled on the following day. Committee members convinced him to take it to Doctor Frederick Wiles at 56 Mile End Road. In his absence, the doctor's assistant Mr F. S. Reed identified the 'meaty substance that gave off a very offensive odour' as 'half of a human kidney, which had been divided longitudinally'.[21] It had been preserved in spirits of wine. Reed recommended taking the kidney to Doctor Thomas Horrocks Openshaw at Whitechapel's London Hospital.

Doctor Openshaw examined it with a microscope and concluded that it was part of the left kidney of an adult human. Given Eddowes' missing left kidney, the gruesome item, along with its accompanying letter and wrappings, was taken to Inspector Abberline at Leman Street police station. Abberline informed the City of London Police, who were leading the Eddowes investigation.[22] The parcel was probably a prank, with the organ part supplied by medical students to the anonymous letter-writer. However, in his memoir, acting City Police Chief Major Henry Smith noted that Eddowes' remaining kidney 'was in an advanced stage of Bright's disease [chronic nephritis]; the kidney [part] sent me was in an exactly similar state … [It] had been put in spirits within a few hours of its removal from the body – thus effectually disposing of all hoaxes in connection with it.'[23]

The day before Lusk received the package, a Miss Emily Marsh had an unsettling visitor at her father's leather shop at 218 Jubilee Street, off Mile End Road. A man described as 'a stranger, dressed in clerical costume, entered, and, referring to the reward bill in the window, asked for the address of Mr Lusk, described therein as the president of the Vigilance Committee'.[24] After some discussion, Marsh found Lusk's address, without its house number, in a newspaper. As the package received by Lusk had no house number on it, the press deduced that the stranger was its sender.[25]

However, his description entirely rules him out as either Lusk's earlier visitor or the Ripper, whom eyewitnesses assessed as a man in his mid-thirties and of middling height:

> … a man of some 45 years of age, fully six feet in height, and slimly built. He wore a soft felt black hat, drawn over his forehead, a stand-up collar, and a very long black single-breasted overcoat, with a Prussian or clerical collar partly turned up. His face was of a sallow type, and he had a dark beard and moustache. The man spoke with what was taken to be an Irish accent.[26]

The unknown man might have been the hoaxer or someone with information – real or imagined – who was tempted by an increase in the reward money, which then totalled £1,200,[27] a sum worth over

£100,000 today. This incident is fascinating for its coincidence of place and timing, occurring at 218 Jubilee Street off Mile End Road, on a date at which Hyams might have been living at No. 217.[28] The shop run by the Marshes was directly opposite his house.

It is not possible to time with precision Hyams' move from Wentworth Court to Jubilee Street. Wentworth Court was a location that offered close access to and from the scenes of the canonical five murders. It could be the case that, in late autumn 1888, when her husband's physical and mental illnesses became acute, Sarah Hyams chose to move the family closer to her brother George Davis, who ran a shop at 82 Mile End Road.

In mid-November, the newspapers started to leak what they called 'authentic descriptions', quoting information 'secretly circulated by the authorities of Scotland Yard since October 26'.[29] The first two of the following descriptions are of a man, or men, seen with Elisabeth Stride at Berner Street. The third, originating from the City of London Police, provides details of a man seen with Kate Eddowes in Church Passage. None of the descriptions suggest that the man was a named individual who was already known to the police.

> At 12.35 a.m., 30th September, with Elizabeth [*sic*] Stride, found murdered at one a.m., same date, in Berner-street – A man, aged 28; height, 5ft. 8 in.; complexion dark, small dark moustache; dress, black diagonial [*sic*] coat, hard felt hat, collar and tie; respectable appearance; carried a parcel wrapped up in a newspaper.
>
> At 12.45 a.m., 30th, with same woman, in Berner-street, a man, age about 30, height 5ft. 5in., complexion fair, dark hair, small brown moustache, full face, broad shoulders; dress, dark jacket and trousers, black cap with peak.
>
> Information to be forwarded to the Metropolitan Police Office, Great Scotland-yard, London, S.W.
>
> At 1.35 a.m., 30th Sept., with Catherine Eddows [*sic*], in Church-passage, leading to Mitre-square, where she was found

> murdered at 1.45 a.m. same date, a man, age 30, height 5ft. 7 or 8 in. complexion fair, moustache fair, medium build; dress, pepper-and-salt colour loose jacket, grey cloth cap, with peak of the same material, reddish neckerchief tied in knot; appearance of a sailor.
>
> Information respecting this man to be forwarded to Inspector M'William [*sic*], 26, Old Jewry, London, E.C.[30]

It is clear that, in the case of Elisabeth Stride's murder, the police were relying on descriptions given by Constable William Smith and Israel Schwartz. The main variances between the two were the newspaper parcel seen by Smith but not by Schwartz, and Smith's description of a man with a 'dark complexion', whereas Schwartz considered him to be fair-skinned. It is a matter of speculation whether a non-Jew and a Jew would have different perceptions of skin tone.

The description of the man in Church Passage must have been provided by Joseph Lawende, the only man of the three who passed him to look in his face. The man's salt-and-pepper jacket, and his fair moustache, do not tally exactly with the earlier descriptions of the man in Berner Street. It is possible that the killer left his coat at a location en route from Dutfield's Yard to Mitre Square, in the half-hour gap between 1 and 1.32 a.m. Even if it took him twelve minutes to walk between the two sites, he could have had a spare twenty minutes to visit his home, a relative's home, or a late-opening bar. It is also possible that the coat is a red herring, wrongly described either by Lawende or the earlier eyewitnesses.

In an undated document, Swanson drew up a table he entitled 'Comparison of the descriptions given of the men who were observed near the scene at the time of the several murders'.[31] As it covers the three murders of Annie Chapman, Elisabeth Stride and Kate Eddowes, one might assume that it pre-dates that of Mary Jane Kelly. There were no sightings of suspects at the scene of Polly Nichols' murder. Swanson compared the physical attributes and clothing of the men as follows:

Murder of					
	Annie Chapman	Elizabeth [*sic*] Stride			Eddowes
	Description of man seen by Mrs. Long at 5.30	[The word 'First' partially removed] man seen at 12.35 by Police Constable	First man seen by Schwartz with woman at 12.45.	Man seen on the opposite side of the street by Schwartz.	Man seen with woman at 1.35.
Age.	40.	28.	30.	35.	30.
Height.		5 ft. 7 inc.	5 ft. 5 inc.	5 ft. 11 inc.	5 ft. 7 or 8 inc.
Complexion.		dark	fair	fresh	
Hair.			dark	light brown	
Moustache.		small dark.	small brown	brown	fair
Face.			full		
Figure.			broad shouldered		medium build
Coat.	qy. [query] dark	black diagonal [meaning a type of twilled fabric]	dark jacket	dark with overcoat.	pepper and salt color [*sic*]; loose jacket
Trousers.			dark		
Hat.		Hard felt.	black cap with peak	Old black hat; hard felt; wide brim.	Grey cloth cap with peak of same color [*sic*].
Collar.		White collar and tie.			

The inconsistencies between the five descriptions are frustrating. All of those descriptions, except that of the 'second' man with a pipe seen by Schwartz on the opposite side of the street, are probably of

Jack the Ripper, and he might have been wearing the same clothes continuously on the night of the double event. Briefly in the wrong place at the wrong time, the 'Pipeman' was not involved in the murder of Stride. If he had come forward to police, he could have provided a description of the man who shouted 'Lipski!' at him, hit Stride, and probably killed her.

Gaps in the official record make it impossible to deduce for whom the police were looking, and what their precise methods were. Both the Metropolitan and City Police put large numbers of men on plain-clothes patrol to watch for the next likely victim frequenting local pubs and walking the streets, in the hope of catching the Ripper as he attacked. Both Forces shared an interest in the prime witness to Eddowes' murder, Joseph Lawende.

The three men who emerged from the Imperial Club on the City's eastern edge, minutes before Kate Eddowes' murder, were part of the tightly knit Ashkenazi Jewish community. Joseph Lawende, an illiterate travelling salesman, was the only recent immigrant among them. Born in Warsaw, he probably emigrated to London in his twenties, before his marriage in January 1873 to Annie Lowenthal, in the City. A cigarette maker by trade, it is not beyond the bounds of possibility that he knew Hyam Hyams.

On 11 December 1876, Lawende had given evidence at a trial of a fellow Jew for murder. On a back street off the thoroughfare of Newington Butts in Walworth, Isaac Marks shot Frederick Barnard three times in the back with a revolver. The two men had history: Barnard's sister had sued Marks for £50 in a case of breach of promise of marriage, and Barnard had claimed that Marks had deliberately set fire to his own shop as part of a fraudulent insurance claim. After shooting Barnard, Marks dropped his revolver, walked to the nearby Kennington Lane police station and gave himself up. He twice came before the Magistrate at Lambeth police court, by his own choice unrepresented by Counsel. He told the court: 'I am like a sheep tied up ready for the slaughter.'[32]

At the Old Bailey, before the eminent Judge Baron Pollock, Lawende testified in Marks's defence:

> I am a cigarette maker, and live at 3, Lenton Street, Goodman's Fields. I have known the prisoner some twelve months as one of the persons frequenting the Camperdown Hotel – I dine there on Sundays – during the time I have known him I have observed that he has been strange in his manner – I never spoke to him in the street – I have played dominoes with him, and in the middle of the game he threw away his bones, and stood up and went out without any reason, and walked out of the house – he used to sit for an hour together with his head in his hands and an empty pipe in his mouth, thinking to himself; he did not move – I have spoken to him many times, and he did not give me any answer.[33]

Other defence witnesses testified that Marks, who was unkindly nicknamed 'Mad Marks' and 'Breach of promise', was 'very strange in his manner … violent, nasty-tempered …', and had tried to stab another man; also, that his parents and brother had suffered from madness.[34]

Unusually, the defence barrister did not call any medical evidence on behalf of the defendant. It was for the jury to decide whether, at the time he committed the murder, he was sane or insane. Prison surgeon John Rowland Gibson had made a two-hour examination of Marks at Newgate Gaol. He stated: 'I could detect no delusions leading up to the commission of the act.' When cross-examined, he said: 'The boundaries of sanity and insanity are very ill-defined – it is a most difficult task to express a scientific opinion as to the state of a man's brain.'[35]

The jury found Marks guilty, as they 'believed him to be of sound mind at the time the act was committed'. He was sentenced to death.[36] If found insane, Marks would have been sent to Broadmoor Criminal Lunatic Asylum 'at Her Majesty's Pleasure', instead of the gallows.

The Jewish community petitioned the Home Secretary for a commutation of Marks's death sentence, while raising over £1,000 for the maintenance of his children. The Home Secretary's response was that 'he was unable to discover any facts that would justify him in recommending the prisoner to the clemency of the Crown'.[37] On the date that was originally set, Marks was hanged by the expert of the day, executioner William Marwood. Marwood developed the technique known as the 'long drop', designed to break the prisoner's neck instantly at the end of the drop. In Marks's case, the 'long drop' was not effective, and he 'died hard', suffering a slow, painful death by strangulation.

The significance of the Marks case is that members of the East End Jewish community came forward, not to defend him, but to testify that he was known to be mentally ill. Their aim was to save him from the death sentence. Not only was their testimony in court unheeded; their post-verdict petition was rejected, and Marks died a slow and horrifying death. This caused widespread shock and regret, and a fresh distrust of the English authorities. Any reluctance to appear in a case that might attract the death sentence must surely be understandable. As a result, Joseph Lawende was willing to testify in a coroner's court investigating Eddowes' cause of death, but not in a murder trial.

When Lawende applied for a Certificate of British Naturalization in early 1889, the Home Office referred his application to the Metropolitan Police CID. Although a customized form existed for that eventuality, not every applicant can have been investigated in such detail. Something triggered the Home Office to instigate an additional check. The completed form stated that the applicant 'is a very respectable man, and is spoken well of by his sureties, who consider him worthy of the certificate he asks for'.[38] Lawende's naturalization was duly granted.

His two fellow eyewitnesses on Duke Street arguably had a connection to Hyam Hyams beyond their Jewish faith, reinforcing any reluctance on their part to testify against him. In fact, Harry Harris did not testify at the inquest into Eddowes' death. His wife Rebecca Benjamin[39] and her family must have known the Davis family, into which Hyams married. In 1861, both families, headed by Angel Benjamin and Henry Davis, lived on neighbouring streets in Aldgate between Harrow Alley and Stoney Lane, which were separated by a narrow alleyway. The Benjamins were at 10 Petticoat Square,[40] while the Davis family lived at 8 Ebenezer Square.[41] They overlapped at those addresses for at least ten years.[42] By coincidence, in 1884 those streets were demolished to make way for the construction of the Artizans' Dwellings,[43] where Hyams' brother Mark and his family later lived.

A connection between Hyam Hyams and the other eyewitness, Joseph Hyam Levy, is also geographical. Levy's wife Amelia Lewis[44] was raised at 21 Mitre Street, which backed on to the Ripper murder location of Mitre Square. Hyams' first cousin Lewis Mordecai was married to Amelia Emanuel,[45] whose family also lived on a road off Mitre Square, at 8 St James's Place, the Orange Market. Both families not only lived in neighbouring streets, but occupied shop premises. They overlapped at those addresses for several decades.[46] Both were fruiterers by trade, as were Hyam Hyams' parents Isaac and Rebecca. The associations between their extended families link Joseph Hyam Levy to Hyam Hyams.

In the early hours of Monday 1 October, approximately twenty-four hours after the double event, a bloodied knife was discovered in a shop doorway on Whitechapel Road. If any connection could be made, the perpetrator's discarding of the knife is an action similar to the dropping of the corner of Eddowes' apron. Its specific location is of potential interest to the case against Hyam Hyams.

The knife was found by Thomas Coram, a 'Cocoa-nut opener' who lived at 67 Plummer's Row, Mile End. With youthful good looks, brilliantined hair and a fashionable quiff, Coram appeared as a witness at the inquest into Elisabeth Stride's murder.

He stated that, at about 12.30 a.m. in the early hours of Monday

1 October, he was returning home from visiting a friend at 16 Bath-gardens, Brady-street, north of Whitechapel Road:

> **Coram:** I was walking [westwards] on the right hand side of the Whitechapel-road towards Aldgate. When opposite No. 253 I crossed over, and saw a knife lying on the doorstep. No. 252 was a laundry business, and there were two steps leading to the front door. I found the knife on the bottom step.
>
> That is the knife I found (witness being shown a long-bladed knife). The handkerchief produced was wrapped round the handle. It was folded, and then twisted round the handle. The handkerchief was blood-stained. I did not touch them. A policeman came towards me, and I called his attention to them.
>
> **The Coroner:** The blade of the knife is dagger-shaped and is sharpened on one side. The blade is about 9 in. or 10 in. long, I should say.
>
> **Coram:** The policeman took the knife to the Leman-street Police-station, and I went with him.
>
> **The Coroner:** Were there many people passing at the time?
>
> **Coram:** I should think I passed about a dozen between Brady-street and where I found the knife.
>
> **The Coroner:** Could it easily be seen?
>
> **Coram:** Yes; and it was light [meaning well lit].
>
> **The Coroner:** Did you pass a policeman before you got to the spot?
>
> **Coram:** Yes, I passed three. It was about half-past 12 at night.[47]

Constable Joseph Drage was called to the stand to continue the narrative.

> **Drage:** At 12.30 on Monday morning I was on fixed-point duty in the Whitechapel-road, opposite Great Garden-street. I saw the last witness stooping down at a doorway opposite No. 253. I was going

> towards him when he rose up and beckoned me with his finger. He then said, 'Policeman, there is a knife down here.' I turned on my light [lantern] and saw a long-bladed knife lying on the doorstep. I picked up the knife and found it was smothered with blood. The blood was dry. There was a handkerchief bound round the handle and tied with string. The handkerchief also had blood-stains on it.
>
> I asked the last witness how he came to see it. He said, 'I was looking down, when I saw something white.' I then asked him what he did out so late, and he replied, 'I have been to a friend's in Bath-gardens.' He then gave me his name and address, and we went to the police-station together. The knife and handkerchief produced are the same.
>
> **The Coroner:** Was the last witness sober?
>
> **Drage:** Yes. His manner was natural, and he said when he saw the knife it made his blood run cold, and added that nowadays they heard of such funny things. When I passed I should undoubtedly have seen the knife. I was passing there continually. Some little time before a horse fell down opposite the place where the knife was found. I assisted in getting the horse up, and during that time a person might have laid the knife down on the step. I would not be positive that the knife was not there a quarter of an hour previously, but I think not …[48]

Reporters who saw the weapon produced in court described it as 'like a carving knife … with a long narrow blade and black bone handle', exactly as depicted in drawings in the press.[49]

Two days later, Doctor Phillips was recalled to testify further, and was asked his opinion of that knife as a possible murder weapon. He expressed doubts about its effectiveness, as it was only sharp on its bottom edge, its upper spine not being used for cutting.

> **Dr Phillips:** On examination I found it to be such a knife as would be used in a chandler's shop, called a slicing knife. It had

> blood upon it, which was similar to that of a warm-blooded being. It has been recently blunted and the edge turned by apparently rubbing on a stone. It evidently was before that a very sharp knife.
>
> Such a knife could have produced the incision and injuries to the neck of the deceased, but it was not such a weapon as I would have chosen to inflict injuries in this particular place; and if my opinion as regards the position of the body is correct, the knife in question would become an improbable instrument as having caused the incision …
>
> I have come to the conclusion that the deceased was seized by the shoulders, placed on the ground, and that the perpetrator of the deed was on her right side when he inflicted the cut. I am of opinion that the cut was made from the left to the right side of the deceased, and therefore arises the unlikelihood of such a long knife having inflicted the wound described in the neck, taking into account the position of the incision …
>
> **The Coroner:** Was there anything in the cut that showed the incision first made was done with a pointed knife?
>
> **Dr Phillips:** No.[50]

Doctor Blackwell, who was also recalled, agreed that 'although it might have possibly inflicted the injury it was extremely unlikely that such an instrument was used. The murderer using a sharp, round-pointed instrument would severely handicap himself, as he could only use it one way.' A juryman spoke up to say that slaughterers always used round-pointed instruments, causing Wynne Baxter to ask: 'Is it your suggestion that this was done by a slaughterer?' Doctor Blackwell replied in the negative.[51]

Newspaper articles consistently reported the knife's total length, including the handle, as 12 inches. That is consistent with Thomas Eade's testimony about the man seen after Annie Chapman's murder, with the blade of a knife 'sticking out about four inches' from his trousers.[52]

The place where the knife was discovered was close to premises used by two of Hyam Hyams' uncles. The shops at 252 and 253 Whitechapel Road were located on the same block as Abraham Mordecai's cigar factory at No. 230, which was itself separated by only a few shopfronts, and across New Road, from Joseph Mordecai's second-hand clothes shop at No. 210. The doorstep in question was on Hyams' regular route along the south side of Whitechapel Road when visiting the family businesses, ten minutes' walk from his home. He might have been alarmed by the police presence and dropped the knife while Drage's attention was on the spooked horse. Despite the reservations expressed by the two police surgeons, it is possible that the Metropolitan Police unwittingly took possession of the murder weapon.

9

THE MURDER OF MARY JANE KELLY

The murder of Mary Jane Kelly on Friday 9 November 1888 between 2 and 10.45 a.m. at 13 Miller's Court, Dorset Street.

Fresh-faced and blue-eyed, with brown hair reaching nearly to her waist, twenty-four-year-old Mary Jane Kelly was the youngest and last of The Five. A delight to the eye, she was also a songbird, and was heard singing in her room shortly before she died. Walter Dew knew Mary Jane Kelly by sight from the streets near Commercial Street police station, recollecting, 'She was usually in the company of two or three of her kind, fairly neatly dressed and invariably wearing a clean white apron, but no hat.'[1]

Those who knew her well traced her background to Ireland, then Wales, where her husband, only referred to as Davies, had been killed in a coal mining accident. After a stint in Cardiff, she embarked on a career as a prostitute in London, not on the streets, but in West End bawdy houses, with even a foray to France. Kelly left that lifestyle after starting a relationship with market porter Joe Barnett, and moved into lodgings at 13 Miller's Court in Dorset Street.

Her landlord was John McCarthy, 'an Irishman, a bully [pimp], a tough guy … [who] owned all the furnished rooms down there'.[2] Among McCarthy's properties were numbers 26 and 27 on the north side of Dorset Street, where he lived with his family. Miller's Court, a courtyard lined with ramshackle housing, was accessed from a passage running between the two houses. The passage was unlit, and doors led off each side of it. The door on the left opened on to a back room behind McCarthy's chandler's, or grocer's, shop, and two doors on the right to 13 and 20 Miller's Court, effectively a back extension of 26 Dorset Street. It was a one-up, one-down in which Kelly lived downstairs at No. 13, and another 'unfortunate' called Elizabeth Prater upstairs at No. 20. The front of the house, called 'the shed', was used as a storeroom.

Eight days before Kelly's murder, Barnett had an argument with her and moved out. Vitally for her killer, this left Kelly alone in premises that suited his purpose; a private double bedroom off a secluded courtyard, where he would not be disturbed. Less than six weeks after the double event, and on the eve of the Lord Mayor's Parade, Kelly was blind to the risk of meeting a punter outside a pub and taking him home with her for paid casual sex. She was the only one of the Ripper's victims to be killed in her own bed, in a brutal act demonstrating the deterioration of his mental state. An eyewitness description of a man seen accompanying Kelly home links her killer to the murders of Annie Chapman, Elisabeth Stride and Kate Eddowes.

On the night of Thursday 8 November, Kelly was motivated to line up as many clients as possible. Her rent of four shillings and sixpence a week was due the next day, and she already owed her landlord nearly thirty shillings.[3] Not all of her comings and goings from 13 Miller's Court on the eve of her death were observed. She was seen hatless and wearing what was variously described as a red cape or maroon shawl, a velvet bodice, and a shabby dark skirt. Two separate eyewitnesses saw her bring a different man home with her, one at 11.45 p.m. and the other after 2 a.m.

At a quarter to eleven on the morning of Friday 9 November, John McCarthy sent his 'man' Thomas Bowyer next door to collect Kelly's rent. Bowyer had the nickname 'Indian Harry' from his past foreign military service. Like McCarthy, he was a sturdy man who would take no nonsense. He knocked twice at the door of No. 13 and received no answer. He went around the corner and saw the window had two broken panes. As Kelly might be inside ignoring his knock, he reached through a chink and pulled the curtain aside to look in.

Despite being an old soldier, and a Dorset Street resident familiar with acts of violence and criminality, he was shocked by the sight of

> two lumps of flesh laying on the table … in front of the bed. The second time I looked I saw a body of some one laid on the bed, and blood on the floor. I at once went then very quietly back to my master … and I told him what I had seen … I and my master went and looked in the window. Then we went to the [Commercial Street] police station and told the police what we had seen.[4]

Police took statements on Friday 9th, working at speed to allow the inquest to be held on Monday 12th. Inspector Abberline and his colleagues in CID and H Division were not the only officials to work over that weekend. On the Saturday, Sir Charles Warren offered a pardon 'to any accomplice, not being a person who contrived or actually committed the Murder, who shall give such information and evidence as shall lead to the discovery and conviction of the person or persons who committed the Murder'.[5]

The inquest into Mary Jane Kelly's death was officiated by Doctor Roderick Macdonald, coroner for North-East Middlesex, at Shoreditch Town Hall. Originating from the Isle of Skye in Scotland's Inner Hebrides, Macdonald was also the Member of Parliament for Ross-shire and police surgeon for K (West Ham) Division. His approach was in direct contradiction to Wynne Baxter's slow, methodical process, taking down everything for the record. His role was solely to determine the cause of death, and to leave the police to deal with the case.

Superintendent Arnold and Inspectors Abberline, Reid and Chandler represented the Metropolitan Police. Unusually, proceedings started with dissatisfied queries from jurors about why, when they were summoned for Shoreditch, they were sitting on a murder that took place in Whitechapel. The coroner for Whitechapel was Wynne Baxter, who had conducted the inquests on Polly Nichols, Annie Chapman and Elisabeth Stride. Macdonald dispatched their complaints with a terse rejoinder: 'Jurisdiction lies where the body lies, not where it was found.'[6] The Commercial Street police officers had taken Kelly's body to their nearest mortuary north of the station at St Leonard's Church, in Macdonald's district. The jury viewed the body at the small brick mortuary in the church grounds, and then visited the murder site, before hearing evidence.

An eyewitness account of the jury visits was published by a journalist. Of Kelly's body, he noted that only her 'scored and slashed' face was visible. He gave a more graphic description of the crime scene at Miller's Court:

> The entrance to the court was held by a couple of policemen, and it was so narrow that we could only pass up in single file. It was only about three yards long, and then we were at the door which is numbered 13. The two windows which look into the little court were boarded up, and had apparently been newly whitewashed. From the windows above a girl looked down upon us quite composedly, and several pots of beer were brought in during our stay to comfort the denizens of the court.
>
> At last the key was procured, and the room was surveyed in batches. The inspector, holding a candle stuck in a bottle, stood at the head of the filthy, bloodstained bed, and repeated the horrible details with appalling minuteness. The little table was still on the left of the bedstead, which occupied the larger portion of the room. A farthing dip [candle] in a bottle did not serve to illuminate the fearful gloom, but I was able to see what a wretched hole the poor murdered woman called 'home'. The only attempts at decoration were a couple of engravings, one, 'The Fisherman's Widow', stuck over the mantelpiece, while in the

corner was an open cupboard, containing a few bits of pottery, some ginger beer bottles, and a bit of bread on a plate …

In twenty minutes the jury filed out again and marched back … to the Town Hall …[7]

The first witness at the inquest was Kelly's former partner Joseph (or Joe) Barnett, aged thirty, a former fish porter at Billingsgate market. Slim and serious-looking, he had the horrendous task of identifying Kelly's mutilated body, and was the main source of information about her past:

Barnett: I have seen the body, and I identify it by the ear and eyes, which are all that I can recognise, but I am positive it is the same woman I knew …

I separated from her on October 30th … because she had a woman of bad character [staying at Miller's Court], whom she took in out of compassion, and I objected to it …

I last saw her alive between half-past seven and a quarter to eight on Thursday night last, when I called upon her. I stayed there for a quarter of an hour … when we parted I told her I had no work, and had nothing to give her, for which I was very sorry … She was quite sober …

[I picked up with her first] in Commercial-street. We then had a drink together, and I made arrangements to see her on the following day – a Saturday. On that day we both of us agreed that we should remain together. I took lodgings in George-street, Commercial-street, where I was known. I lived with her, until I left her, on very friendly terms.

Coroner: Have you heard her speak of being afraid of anyone?

Barnett: Yes, several times. I bought newspapers, and read her everything about the murders, which she asked me about. [Suggesting that Kelly was illiterate.]

Coroner: Did she express fear of any particular individual?

Barnett: No, sir. Our own quarrels were very soon over.[8]

To assist the police in fully identifying Kelly, and possibly locating her family, Barnett repeated what she had told him about her past:

> She said she was born in Limerick ... & from there went to Wales when very young ... she came to London about 4 years ago. Her father's name was John Kelly, he was a Gauger [inspector; alternatively reported as a 'gaffer' or foreman] at some iron works in Carnarvonshire. She told me she had one sister ... [and] 6 brothers at home and one in the army, one was Henry Kelly ...
>
> She told me she had been married when very young in Wales. She was married to a Collier, she told me the name was Davis or Davies ... She told me she was lawfully married to him until he died in an explosion ... she was married at the age of 16 years ...[9]

Once widowed, according to Barnett, Kelly started to follow 'a bad life' under the influence of a cousin who 'was the cause of her downfall'. She was in a Cardiff infirmary for eight or nine months before moving to 'a gay house', meaning a brothel, in the West End. She was persuaded to spend a couple of weeks in France, but returned because she did not like it. After a stint at 'a bad house' near the London Docks, she lived with a man named Morganstone opposite the Commercial Gas Works in Stepney. She lodged with another man, a mason's plasterer named Joseph Fleming, in Bethnal Green Road, before starting a relationship with Barnett. The coroner thanked Barnett for his evidence, reassuring him that he had given it 'very well indeed'.[10] Despite the efforts of the authorities, none of Kelly's family came forward, not even to attend her funeral. Her identity has never been proved conclusively.

Thomas Bowyer was the next witness, who described viewing the body from the side window with reference to a plan of the room put in by Inspector Charles Ledger. He had last seen Kelly alive on the Wednesday afternoon before her murder. Bowyer was followed by

John McCarthy, who despite his tough exterior reported that on first seeing the body, he 'could say nothing for a little time'.[11] He confirmed that she was twenty-nine shillings in arrears and added: 'I very often saw deceased worse for drink she was a very quiet woman when sober but noisy when in drink she was not ever helpless when drunk.'[12]

Mary Ann Cox, a streetwalker aged thirty-one, was the first occupant of Miller's Court to testify. Her downstairs room at No. 5 occupied the last house on the left-hand side of the courtyard. It was the furthest from No. 13, explaining why she heard nothing on the night of Mary Jane Kelly's murder. Her statement is significant, however, in terms of what she saw as she left and returned to the courtyard three times that night, passing No. 13, which guarded its entrance: 'I last saw her alive on Thursday night, at a quarter to twelve, very much intoxicated … in Dorset-street. She went up the court, a few steps in front of me … [with] a short, stout man, shabbily dressed. He had on a longish coat, very shabby, and carried a pot of ale in his hand.'[13]

Cox further described the man as wearing a dark coat, a round hard billycock hat, and having a blotchy face and full carroty, or orange-red, moustache. His chin was shaven and she saw him by the light of the lamp that faced the door. She saw them turn right into No. 13.

> **Cox:** I said 'Good night, Mary,' and she turned round and banged the door … She said, 'Good night, I am going to have a song.' As I went in she sang 'A violet I plucked from my mother's grave when a boy.' I remained a quarter of an hour in my room and went out.
>
> Deceased was still singing at one o'clock when I returned. I remained in the room for a minute to warm my hands, as it was raining, and went out again. She was singing still, and I returned to my room at three o'clock. The light was then out, and there was no noise …
>
> I was upset. I did not undress at all. I did not sleep at all. I must have heard what went on the court. I heard no noise or cry of 'Murder!' but men went out to work in the market.

Coroner: How many men live in the court who work in Spitalfields market?
Cox: One. At a quarter-past six I heard a man go down the court. That was too late for the market...
Coroner: What would you take the stout man's age to be?
Cox: Six-and-thirty.
Coroner: Did you notice the colour of his trousers?
Cox: All his clothes were dark ...
Coroner: What clothes had Mary Jane on?
Cox: She had no hat; a red pelerine [cropped cape] and a shabby skirt.
Coroner: You say she was drunk?
Cox: I did not notice she was drunk until she said good night. The man closed the door ... There was a light in the window, but I saw nothing, as the blinds were down. I should know the man again, if I saw him ... I feel certain that if there had been the cry of 'Murder!' in the place I should have heard it; there was not the least noise. I have often seen the woman the worse for drink.[14]

Mary Ann Cox's man in a billycock hat would metaphorically go head to head with a statement to the police by an acquaintance of Kelly's, who claimed to have seen her returning to Miller's Court from Dorset Street, after 2 a.m., with a different man.

The next witness was twenty-eight-year-old Elizabeth Prater, a garrulous young woman,[15] who lived alone in Room 20, the room above Kelly's, accessed by a staircase from the court's main passageway. The door to that staircase was approximately four feet to the right of the door to Kelly's room.

Prater testified to hearing a voice from the room below in the early hours:

Prater: I left the room on the Thursday at five p.m., and returned to it about one a.m. on Friday morning. I stood at the corner [of the entrance to the court] until about twenty minutes past one. No one spoke to me.

McCarthy's shop was open, and I called in, and then went to my room. I should have seen a glimmer of light in going up the stairs if there had been a light in deceased's room, but I noticed none. The partition was so thin I could have heard Kelly walk about in the room. I went to bed at half-past one, and barricaded the door with two tables. I fell asleep directly, and slept soundly. A kitten disturbed me about half-past three or a quarter to four. As I was turning round I heard a suppressed cry of 'Oh – murder!' in a faint voice. It seemed to proceed from the court.

Coroner: Do you often hear cries of 'Murder'?

Prater: It is nothing unusual in the street. I did not take particular notice.[16]

Whether or not the coroner's question had a barbed edge, implying that Prater should have paid more attention to a cry of murder, it is accurate to say that Prater's room was within earshot of at least two common lodging houses that had people coming and going at all hours.

Coroner: Did you hear it a second time?

Prater: No.

Coroner: Did you hear beds or tables being pulled about?

Prater: None whatever. I went asleep, and was awake again at five a.m. I passed down the stairs, and saw some men harnessing horses. At a quarter to six I was in the Ten Bells [pub].

Coroner: Could the witness, Mary Ann Cox, have come down the entry between one and half-past one without your knowledge?

Prater: Yes, she could have done so.

Coroner: Did you see any strangers at the Ten Bells?

Prater: No. I went back to bed and slept until eleven.

Coroner: You heard no singing downstairs?

Prater: None whatever. I should have heard the singing distinctly.

> It was quite quiet at half-past one o'clock.[17]

Elizabeth Prater's disregard of her housemate's cry might not have cost Kelly her life, but could have cost the police an opportunity to catch her killer. Prater must have been a deep sleeper. Despite her room being located directly above Kelly's, she heard only a faint cry in the early hours, and did not perceive any signs of what Inspector Abberline reported as a large fire burning in the fireplace beneath her own, its traces visible to police on their entry. Prater remained unaware of its heat, excessive smoke and the acrid smell of burning from the melting spout of the kettle.[18]

Sarah Lewis, a laundress in her mid-thirties residing at 24 Great Pearl-street, Spitalfields, testified that, on the night in question, she stayed with her friend Mrs Keyler at No. 2, Miller's Court. An upstairs room, No. 2 was on the opposite side of the courtyard to Nos 13 and 20.

> **Lewis:** [I] went to her [Mrs Keyler's] house at 2, Miller's-court, at 2.30 a.m. on Friday. It is the first house. I noticed the time by Spitalfields' Church clock. When I went into the court … I saw a man with a wideawake [a hat with a low crown and very wide brim]. There was no one talking to him. He was a stout-looking man, and not very tall. The hat was black. I did not take any notice of his clothes. The man was looking up the court; he seemed to be waiting or looking for some one.
>
> Further on [in Dorset Street] there was a man and woman – the latter being in drink. There was nobody in the court. I dozed in a chair at Mrs Keyler's, and woke at about half-past three. I heard the clock strike.
>
> **Coroner:** What woke you up?
>
> **Lewis:** I could not sleep. I sat awake until nearly four, when I heard a female's voice shouting 'Murder' loudly. It seemed like the voice of a young woman. It sounded at our door. There was only one scream … I took no notice, as I only heard the one scream …

> [I stayed until] half-past five p.m. on Friday. The police would not let us out of the court.[19]

Her testimony confirms that of Prater, of one scream at around 4 a.m., and appears to fix the time of the murder. Another item of interest is her possible sighting, close to the time of the murder, of a lone man who might be George Hutchinson. Hutchinson later made a statement to police that he waited outside the entrance to Miller's Court as Mary Jane Kelly hosted a male visitor.

At the advice of the coroner, Doctor Phillips testified in brief about the layout of the crime scene and cause of death, without describing the mutilation of the body:

> I was called by the police on Friday morning at eleven o'clock, and on proceeding to Miller's-court, which I entered at a quarter past eleven, I found a room the door of which led out of the passage at the side of 26, Dorset-street, photographs of which I produce. It had two windows in the court. Two panes in the lesser window were broken, and, as the door was locked, I looked through the lower of the broken panes and satisfied myself that the mutilated corpse lying on the bed was not in need of any immediate attention from me, and I also came to the conclusion that there was nobody else upon the bed, or within view, to whom I could render any professional assistance.
>
> Having ascertained that probably it was advisable that no entrance should be made into the room at that time, I remained until about 1.30 p.m., when the door was broken open by M'Carthy [*sic*], under the direction of Superintendent Arnold. On the door being opened, it knocked against a table which was close to the left-hand side of the bedstead, and the bedstead was close against the wooden partition.
>
> The mutilated remains of a woman were lying two-thirds over, towards the edge of the bedstead, nearest the door.

> Deceased had only an under-linen garment [a chemise, or thin smock] upon her, and by subsequent examination, I am sure the body had been removed, after the injury which caused death, from that side of the bedstead which was nearest to the wooden partition previously mentioned.
>
> The large quantity of blood under the bedstead, the saturated condition of the palliasse [mattress], pillow, and sheet at the top corner of the bedstead nearest to the partition leads me to the conclusion that the severance of the right carotid artery [in the neck], which was the immediate cause of death, was inflicted while the deceased was lying at the right side of the bedstead and her head and neck in the top right-hand corner.[20]

After a brief adjournment, Julia Venturney at No. 1 Miller's Court was called as a witness. Like No. 2, it was directly opposite Nos 13 and 20. Despite claiming that she went to bed about 8 p.m., and 'could not rest at all during the night', she did not see nor hear anything, neither singing nor screams. She commented: 'Deceased often got drunk.'[21]

Venturney was followed on the stand by Kelly's friend Maria Harvey, the woman of ill-repute complained of by Joe Barnett. Harvey had spent the whole of the Thursday afternoon with Kelly, and had slept at her room on the Monday and Tuesday nights. She had left several items of clothing there, 'two men's dirty shirts, a little boy's shirt, a black overcoat, a black crepe bonnet with black satin strings, a pawn-ticket for a grey shawl … and a little girl's white petticoat'. Kelly had not spoken to her about being afraid of any man.[22]

The final witnesses were two policemen. Inspector Walter Beck from Commercial Street police station 'deposed that, having sent for the doctor, he gave orders to prevent any person leaving the court, and he directed officers to make a search'.[23] Inspector Abberline explained that a fruitless wait for bloodhounds was the reason for the delay in entering No. 13, adding that he agreed with the medical evidence as to the condition of the room, aspects of which he described:

> I subsequently took an inventory of the contents of the room. There were traces of a large fire having been kept up in the grate, so much so that it had melted the spout of a kettle off. We have since gone through the ashes in the fireplace; there were remnants of clothing, a portion of a brim of a hat, and a skirt, and it appeared as if a large quantity of women's clothing had been burnt … I can only imagine that it was to make a light for the man to see what he was doing. There was only one small candle in the room, on the top of a broken wine-glass …
>
> [Joseph] Barnett informed me that [the key] has been missing for some time, and since it being lost they have put their hand through the broken window and moved back the catch. It is quite easy.[24]

The coroner cut short the proceedings by inviting the jury to decide whether they wished to adjourn for further evidence, or whether they could perform their role, to 'come to a decision as to the cause of death'.[25] The jury confirmed that they had 'quite sufficient evidence' and returned the verdict of 'Wilful murder by some person or persons unknown'.[26]

While examining Kelly's body at the scene of the crime, Doctor Phillips had called for two senior fellow surgeons to join him. They were Thomas Bond and the City's Doctor Gordon Brown. Bond carried out the post-mortem examination together with Phillips' assistant Doctor William Profit Dukes. Bond's post-mortem report reads as follows:

> **Position of body.**
> The body was lying naked in the middle of the bed the shoulders flat, but the axis of the body inclined to the left side of the bed. The head was turned on the left cheek. The left arm was close to the body with the forearm flexed at a right angle & lying across the abdomen, the right arm was slightly abducted from the body & rested on the mattress, the elbow bent & the forearm supine with the elbow bent & the forearm supine with the fingers clenched. The

legs were wide apart, the left thigh at right angles to the trunk & the right forming an obtuse angle with the pubes.

The whole of the surface of the abdomen & thighs was removed & the abdominal cavity emptied of its viscera. The breasts were cut off, the arms mutilated by several jagged wounds & the face hacked beyond recognition of the features. The tissues of the neck were severed all round down to the bone.

The viscera were found in various parts viz; the uterus & kidneys with one breast under the head, the other breast by the right foot, the liver between the feet, the intestines by the right side & the spleen by the left side of the body.

The flaps removed from the abdomen and thighs were on a table.

The bed clothing at the right corner was saturated with blood, & on the floor beneath was a pool of blood covering about 2 feet square. The wall by the right side of the bed & in a line with the neck was marked by blood which had struck it in a number of separate splashes.

Postmortem Examination.

The face was gashed in all directions the nose, cheeks, eyebrows & ears being partly removed. The lips were blanched & cut by several oblique incisions running obliquely down to the chin. There were also numerous cuts extending irregularly across all the features.

The neck was cut through the skin & other tissue right down to the vertebrae the 5th & 6th being deeply notched. The skin cuts in the front of the neck showed distinct ecchymosis [discoloration of the skin resulting from bleeding underneath, typically caused by bruising].

The air passage was cut through at the lower part of the larynx through the cricoid cartilage [a ring of cartilage around the trachea or windpipe].

Both breasts were removed by more or less circular incisions,

> the muscles down to the ribs being attached to the breasts. The intercostals between the 4 5 & 6 ribs were cut through & the contents of the thorax visible through the openings.
>
> The skin & tissues of the abdomen from the costal arch [bottom edge of the ribcage] to the pubes were removed in three large flaps. The right thigh was denuded in front to the bone, the flap of skin, including the external organs of generation & part of the right buttock. The left thigh was stripped of skin, fascia & muscles as far as the knee.
>
> The left calf showed a long gash through skin & tissues to the deep muscles & reaching from the knee to 5 ins above the ankle.
>
> Both arms & forearms had extensive & jagged wounds.
>
> The right thumb showed a small superficial incision about 1 in long, with extravasation of blood in the skin & there were several abrasions on the back of the hand moreover showing the same condition.
>
> On opening the thorax it was found that the right lung was minimally adherent by old firm adhesions. The lower part of the lung was broken & torn away.
>
> The left lung was intact; It was adherent at the apex & there were a few adhesions over the side. In the substances of the lung were several nodules of consolidation.
>
> The Pericardium [membrane enclosing the heart] was open below & the Heart absent.
>
> In the abdominal cavity was some partially digested food of fish & potatoes & similar food was found in the remains of the stomach attached to the intestines.[27]

Photographs of Kelly's body can be found online, capturing the state of her room as witnessed by the men who found her. Their black-and-white rendering marginally reduces their terrible impact. It is clear why they and the post-mortem report were not produced at the inquest. The extent of the injuries made after her death is sickening, with the whole of the organs in her abdominal cavity excised. Her murderer left his bloody fingerprints on her chemise and his left hand-print on her right calf, a gift to modern forensics.

In his previously quoted profile of the killer, Bond flagged the similarities between the series of murders: 'The mutilations in each case excepting the Berner's [*sic*] Street one were all of the same character and showed clearly that in all the murders the object was mutilation.'[28] He drew attention to the corner of Mary Jane Kelly's sheet, 'much cut and saturated with blood',[29] which may have covered her savaged face. His description evokes one of the Colney Hatch medical notes about Hyams, where he was 'Distructive [*sic*] and often tearing his clothes and blankets to pieces'.[30]

At 6 p.m. on the day of the inquest into Mary Jane Kelly's death, groom-turned-labourer George Hutchinson walked into Commercial Street police station to make a statement. Currently unemployed, he was lodging at the Victoria Working Men's Home on the same street as the police station. If not her pimp, he often loaned her money in expectation of a return. He had information about Kelly's movements on the night of her murder, when he saw her with a well-dressed stranger. Hutchinson's statement was taken by Sergeant Edward Badham, who had escorted Kelly's coffin to Shoreditch mortuary:

> About 2 am 9th I was coming by Thrawl Street, Commercial Street, and ... just before I got to Flower and Dean Street I saw the murdered woman Kelly, and she said to me Hutchinson will you lend me sixpence. I said I can't I have spent all my money going down to Romford. she said Good morning I must go and find some money, she went away towards Thrawl Street, a man coming in the opposite direction to Kelly tapped her on the shoulder and said something to her. they both burst out laughing. I heard her say alright to him, and the man said you will be alright for what I have told you. he then placed his right hand around her

> shoulders. He also had a kind of small parcel in his left hand with a kind of strap round it.
>
> I stood against the lamp of the … Queens Head Public House [on the corner of Fashion Street] and watched him. They both then came past me and the man hid down his head with his hat over his eyes. I stooped down and looked him in the face. He looked at me stern. They both went into Dorset Street I followed them. They both stood at the corner of the Court for about 3 minutes. He said something to her. she said alright my dear come along you will be comfortable He then placed his arm on her shoulder and gave her a kiss. She said she had lost her handkerchief he then pulled his handkerchief a red one out and gave it to her. They both then went up the Court together. I then went to the Court to see if I could see them but could not. I stood there for about three quarters of an hour to see if they came out they did not so I went away.
>
> Description age about 34 or 35. height 5ft6 complexion pale, dark eyes and eye lashes … slight moustache, curled up each end, and hair dark, very surley [*sic*] looking dress long dark coat, collar and cuffs trimmed astracan. [*sic*: meaning astrakhan black or grey fur] and a dark jacket under. light waistcoat dark trousers dark felt hat turned down in the middle. button boots and gaiters with white buttons. wore a very thick gold chain white linen collar. black tie with horse shoe pin. respectable appearance walked very sharp. Jewish appearance. can be identified.[31]

The CID report written by Inspector Abberline, dated 12 November 1888, lends credibility to Hutchinson's statement:

> An important statement has been made by a man named George Hutchinson which I forward herewith. I have interrogated him this evening and I am of opinion his statement is true. He informed me that he had occasionally given the deceased a few shillings, and that

> he had known her about 3 years. Also that he was surprised to see a man so well dressed in her company which caused him to watch them. He can identify the man, and arrangement was at once made for two officers to accompany him round the district for a few hours tonight with a view of finding the man if possible ... He has promised to go with an officer tomorrow morning at 11.30. am. to Shoreditch mortuary to identify the deceased.
>
> Several arrests have been made on suspicion of being connected with the recent murders, but the various persons detained have been able to satisfactorily account for their movements and were released.[32]

Scotland Yard was concerned that the killer might take evasive action to avoid coming into contact with Hutchinson for that crucial identification. It was reported in the press that

> the police are now to a great extent concentrating their efforts upon an endeavour to find the man so vividly described by George Hutchinson, and they do not doubt that they will be successful. It is understood that the police authorities are somewhat annoyed at the widespread publicity given to Hutchinson's statement, and complain that its immediate effect will be to put the assassin on his guard ... [33]

In his profile of the killer, Bond had estimated that 'one or two o'clock in the morning would be the probable time of the murder'.[34] His early timing fitted the ginger-haired man seen with Kelly by Mary Ann Cox. In contradiction, Hutchinson's statement implied that Kelly had already dispatched the man seen by Cox, and returned with another customer. A witness at the inquest, Sarah Lewis, provided corroboration that, at 2.30 a.m., a man who might have been Hutchinson was waiting outside the entrance to Miller's Court.

George Hutchinson's description was an exact match to Hyams

in age, height and ethnicity. He was clear that the man he saw walked with an unusual gait. In his official police statement taken down by Badham, Hutchinson said that the smartly dressed man 'walked very sharp', meaning fast. Yet over sixteen newspaper reports contain the phrase: 'he walked very softly'.[35] Hyams' stiff knees and asymmetric foot dragging might have contributed to a quiet step, moving gingerly, and taking considerable effort to lift his feet off the ground. It could explain the mystery of how the Ripper was rarely heard entering or leaving the crime scenes.

A question is raised by the disparity in the man's appearance, elevated from 'shabby genteel' to 'well dressed'. The answer may lie in his horseshoe tiepin. Thursday 8 November was the eve of the Lord Mayor's Show, a ceremonial event viewed by thousands, with the streets of the City of London packed with sightseers and police. It was also the day of the Liverpool Autumn Cup at Aintree, run at 3 p.m., with a prize of 1,000 sovereigns. Midland Railway ran a service to get racegoers back to London, which left Aintree at 4.15 p.m., arriving at 9.40 p.m. at St Pancras railway station.[36] Hyam Hyams could have had a day at the races, like his brother Mark in 1882, and returned to London in time to toast his winnings and hook up with Mary Jane Kelly.

It may be that George Hutchinson exaggerated or over-emphasized the man's apparent wealth, as he waited in hope for a good payout for Kelly. A man such as Hyams, dressed to the best of his ability for a day at the races, with a cutaway frock coat as seen by Ripper eye witnesses, may not have worn the finer trimmings of spats, kid gloves and so on. His sister Sarah, a tailoress,[37] may have contributed to his smartish threads. His lucky horseshoe tiepin may have been made of brass, not gold, and the thick chain with a seal and red stone nothing more than an admission pass to a racecourse.

Then, as now, such passes were usually made up of a cardboard fob attached to a thick cord, and displayed on a racegoer's clothing. The Aintree emblem was a Liver bird in turquoise or yellow, on a white background. A blue surround at the top bore a legend such as 'Liverpool county stand' and a red border at the bottom bore the date in brass. It is possible that George Hutchinson could have seen the red-bottomed pass with its thick cord and perceived it as a watch chain, seal and red stone. The answer to the perpetrator's 'disappearing' moustache might also be provided by Hutchinson, who described it as 'slight'. It may be that he trimmed it down on race days and left it to grow between times.

A race-going theory can be applied to the dates of other Ripper murders, although on some occasions the killer might only have placed bets on the races, and not attended them. Polly Nichols' murder was in the early hours after a day's racing at York's Great Yorkshire Stakes,[38] but the journey may have been too far or expensive to attempt. Annie Chapman was killed after the Sandown Park September meeting, when both ordinary and special trains ran between London and Esher.[39] The Plumpton steeplechase meeting, near Lewes in East Sussex, was on the day before the double event, with cheap and fast day returns from London Bridge.[40] Hyams might have been carrying his race programme or a copy of *The Sportsman*,[41] and given Elisabeth Stride his floral buttonhole as a corsage. As detailed in the next chapter, Martha Tabram's earlier murder coincided with the Croydon August Bank Holiday meeting.[42]

In addition to his knife, and his bloodstained hands and clothing, the killer took the incriminating trophies of his victims' possessions and body parts away with him. Police were unable to locate Annie Chapman's missing rings at the local pawnshops. Nor does anyone know what he did with the body parts, or the extent to which he gloated over or played with them. At some point, he must have disposed of them. He could hypothetically have discarded them in a gutter, dustbin or down a privy. He could have buried or burned them, or thrown them to a dog.

Hyams' activities as recorded at Colney Hatch in November 1904 might help to form an assumption. He swallowed some stones and was found lying in a state of collapse on the floor of the infirmary.

Over the next two days, he started to pass the stones – which varied in size from a walnut to a hazelnut, some with sharp edges and angles – along with some pieces of rag.[43] Suffering from *pica*, the desire to eat non-nutritive objects, he may also have had the more severe disorder of sexual cannibalism. It was the ultimate expression of possessing another human being.

The Ripper's violence reached its peak with Kelly's death in November 1888. The final murder of the canonical five, it demonstrated a logical escalation after the injuries and disfigurements inflicted on Eddowes. Despite a huge police operation, the Ripper bypassed observation on the busy streets by taking the simplest approach of all: chatting up Kelly and accompanying her on the short walk to her private room.

CRIME RECONSTRUCTION FOR THE MURDER OF MARY JANE KELLY

At two o'clock in the morning, Hyam Hyams encounters Mary Jane on Commercial Street, as she is going in the opposite direction. He taps her on the shoulder and says something that makes them both laugh – maybe *I've had a win on the horses*, or even *I'm not Jack the Ripper*. He must promise her a generous payment, reassuring her: *You will be all right for what I have told you.*

Followed by George Hutchinson, they walk in the direction of Miller's Court, stopping on the street outside. When Hyams asks to stay the night in her room, Mary Jane agrees: *All right my dear, come along; you will be comfortable.* He places his arm on her shoulder and gives her a kiss. Mary Jane says, *I've lost my handkerchief*, whereupon Hyams pulls his out and hands it to her. They walk under the arch into Miller's Court and down its passageway to the doorway on the right. Mary Jane puts her arm through the broken window to lift the latch and let them both into No. 13.

George Hutchinson takes up a position opposite, under the arched entry to Crossingham's lodging house, where he stands guard for forty-five minutes. Tired of waiting for Mary Jane's customer to leave, when he might levy his cut of her earnings from her before McCarthy takes it for rent, he moves on.

By darkness or candlelight, Mary Jane undresses, putting her clothes on a chair at the bottom of the bed, and her boots underneath it. She clambers into bed, moving across to the far side next to the wall. Hyams joins her on the bed but does not remove his clothes. It is half past two in the morning. Whether they have a sexual interlude or not, by a quarter to four, Mary Jane is deeply asleep. Hyams quietly takes hold of his knife and leans over her. When he moves to cut her throat in the dark, Mary Jane awakes suddenly and cries out: *Murder!* He draws his knife across her throat to silence her. He pauses to listen for any reaction from overhead or elsewhere in the yard, but there is none.

He lights the fire and starts to burn the clothes that are piled up around the room. Light and warmth assured, he sets to work on Mary Jane's body. He has sourced a shorter, sharper, pointed knife to cut surgically through skin and bone. Hyams pulls her away from the wall towards the edge of the bed and pushes her legs apart, leaving a bloody left hand-print on her right calf. He takes his time cutting her up, slashing her sheets as he works.

Two hours later, he wipes his knife and hands on a shirt and throws it on the fire. He puts his coat and hat back on, stows his knife away, and picks up the package that contains his new trophies. He walks out into the yard, firmly closing the door behind him.

He turns right out of Miller's Court, in the opposite direction to Commercial Street and its police station, and, at the end of Dorset Street, doubles back on himself to take a cut-through between White's Row and Tenter Street. Its apparent dead end at Tilley Street leads through to Ann's Place. Ann's Place runs down to Wentworth Street, where a turn to the right takes him home to Wentworth Court. He needs to make himself presentable. It is six o'clock in the morning and the pubs are open.

10

THE FIRST TWO MURDERS IN THE WHITECHAPEL MURDERS FILES:

EMMA ELIZABETH SMITH AND MARTHA TABRAM

The fatal attack on Emma Elizabeth Smith on Tuesday 3 April 1888, at 1.30 a.m. and the murder of Martha Tabram on Tuesday 7 August 1888, between 2 and 4.45 a.m., inside George Yard Buildings.

While Mary Jane Kelly was the last of the Ripper's kills, the first victim recorded on the Metropolitan Police 'Whitechapel Murders' files was forty-five-year-old widow Emma Elizabeth Smith, who died of abdominal injuries on the morning of Wednesday 4 April 1888. She was attacked over twenty-four hours earlier, on Easter Tuesday, on Osborn Street, a short distance from Whitechapel Road. That location was where Polly Nichols was last seen alive by her fellow lodger Ellen Holland. An 'unfortunate' like the Ripper victims, Smith also frequented the local pubs and lodging houses. Her age and height were in line with the canonical five, as the police post-mortem description of her read: 'Aged 45 years, 5' 2" high, complexion fair, hair light brown, scar on right temple.'[1] However, in crucial differences from the Ripper murders, her throat was not cut, and she made a deathbed statement that she had been attacked by a gang of youths who forced a blunt object into her vagina, causing fatal internal injuries.

H Division detective Walter Dew declared in his memoir that

he considered Smith a Ripper victim, while omitting the fact that several men were involved. He emphasized the effort made by police to identify the perpetrator:

> As in every case of murder in this country, however poor and friendless the victim might be, the police made every effort to track down Emma Smith's assailant. Unlikely as well as likely places were searched for clues. Hundreds of people were interrogated, many of them by me personally. Scores of statements were taken. Soldiers from the Tower of London were questioned as to their movements. Ships in the docks were searched and sailors questioned.
>
> All this led nowhere. Not a single clue was discovered.
>
> No one appeared to have seen the fatal blow struck, and no one seemed able to give a description of any man with whom the victim might have been seen.
>
> The silence, the suddenness, the complete elimination of clues, the baffling disappearance all go to support the view which I have always held that Emma Smith was the first to meet her death at the hands of Jack the Ripper.[2]

Another protagonist in the Ripper investigation, Coroner Wynne Baxter, drew similarities between the four murders of Smith, Tabram, Nichols and Chapman during his summing-up at the inquest into Nichols' death:

> All four victims were women of middle age, all were married and had lived apart from their husbands in consequence of intemperate habits, and were at the time of their death leading an irregular life, and eking out a miserable and precarious existence in common lodging-houses. In each case there were abdominal, as well as other injuries. In each case the injuries were inflicted after midnight, and in places of public resort, where it would appear

> impossible but that almost immediate detection should follow the crime, and in each case the inhuman and dastardly criminals are at large in society.[3]

After that acknowledgement that all four murders might not have been committed by the same hand, he split out the last two cases from the first. Nichols and Chapman had been killed by instruments that were 'not so different', and he considered it 'a possibility that [they] … may have been murdered by the same man with the same object'.[4] From September 1888 onwards, however, the press frequently included Smith as the first of the 'Whitechapel Murders', with the inference that the growing list of victims could be attributed to one man.

The volume on Smith went missing from the set of New Scotland Yard files before 1983, when they were passed en masse to The National Archives at Kew for the public record.[5] There are, however, two surviving contemporary police reports, supplemented by the press coverage. The inquest into the death of Emma Elizabeth Smith took place on the morning of Saturday 7 April 1888, at the London Hospital in Whitechapel. Coroner Wynne Baxter presided over the proceedings, as yet unaware of the series of sensational murders that would come to his professional attention over the remainder of the year.

The first witness was Mary Russell, the keeper of a lodging house at 18 George Street, Spitalfields. That address was next door to Satchell's at No. 19 where Martha Tabram, probably the first Ripper victim, had lodged. Russell related what she knew of the assault on Smith that caused her death:

> Deceased had been a lodger there for some months … [She] got her living on the streets, and when she returned home one night she told Witness that she had been thrown out of a window. When she had had drink, the Deceased acted like a mad woman.
>
> On Bank Holiday [Monday] the Deceased left the house in the evening, apparently in good health. She returned home

> between four and five o'clock the next morning severely injured, and she said she had been shockingly treated by some men. Her face was bleeding, and she said that she was also injured about the lower part of the body. Witness took her at once to the hospital.
>
> Deceased further said that she was coming along Osborne-street [*sic*], Whitechapel, when she was set upon and her money taken from her. On the way to the hospital Deceased pointed out the spot, and said she did not know the men nor could she describe them. Witness believed that the statements made by the Deceased were to be relied upon …
>
> [In answer to a question from the coroner] Deceased had often come home with black eyes that men had given her. She was not so drunk as not to know what she did.[6]

In an official report, Inspector Reid identified the exact location of the attack, as 'on the pathway opposite No. 10 Brick Lane, about 300 yards from 18 George Street, and half a mile from the London Hospital to which deceased walked. She would have passed a number of Pc's [*sic*: Police Constables] en route but none was informed of the incident or asked to render assistance.'[7]

Smith's fellow lodger Annie Lee helped Russell to walk Smith to the hospital in a slow and painful journey. It says something about the attitude of the three women towards the police that none of them approached a policeman at any time, not even when passing him on the street. According to Reid, 'None of the PC's [*sic*] in the area had heard or seen anything at all, and the streets were said to be quiet at the time.'[8] And no policeman regarded the women's movements as unusual. Smith's awkward, painful gait and use of the other two women for support might have been attributed to drunkenness.

A hospital doctor, George Haslip, testified that Smith had told him before her death that

> at half-past one that morning she was going by Whitechapel

> Church [St Mary Matfelon],[9] when she saw some men coming, and she crossed the road to get out of their way, but they followed her. They assaulted her, robbed her of all the money she had, and then commenced to outrage [rape] her. She denied soliciting them. She could not say if they used a knife. She could not describe them except that one appeared to be a youth of 19.[10]

Emma Smith died at 9 a.m. on Wednesday 4 April, without providing any further description of her attackers. Doctor Haslip confirmed that her death had been caused by a blunt instrument inserted into her vagina 'with great force. Peritonitis [an inflammation], a result of the injuries, had caused death.'[11] He added that she had been drinking, but was not intoxicated. Her friendless status was exposed as he reported, 'The deceased stated that she had not seen any of her friends for 10 years.'[12]

The next witness was Smith's fellow lodger Margaret Hames, who testified 'to seeing Smith about a quarter-past twelve on Tuesday morning, near the Burdett-road, talking to a man dressed in dark clothes with a white neckerchief round his neck …'[13] Burdett Road in Poplar was almost 2 miles away from where Smith was attacked, a distance that would take forty minutes to walk. If Smith were seen in Poplar by her fellow lodger, she had sufficient time to reach Osborn Street before 1.30 a.m. Hames had been

> hurrying away from the neighbourhood, as she had herself been struck in the mouth a few minutes before by some young men. She did not believe the man talking to Smith was one of them. The quarter was a fearfully rough one. Just before Christmas last she had been injured by men under circumstances of a similar nature, and was a fortnight in the infirmary.[14]

Chief Inspector West, who would be the first senior officer at the scene of Elisabeth Stride's murder, was the final witness. He stated that 'he had made inquiries of all the constables who were on duty anywhere near the place, but failed to find anyone who saw it or heard of it'.[15] In summing up, Baxter was firm in his disapprobation: 'From the medical evidence it was clear the woman had been barbarously murdered. Such a dastardly assault he had never heard of, and it was impossible to imagine a more brutal case.'[16] After a short consultation, the jury returned a verdict of 'Wilful murder by some person or persons unknown'.

Emma Smith's death is significant as it indicates the high risk in Whitechapel of falling foul of casual street violence, and in its time, the serious consideration given to the case as the first of the Ripper murders. Smith's own statements about her attackers must be conclusive, and they rule her out as a Ripper victim.

Almost four months later, in the early hours of Tuesday 7 August 1888, Martha Tabram's body was found on the first-floor landing of a shabby apartment block. By the autumn, as the body count of the Whitechapel Murders increased, so did observations that this murder was the first, or even the second, in a series, if counting Smith. Walter Dew observed: 'Whatever may be said about the death of Emma Smith, there can be no doubt that the August Bank Holiday murder, which took place in George Yard Buildings … was the handiwork of the dread Ripper …'[17] Dew was joined in his conviction that Tabram was a Ripper victim by Robert Anderson and Inspectors Abberline and Reid. Further weight is given to Tabram as the first fatality preceding The Five by its location at the epicentre of the murder sites and its immature 'signature' of a sexually motivated violent crime.

Thirty-nine-year-old Tabram had lived apart from her husband and two young sons for thirteen years. Her heavy drinking had caused the split, and she moved from her native Southwark to Whitechapel, with occasional admissions to the workhouse. At the time of her death, less than a month before Nichols', she was in a relationship with carpenter Henry Turner. She ostensibly made her living as a hawker of cheap trinkets, menthol cones, matches, and pins and needles, while also earning money from casual prostitution.

A sensational interpretation of the discovery of Martha Tabram's body on the staircase of George Yard Buildings. Hidden by darkness, her apparently sleeping body was passed closely by at least one witness in the middle of the night.

On the night of the August Bank Holiday Monday, Tabram was out with another streetwalker, picking up a couple of men in the pubs and back alleys of Whitechapel. Her body was discovered the next morning on a lodging house stairway, stabbed thirty-nine times. The difference in the method of her killing is sufficient for many analysts to discount her from the canon. But the sexual pleasure implicit in the act of repeated stabs, or *piquerism*, substituting for intercourse, and, crucially, its date and location, signpost it as a Ripper murder. It also fits with the clear escalation in violence across the Ripper's kills.

Monday 6 August was the day of the Croydon Bank Holiday horse racing meeting. Perennially popular with metropolitan racegoers, it was located less than 9 miles from London. Despite heavy clouds, the races were very well attended, and 'simply overrun with holiday makers ... in thousands'.[18] Transport arrangements from London to Croydon were inadequate, despite cheap special trains running between at least three London railway stations and Norwood Junction.[19] 'The avalanche of moral sewage'[20] was impeded in its descent from the metropolis on to the racecourse, with attendance reaching its peak only after the first race had started.

Whether or not Hyam Hyams was out on a bender that evening after the races, thirty-nine-year-old Martha Tabram and her 'partner in crime' Mary Ann Connolly, known as 'Pearly Poll', were definitely on a Bank Holiday spree. The women picked up two guardsmen and went on a pub crawl, finishing up in the White Swan on Whitechapel High Street. At around 11.45 p.m. the foursome split into two couples. Pearly Poll went into Angel Alley with her Corporal, while Tabram took her Private into George Yard. All we know for certain about what happened next is that John Reeves – a resident of a large tenement at its northern end, George Yard Buildings – discovered Tabram's body at a quarter to five the next morning, on the first-floor landing. Two days later, the inquest into her death was held by Coroner Wynne Baxter's deputy, George Collier, at the Working Lads' Institute. Detective Inspector Edmund Reid was in charge of the case and attended each of the inquest's sittings.

On the first day of the inquest, the victim's name remained unknown, as three women had identified the body under three different names. It took as long as a week to confirm the identification of Martha Tabram or Turner, during which newspapers continued to run the description of a woman 'age 37, length 5ft 3, complexion and hair dark: dress, green skirt, brown petticoat, long black jacket, brown stockings, side-spring boots, black bonnet – all old'.[21]

The first witness was Elizabeth Mahoney, a young woman in her mid-twenties, who resided at 37 George Yard Buildings with her husband Joseph. She spoke so quietly that, after a complaint from a juror, she was 'made to stand immediately next to the jury'.[22] Mahoney related that she and her husband had arrived home at twenty minutes past two on the Tuesday morning. She then popped out to a chandler's shop in Thrawl Street to buy some provisions for their supper, and was only gone for about five minutes. After having supper, they went to bed.

Mahoney expressed doubt about whether, in the darkness, she could have seen a body on the stairs:

> On no occasion, either in coming up or going down the stairs, did I see the body of a woman lying there. It is quite possible that a body might have been there, and that I did not notice it, because the stairs are very wide, and were completely dark, all the lights having, as usual, been turned out at eleven o'clock. I did not get up till half-past eight in the morning, and during the night my attention was not attracted by a noise or disturbance of any kind.[23]

The next witness was a fellow resident, Alfred George Crow, in his early twenties, who worked as a cab driver. Crow testified that he returned home at half past three on Tuesday morning, and that he did see a person on the stairway:

> I went straight up to my lodgings. I had no light with me, and went up the same staircase as the last witness. On my way up I noticed that there was somebody lying on the first landing. My eyesight is very good, and I noticed a body lying there just as I turned the landing.
>
> I am accustomed, however, to find people lying sleeping there, and took no notice at the time – not even to ascertain

whether the body was that of a male or female. I don't know, therefore, whether the deceased was alive or dead at the time I saw her. I went to bed, and did not come out again before half-past nine, and up to that time I heard no noise at all of any kind.[24]

The third resident of George Yard Buildings to be called as a witness was John Reeves, a short, pale waterside labourer, who discovered the body.

> On Tuesday morning [I] proceeded to go out to work at a quarter to five in the morning. On reaching the first-floor landing … I found a female there lying on her back, in a pool of blood. I did not stop to examine her further, but gave information to a police-constable whom I met in the street.
>
> I went up to my room on Monday night at six o'clock, and remained there all night til I went down at a quarter to five, and during that time I heard no unusual noises. I made no examination whatever of the body when I first saw it, but I did notice that all the clothes were disarranged, being open in front.
>
> I did not notice any foot-marks on the staircase, nor did I find a knife or any other instrument lying there. The hands of the deceased were clenched, but contained no hair or anything else; nor was there any blood coming from the mouth.[25]

When questioned by a juryman, he added: 'I believe it is quite possible for anybody coming up the stairs in the dark to have passed the body without noticing it.'[26]

Police Constable Thomas Barrett was the next witness to take the stand, 'a young constable who gave his evidence very intelligently'.[27] Barrett testified as follows:

> On Tuesday morning I was on duty at about a quarter to five, when my attention was called to George-yard-buildings by Reeves, the last witness. I followed him up the stairs, and found

> the deceased lying on her back. She was dead, but I at once sent for a doctor. The body was not moved by me or Reeves before the doctor came. I noticed that the hands were clenched, but that there was nothing in them.
>
> The clothes were turned up as far as the centre of the body, leaving the lower part of the body exposed: the legs were open, and altogether her position was such as to at once suggest in my mind that recent intimacy had taken place. The deceased was not known on the streets.[28]

At about half past five on the morning of the murder, local doctor Timothy Killeen was called out from his surgery at 68 Brick Lane to pronounce Tabram dead. In his evidence, he contradicted Barrett by expressing the view that there was no evidence of recent sexual intercourse. Killeen testified about Tabram's injuries and cause of death, stating that she had been dead some three hours:

> On examining the body externally I found no less than thirty-nine punctured wounds. From my examination of the body it seemed to be that of a woman about 36 years of age, and was well nourished. I have since made a *post mortem* examination of the body. The brain was healthy; the left lung was penetrated in five places, and the right lung in two places, but the lungs were otherwise perfectly healthy. The heart was rather fatty, and was penetrated in one place, but there was otherwise nothing in the heart to cause death …
>
> The liver was healthy, but was penetrated in five places, the spleen was perfectly healthy, and was penetrated in two places; both the kidneys were perfectly healthy; the stomach was also perfectly healthy, but was penetrated in six places; the intestines were healthy, and so were all the other organs. The lower portion of the body was penetrated in one place, the wound being three inches in length and one in depth. From appearances, there was no reason to suppose that recent intimacy had taken place.

> I don't think that all the wounds were inflicted with the same instrument, because there was one wound on the breast bone which did not correspond with the other wounds on the body. The instrument with which the wounds were inflicted, would most probably be an ordinary knife, but a knife would not cause such a wound as that on the breast bone. That wound I should think would have been inflicted with some form of a dagger.
>
> I am of opinion that the wounds were inflicted during life, and from the direction which they took it is my opinion, that although some of them could have been self-inflicted, yet, there were others which could not have been so inflicted. The wounds generally would have been inflicted by a right-handed person. There was no sign whatever of any struggle having taken place; and there was a deal of blood between the legs, which were separated.
>
> Death was due to hemorrhage and loss of blood.[29]

The doctor's view that the deep cut through Tabram's breastbone required a stronger blade than an ordinary knife, such as a bayonet or dagger, suggested that she was killed by her soldier client. Later commentators, though, have observed that a knife wielded with force could have penetrated Tabram's breastbone, demoting her killer to civilian ranks.

The inquest was adjourned for a fortnight to allow the police time to confirm the dead woman's identity and 'ascertain the assailant'.[30] The coroner concluded by saying it was 'one of the most terrible cases that anyone can possibly imagine. The man must have been a perfect savage to have attacked the woman in that way.'[31]

At the inquest's resumption on Thursday 23 August, Henry Tabram of East Greenwich identified Martha Tabram as his estranged wife, from whom he had been separated for thirteen years. He was a sallow-complexioned man with iron-grey hair, a moustache and an imperial, or small tufted beard, who despite losing one eye was still able to work as a furniture packer and porter.

Speaking with deep emotion, he testified that he had left Martha in March 1875 because of her drinking. He paid her a maintenance allowance of varying amounts for three years, until she took up with another man, Henry Turner. Tabram then reduced the allowance from twelve shillings a week to half a crown (two shillings and sixpence), as 'I did not think it my place to support her then'.[32] He last saw her eighteen months before her death, in Whitechapel Road.

Henry Turner was a younger man dressed in a light tweed suit, with a pale face, who, like Henry Tabram, wore a moustache and imperial. A carpenter, who when out of work traded as a street hawker, he testified as follows:

> I have been … living with deceased up to three weeks ago. On and off I have lived with her for nearly nine years. Occasionally she had given away to drink, and then I had to leave her. I was living with her for three weeks previous to the occurrence. She used to sell in the streets some times, usually selling the same things as I did.
>
> I last saw her alive on the Saturday before Bank Holiday, when I met her in Leadenhall-street, just against the Aldgate pump … It was about two o'clock in the afternoon … and I was with her about 20 minutes altogether. I gave her 1s. 6d. [one shilling and sixpence] to purchase stock, with which to earn a few ha'pence. Since she has been living with me her character for sobriety was not good. If I gave her any money she generally spent it in drink. In fact, it was always drink.
>
> She was in the habit of staying out late at night. I could'nt [*sic*] say for certain what time she usually came home. When I was with her, it was usually eleven o'clock, except on Saturday night when it was usually twelve … When she took to drink, however, I generally left her to her own resources, and I can't answer for her conduct then.
>
> She had no regular companions that I am aware of. I am not

> accountable for whether she walked the streets or not, but she certainly never did so to my knowledge while I was with her … I never knew she was acquainted with the woman 'Pearly Poll', until I read the account of her death in the papers. I am a man of sober habits as a rule, and we usually agreed well enough together, as long as she remained sober, but when she got the worse for drink I left her. There was no quarrel then, I simply left her.[33]

When questioned by Inspector Reid, he added: 'There were times when she stayed out all nights, but her excuse was invariably that she was subject to hysterical fits, and had been overtaken with one and taken to a police-station or hospital. I, myself have seen her in these fits, but it was as a rule, when she was under the influence of drink …'[34]

Mary Bousfield was the next witness, who said that Tabram was her former lodger and a hawker, and left owing some rent about three weeks before her death. She went on to say: 'I have known her for about four months, but I have formed no opinion as to whether she was of intemperate habits. She would rather have a glass of ale than a cup of tea, however …'[35] It was a delicate way of expressing Tabram's fondness for the booze.

Tabram's sister-in-law Ann Morris, 'a pale looking woman, whose pallor was increased by her totally black, but neat, attire',[36] said that she last saw Tabram alive outside the White Swan pub on Whitechapel Road at 11 p.m. on the night of her murder: 'She was alone at the time, but I didn't follow her in, and I saw no more of her after that. She drank very heavily, and was a very bad woman in other respects. She was, I believe, on the streets … She used to apply to me for money, but not lately.'[37] Her evidence confirmed Tabram's status as a sex worker. When questioned by Inspector Reid, she added that Tabram had been charged three times by the police 'with annoying me by using bad language and threats. On the last occasion she was sentenced to seven days. She was never sober on these occasions …'[38]

The final witness was Mary Ann Connolly, otherwise known as

Pearly Poll, described as 'wearing simply an old green shawl and no hat, her face being reddened and soddened [made dull or expressionless] by drink'.[39] She said that her chest was 'queer', affecting her voice, so the officer of the court relayed what she said. The coroner cautioned her before she testified, 'that she was not bound to answer any questions unless she pleased, but that if she did answer them they would be put in writing, and perhaps used against her'.[40]

She started by saying that she had been living for the past two nights at Crossingham's lodging house on Dorset Street (opposite Mary Jane Kelly's lodgings at Miller's Court). As the last known person to see Tabram, whom she called 'Emma', alive, her testimony is of particular interest:

> I am single … and follow no occupation, being an unfortunate. I knew the deceased for about five months as 'Emma'. I last saw her alive at 20 minutes past eleven on Bank Holiday night, at the corner of George-yard, Whitechapel. I was with her for some time, and we separated at a quarter to twelve. I was with her and two soldiers at the time, one of whom was a private and the other a corporal. I don't know what regiment they belonged to, but one had a white band round his cap. The corporal had no side arms [weapons] on.
>
> During the three-quarters of an hour I was with the deceased we were all [four] in the public house … After she and I separated she went away with the private, and I went with the corporal up Angel-alley. Before we parted there was a quarrel about money, but not with the deceased. We parted all right, however, and with no bad words; indeed, we were all good friends. I know nothing of what became of deceased after we left her – not until I heard of her death …
>
> I have tried to identify the two soldiers, and have been to the barracks for that purpose. When I picked out two after the men had been paraded, I believed at the time that they were

> the men we saw on the Bank Holiday night. For the purpose of identifying them, I went to Wellington Barracks. I had not seen the men before …[41]

In response to a question from Inspector Reid, she went on to say:

> I left the corporal at the corner of George-yard about five-and-twenty minutes past twelve. I went towards Whitechapel, and he went Aldgate way.
>
> I first heard of the death of 'Emma' on the Tuesday – the day after the Bank Holiday – and I said at once that she was the woman I was with on the previous night. I may have threatened to drown myself after the murder, but it was only in a 'lark' [a joke]. If I did not attend the parade of men at the Tower on two occasions, it was because I was with my cousin at Drury Lane.[42]

Although it was not expanded upon at the inquest, Inspector Reid had arranged as many as seven identity parades on separate dates at two barracks in central London, Wellington Barracks, and the Tower of London. It was a failed effort to secure an identification from either Pearly Poll or Constable Barrett, who had also sighted a soldier on the night of the murder.

The coroner briefly summed up, concluding: 'It was a most horrible crime, and showed that the deceased had been the victim of a fiend … [The jury] could only come to the conclusion that the woman had been foully and brutally murdered by some person or persons unknown. That must be their verdict, and the police would do what they could still to endeavour to trace the murderer.'[43]

The jury returned the requested verdict – one that would become all too familiar in the coming months. They added a recommendation that the stairs at George Yard Buildings, and other artisans', or workers', dwellings, should be lit until after eleven o'clock at night.

The window of opportunity to commit the murder spanned from

approximately 2 a.m., as Doctor Killeen put the time of death as 'some three hours' before its discovery, to around 4.45 a.m., when the body was seen by Reeves. Inspector Swanson, in a summary report on the case, attempted to specify that window:

> It will be observed that from the statement of Mrs Mahoney that the murder took place between 2am and 4.50am 7th. Augt., but as the soldier was last seen with deceased at 11 3/4 pm 6th. two and a quarter hours had elapsed. It is not an uncommon occurrence for tramps and others to sleep on a common stairs in the East End, and I venture to think that the something which the cabman Alfred George Crow saw [at 3.30 a.m.] was the body of Martha Tabram.[44]

Swanson commented further that the 'lapse of time' between Tabram going off with the soldier and her body being discovered meant it was possible that she might have been with someone else after him. He mentioned that Tabram had also received a stab wound to the neck.

Constable Barrett reported to his superiors that he had encountered a soldier on Wentworth Street, presumably not far from its junction with the north end of George Yard:

> 2am. 7th. Augt. Police Constable 226H [his divisional collar number] Barrett saw a soldier – a grenadier [Guard] age 22 to 26. height 5 ft 9 or 10. compl. [complexion] fair, hair dark small dark moustache turned up at ends. with one good conduct badge. no medals. in Wentworth Street; and in reply to the PC he stated he was waiting for a *chum*, who had gone with a girl.[45]

Barrett's sighting puts Tabram's liaison with the soldier – or possibly a second soldier – far later than stated by Pearly Poll, who was finished with her own corporal by twenty-five minutes past midnight. A parade of Scots Guards was arranged at the Tower of London for Constable

Barrett. He identified two men who had alibis, leading Reid to report: 'I felt certain in my own mind that P.C. had made a great mistake …'[46]

Two further parades of Scots Guards were organized for Pearly Poll. Having evaded the police for the first one, at the second she provided information previously unknown: the soldiers she and Tabram consorted with 'had white bands round their caps',[47] meaning they were from the Coldstream Guards based at Wellington Barracks. Reid, whose patience must have been tried, arranged a further parade at Wellington Barracks, at which Pearly Poll, like Barrett, identified two men who had firm alibis.[48]

Reid noted his next steps: 'Inquiries were made to find some other person who saw the deceased and Pearly Poll with the privates on the night of the 6th but without success, and Pearly Poll and the P.C. having both picked out the wrong men they could not be trusted again as their evidence would be worthless.'[49] The police had nothing to work on.

It is possible that Tabram's assailant was someone other than a soldier. Doctor Killeen's suggestion that a bayonet was used in her murder partnered well with other testimony that Tabram had a soldier client on the fatal night. It is plausible that Tabram argued with her soldier client, perhaps over money, or that he never intended to pay and the booze and argumentation caused him to kill. However, the long, sharp knife used by the Ripper would be capable of causing the injury to the breastbone attributed to a bayonet, particularly if a man leant his body weight against it.

At an undetermined time after midnight, her encounter with the soldier at an end, Tabram could have returned to the White Swan to spend her earnings, or stopped at a pub that was directly on her way home to her lodgings at Satchell's at 19 George Street, north of George Yard. Either way, she was perilously close to Hyams' home at Wentworth Court, off Wentworth Street, which was two minutes' walk from George Yard Buildings.

Experts on serial killers state that the first murder is staged invariably at a comforting location to the killer, where he feels safe.

The FBI profile of the Ripper placed the first murder as occurring close to either his home or workplace. Former police officer Ian Oldfield mapped the overlapping zones of each of the canonical five murder sites, resulting in a 'red zone' where the perpetrator was most likely to have lived. It falls one block immediately east of Wentworth Court, the notorious area of Flower and Dean, and Thrawl Streets.[50] If the murder location of George Yard Buildings were added to those of the canonical five, the red zone would shift west on to the block between Commercial Street and Bell Lane, comprising Wentworth Court.

Literally around the corner from his home, the location of George Yard could not be more appropriate for Hyams' first murder. He could even have encountered Tabram before, when cutting through George Yard on his way home from Whitechapel Road to Wentworth Street. The proximity of her murder location to his lodgings places Martha Tabram as the first of six Ripper victims.

The stabbing 'signature' left on Tabram fits with the non-fatal attack on another casual prostitute, Annie Millwood, who received several stabs on the lower part of her body. The Millwood attack took place in February 1888, six months before Tabram's murder, at a lodging house at Spitalfields Chambers at No. 8 White's Row. If the Ripper's canon is extended to eight, including Tabram and two non-fatal attacks on Annie Millwood and Annie Farmer covered in the next chapter, then four of the eight incidents took place inside. The indoor assaults on Millwood and Tabram start a new series that precedes The Five and ends with two further indoor attacks on Kelly and Farmer. A residential setting provided privacy and mitigated against casual interruption, while increasing the risk of being trapped in the act or overheard by someone nearby. Those were risks the Ripper was willing to take. Several residents of George Yard Buildings had a room within hearing of the Tabram murder spot, yet heard nothing.

The fact that as many as half of his attacks were indoors demonstrates that the Ripper had no real fear of being cornered, wherever he operated. The unlit staircase of a tenement block was the same to him as the double compartment of a lodging house or a dark semi-residential City Square. This thinking highlights the similarities between the indoor attacks and two of the four that took place outside. Annie Chapman's murder in an enclosed back yard, and Elisabeth Stride's in Dutfield's Yard, were both dead ends, which her killer exited by retracing his steps, first through the narrow corridors of a house, and second through a wicket gate. His sole focus was on his victims, and once satisfied, he hurried from traps that were never sprung. If Hyams were the Ripper, he evaded detection because many of the locations of his crimes, in addition to being dark and secluded, were extremely close to home.

The Ripper's method of killing and 'signature' would develop over time. The darkness of the first-floor landing, and the sporadic comings and goings of its residents, prevented him from doing more than stabbing Tabram in a frenzied attack. Her injuries point to a killer who felt a real 'hatred and disgust for women'.[51] They also suggest a likely escalation in violence, as, in the following murder of Polly Nichols, *piquerism* was replaced by a direct kill by cutting her throat, and the stabs to her abdomen by an attempted removal of her organs of generation.

CRIME RECONSTRUCTION FOR THE MURDER OF MARTHA TABRAM

It is almost closing time and, after a heavy night, her business done in George Yard, Martha starts to make her way home. Walking northwards up the yard on to Wentworth Street, she finds herself facing the Norwich Arms pub, with money in her pocket. A few yards further on lie George Street and the safety of her bed. *A quick drink or two won't hurt, and I'll get a punter to pay for them.*

Inside the pub, it is easy enough for Hyam Hyams to pick up Martha. All he needs to do is buy her a gin and make it clear what he wants. Enjoying her drink, and the rest, she is slow to agree to his terms and state her price. Over half an hour later, Martha leaves with him. If anyone halfway sober sees them together, it is a commonplace sight, a man and a woman disappearing off into the night.

George Yard is a quiet alley at this hour, and convenient for their purposes. Martha wants more comfort than the cobblestones or a brick wall, and simply takes him back to the first-floor landing in the tenement that hosted her last liaison. She had no trouble with her soldier, and is expecting none from this inoffensive stranger, with his funny arm and walk. Unobserved by them, Elizabeth Mahoney is just ten yards ahead, moving quickly to get home with her husband's supper.

The staircase is very dark, but it is not too dark to feel your way up each tread. Just one flight leads to a landing. Hyams backs Martha against a wall, and blocks her nose and mouth with his hands. As she drops to her knees, he grabs the front of her dress to move her on to the floor, lifts her skirts, pushes her legs apart and stabs her with a knife over and over again, moving up and down her torso from her neck, and sliding the blade into her vagina. Tearing open her bodice, he leans his body weight against his weapon to pierce her breastbone. Satisfied, and breathing heavily, he pauses to listen for any movement from the stairwell or its adjoining tenements.

Job done, he gets down the stairs as quickly as he can, and nobody sees him exiting the building. In a fast walk that takes less than two minutes, he retraces his steps to Wentworth Street and, from there, across the road to home. It is his first kill, but it will not be his last.

An hour later, Alf Crow walks up the stairs and notices somebody lying on the first landing. Some drunk has passed out and is sleeping it off. He has seen it all before and can't be doing with any of it. But even if he were to raise the alarm, one hour and fifteen minutes before his neighbour does, the outcome would be the same. Nobody reports seeing Martha with anyone but her soldier, who cannot be traced.

11

OTHER POSSIBLE RIPPER VICTIMS

'We are but shadows.'

EPIGRAM BY HORACE INSCRIBED ON
A FOURNIER STREET SUNDIAL

After Mary Jane Kelly's murder in early November 1888, Hyam Hyams remained free to roam the streets of Whitechapel. Sir Charles Warren, at a low point in his beleaguered relationship with Home Secretary Matthews and with public opinion against him, had resigned and was replaced as Commissioner by one of his Assistant Commissioners and former CID Chief, James Monro. Both the Metropolitan and City Forces made appropriate inquiries 'to all the lunatic asylums in London … respecting persons recently admitted or discharged: many persons being of opinion that these crimes are of too revolting a nature to have been committed by a sane person'.[1]

Walter Dew, writing in 1938, retained vivid memories of a nationwide search:

> One of the strongest inferences to be deduced from the crimes was that the man we were hunting was probably a sexual maniac. This angle of investigation was pursued relentlessly. Inquiries were made at asylums all over the country, including the Criminal Lunatic Asylum at Broadmoor, with the object of discovering whether a

> homicidal lunatic had been released as cured about the time the Ripper crimes commenced. No useful evidence was obtained.[2]

A man as insubstantial as a shadow, his mania having scraped away his essential self, Hyams could not stop himself from killing. The murder of Kelly was the Ripper's ultimate crime, demonstrating the extent of his decline. To quote the FBI's John E. Douglas: 'The escalation of mutilation and depravity in the murders was dramatic, and the Mary Jane Kelly kill certainly strikes me as the work of a guy pretty much at the end of his mental rope. That is not to say that he'd turn himself in … or kill himself. Rather, it suggests that he might not be able to continue functioning on his own much longer.'[3]

A non-fatal attack on Wednesday 21 November 1888, less than two weeks after the murder of Mary Jane Kelly, provides a possible, and illuminating, parallel. Its subject, Annie Farmer, was thirty-four years of age and 'a married woman of good appearance',[4] who was estranged from her husband. Two press clippings about the attack feature in the official police file, and the detail of this attempted murder can be pieced together from broader press coverage:

> [Annie Farmer] has been in the habit of frequenting common lodging-houses in the locality, and had known the man who attacked her for about twelve months … About seven o'clock this morning she met him near Spitalfields Church … and went with him into several 'early' public-houses, where they had drink. The man did not take much liquor, but the woman partook so freely of hot rum that she became intoxicated.
>
> The couple went to the common lodging house at No. 19 George Street, and engaged a double bedroom, or rather a boarded-in compartment containing a large-sized bed.[5]

In an alternative version of events, the man accosted Farmer in Commercial Street, asking after the reason for her 'early appearance', and on being told she had been walking the streets as she had no money for lodgings, asked the price of a double bed, which was eightpence.[6] Satchell's lodging house at 19 George Street was within a few hundred yards of Mary Jane Kelly's lodgings at Miller's Court on Dorset Street. Like Mary Jane Kelly, Annie Farmer took her assailant back to her lodgings for paid sex. Notably, possible Ripper victim Martha Tabram had also lodged at Satchell's.

The press did not comment on what occurred between the couple in the ensuing one to two hours after they had entered their double compartment, simply stating, 'Nothing more was heard of them until about half-past nine, when the man was heard to run downstairs, and presently the woman was heard following him and screaming out that he had tried to murder her.'[7] A fellow lodger, Esther Hall, went to her aid, helped her dress and wrapped a sheet around her throat, where blood was flowing from two wounds. Hall told the press the following: 'I asked her how it happened, and she said she was just dropping off to sleep when she felt her throat was being cut. She called out, "Oh, my throat!" and the man she had gone to bed with "bolted". She stated that he had not undressed at all, and that previous to going to bed they had been drinking at a public-house in Brick-lane.'[8] Although the pub was not named, an educated guess would suggest the Frying Pan, on the corner with Thrawl Street, where Polly Nichols was drinking on the day of her murder.

Farmer was seen at her lodgings by Doctor Phillips, and he described her injuries as 'two wounds in her throat, one across the throat and one underneath it, which was straight down and met the other'. The Doctor 'stitched up the wound',[9] while he 'announced that the wound was little more than superficial'.[10] She was, nevertheless, taken to Commercial Street police station by stretcher:

> The woman was covered up, and it could not be seen whether the police were conveying a live person or a corpse. This, of course, added to the popular excitement, and strengthened the belief that

> another horrible murder and mutilation had been committed. Commercial-street was, in consequence, completely blocked, and the police had great difficulty in reaching their destination.[11]

Once at the police station, Farmer caused some frustration to her interviewing officers, perhaps owing to the effects of alcohol and shock:

> [She] was placed in a warm comfortable room, and interrogated. She was suffering, however, from the effects of drink … [and] neither a coherent narrative nor a satisfactory description of her assailant could be extracted from her. It was not, indeed, until the evening that the woman had sufficiently recovered … to answer questions with anything like clearness, and the description which she ultimately gave of the attempt on her life and the appearance of the would-be murderer was somewhat confusing.
>
> It seems certain, however, that the man was not a stranger to Farmer, and that she had known him as a casual acquaintance for about twelve months. This, together with the evidence of some of the men who pursued the fugitive, has furnished the police with a clue …
>
> The description of Farmer's assailant, as circulated by the police, is as follows: – 'Wanted, for attempted murder, on the 21st … a man, aged thirty-six years; height 5 ft. 6 in.; complexion dark, no whiskers, dark moustache; dress, black jacket, vest, and trousers, round black felt hat; respectable appearance; can be identified.'[12]

It was an accurate description of Hyam Hyams. No name was circulated, suggesting that either Farmer did not know it, or the police suppressed it for fear of disrupting their investigation or triggering reprisals.

Several local men followed Farmer's attacker 'for about 300 yards' from George Street into Thrawl Street, where he must have crossed Brick Lane, as they 'lost him in the direction of Heneage-street'.[13]

Whoever he was, he was heading east, the correct direction for Hyams' lodgings at Jubilee Street if he relocated there in late 1888. The men who chased him were variously named as Farmer's fellow lodger and hawker Philip Harris, John Whitehead, his mate 'Bones', the carter Frank Ruffell, and a milkman.

At four o'clock in the afternoon, Farmer was moved to the Whitechapel Infirmary at Baker's Row, which was situated between the murder sites of Annie Chapman and Polly Nichols. The press recorded, 'The object of this removal was primarily to place the woman beyond the reach of the reporters, against whom the police are curiously incensed.'[14] Police banned the infirmary staff from 'allowing any person to see the woman, and to give any information whatever respecting her'.[15]

However, a Central News Agency reporter managed to speak to its chief medical officer, Doctor Herbert Larder, who

> declined to give information except as to the condition of his patient. Dr Larder stated that the wounds were not dangerous in themselves, and that should no unforeseen complications arise the woman would be convalescent in from ten to fourteen days. The throat was cut in two places, one wound being across and the other up and down, but the latter cut is merely superficial.[16]

The infirmary's records state that she was discharged on 1 December.[17] Hyam Hyams was at liberty until 29 December, when by coincidence Larder admitted him to the same infirmary, where he briefly stayed until early January 1889, being briefly readmitted in early April.[18]

The police response to the attack on Farmer was swift:

> A large force of detectives was immediately drafted into the district, and inquiries were prosecuted diligently throughout the day, but, up to a late hour last evening [Monday 26 November] the man had not been arrested. The general opinion, as well as

that of the police, is that the author of Wednesday's outrage is not the murderer of the previous cases. Great excitement, however, prevailed in the locality.[19]

No arrests were made, not even on suspicion, and insufficient information is available to assess whether the attacker were the Ripper. Regardless of the perpetrator, Annie Farmer's experience elucidates what might have happened to Mary Jane Kelly. Both were accosted by a man on the street, who was intent on securing privacy indoors with his victim. Both were already or soon became drunk, took him inside to a private double room and spent between one and two hours in bed with him. Once she was dropping off or actually asleep, he attempted to cut her throat. The *modus operandi* of the Farmer wounds, with a vertical cut intersecting a deeper horizontal one, was a slight variation to that used by the Ripper.

In the case of Mary Jane Kelly, her killer spent considerable time after her death mutilating her body. Farmer was more fortunate and was lucky to get away with minor injuries. If Kelly's killer, like Farmer's attacker, kept his clothes on while the woman undressed, he was ready to make a quick exit.

The date of the attack on Farmer, Wednesday 21 November 1888, was the final day of the Warwick and Leamington Races, which had started that Monday, and there was active betting on the Manchester November Handicap fixed for Saturday 24 November.[20] Another possible connection to Jack the Ripper was the location where Farmer was picked up, close to where Annie Chapman was probably accosted. The side streets adjacent to Christ Church Spitalfields housed respectable people, including the vicar, leading Chapman and her killer to walk eastwards on to Hanbury Street, where the multi-occupancy households left their doors unlocked and their yards unattended. If the attack on Annie Farmer might be regarded as a final, unsuccessful Ripper attack on an unfortunate, then a similar assault in February 1888 could be considered as his first.

February 1888 was when Hyams received his arm injury: a triggering event for his increasingly erratic behaviour. It was in the same month that his uncle Abraham Mordecai claimed that an apprentice at his cigar factory threatened him, and received a counter-summons for assault. On Saturday 25 February, the Waterloo Cup at Aintree was postponed owing to the severity of the weather. At a late hour, Annie Millwood was attacked and injured at her lodging house at Spitalfields Chambers,[21] one road south of Dorset Street. A soldier's widow, she died over a month later of natural causes, although press reporting speculated that her injuries led to her demise.

There are no surviving police documents, and newspaper coverage of the incident is slim:

> Annie Millwood, aged 38, a single woman … is alleged to have been the victim of a most violent and brutal attack, and whose death is supposed to be due to the injuries inflicted. It appears that a few weeks ago the deceased was admitted to the Whitechapel Infirmary, suffering from numerous stabs in the legs and lower part of the body.
>
> She stated that she had been attacked by a man whom she did not know, and who stabbed her with a clasp knife. No one appears to have seen the attack, and so far as at present ascertained there is only the woman's statement to bear out the allegations of an attack, although that she has been stabbed cannot be denied.[22]

The attack took place less than two months before that on Emma Smith, and five months before Martha Tabram's murder, which was probably the Ripper's first kill. Although dissimilar to the method of attack on Annie Farmer, it is similar to that on Tabram, involving a series of stab wounds below the ribcage and a location close to that of George Yard. It might have been an early attempt by the future serial killer to murder an 'unfortunate'. Spitalfields Chambers, which permitted men and women to sleep together in double compartments, was on White's Row, a convenient cut-through for Hyam Hyams between Spitalfields and his home at Wentworth Court.

Millwood was discharged from Baker's Row Infirmary, where Farmer had also been treated for her injuries, to the Whitechapel Union's workhouse on South Grove Road. She died there on 31 March, when a workhouse messenger found her lying down at the workhouse door, with her face on the step.[23] Dr Wheeler 'came at once and pronounced life to be extinct'.[24] Coroner Wynne Baxter ordered a post-mortem examination to determine whether her death might be 'criminally responsible',[25] though it was ultimately attributed to the 'sudden effusion into the pericardium [the membrane enclosing the heart] from the rupture of the left pulmonary artery through ulceration'.[26] If she had survived, she could have informed the police investigation into the subsequent murders, not least by providing a description and viewing identity parades.

Millwood and Farmer were both victims of non-fatal attacks by a man who could have been Jack the Ripper, but they are not the only cases recorded. The last four unsolved murders on the police Whitechapel Murders files continue to be scrutinized as possible additions to the canon. Shortly before Christmas 1888, a prostitute named Rose Mylett met an extraordinary end in Poplar, further east than the usual Ripper locations. Notably, at the date of her demise Hyam Hyams was at large, not yet having come to the attention of the authorities. At 4.15 a.m. on Thursday 20 December 1888, two K Division policemen, Sergeant Robert Golding and Constable Thomas Costello, discovered the body of a young woman in Clarke's Yard, off Poplar High Street.

Assistant police surgeon Doctor George Harris was called out to confirm her death. Neither Harris nor the Constable who took the body to the mortuary observed any mark on her neck. Coroner Wynne Baxter's assistant, Courtain Chivers, brought the mark to Harris's attention some hours later. The nature of that mark, and whether it indicated misadventure, suicide or murder, became a political issue between the Metropolitan Police, their surgeons and the coroner.

At the first hearing of the inquest, at Poplar Town Hall, Sergeant Golding described the discovery of Mylett's body, noting that her clothes were not disarranged, and there were no signs of a scuffle. K Division's principal police surgeon, Doctor Matthew Brownfield, had conducted the post-mortem examination and was clear in his testimony about the mark on Mylett's neck and its effect:

> On the neck he found a mark which had evidently been caused by a cord drawn tightly round from the spine at the back to the lobe of the left ear. He had since found that the mark could be produced by a piece of four-told cord [*sic*: four-fold was strong cord]. Beside that mark, the impression of thumbs and middle and index fingers was plainly visible on each side of the neck …
>
> The cause of death … was suffocation by strangulation.[27]

In response to a question from the coroner, Brownfield clarified that he thought that the fingermarks around Mylett's neck were made by her, in her own efforts to pull off the cord.[28] He stated that 'the murderer must have stood at the left rear of the woman, suddenly thrown a cord round her throat, and crossing his hands so killed her'.[29]

The coroner announced an adjournment, commenting that the police needed more time to make inquiries, as it looked very much as if a murder had been committed. In fact, Commissioner Monro reported the case to the Home Secretary as a murder: 'The woman had been strangled with a four lag cord (equal to packing string of very moderate thickness!) and … the marks of strangulation were plainly visible on the throat and neck.'[30]

Less than a fortnight passed before the inquest resumed, punctuated by public holidays for Christmas and the New Year. In that period, CID Chief Robert Anderson, who had himself viewed the body, intervened in the case. His memoir stated: 'The Poplar case of December, 1888, was a death from natural causes, and but for the "Jack the Ripper" scare, no one would have thought of suggesting that it was a homicide.'[31]

At the second hearing, Anderson ensured that police interests were represented by a solicitor, St John Wontner, and by his Ripper profiler, Thomas Bond. Doctor Harris, who had seen the body *in situ* and helped with the post-mortem examination, testified, like Brownfield, that Mylett had been strangled. He suggested that the weapon was 'a piece of string similar to that with which soap is cut'.[32] When questioned by Wontner, Harris conceded that he did not see the mark on the neck the first time he saw the body, and thought the 'death was due to asphyxia [lack of oxygen], or drunkenness, or some other natural cause. The eyeballs and tongue did not protrude. In his opinion the appearances showed that strangulation had been rapid.'[33]

Bond testified that, on 22 December, Anderson had sent a note to his Westminster home asking him to examine the body. On Christmas Eve, assisted by notes provided by his colleague Charles Hebbert, he carried out that task, reaching the following conclusions:

> When he saw the body, the mark described as made by a cord had disappeared, but those described as finger marks remained. He agreed with the deductions of Drs Brownfield, Hibberd [*sic*: Hebbert], and Harris, that the deceased died from strangulation, but his opinion was that it was not murder, for the reason that the amount of violence required to strangle an able-bodied woman would leave a mark which would not disappear during five days.
>
> He thought the woman fell while in a state of drunkenness, and that [her] larynx [voice box] was compressed against the neck of her jacket. He believed the mark on the neck was due to the collar of the jacket. He might say his colleague, who was a very experienced man, did not agree with him … so this was a critical case. A tablespoonful of the contents of deceased's stomach had been analysed, and found to contain a teaspoonful of whisky.[34]

After a week's adjournment, Doctor Brownfield testified that the chief surgeon of the Metropolitan Police, Doctor Alexander McKellar, had seen the body, and agreed with his opinion about the cause of death. When examined by Wontner, Brownfield was firm that death was caused by 'homicidal violence' and that 'the mark on the neck was too straight and too even all along its course to have been caused by the collar of the jacket'.[35]

The coroner's assistant, Chivers, testified that he had seen the body on the morning of its death. He seemed to contradict Bond's assessment that the mark on the neck had worn off, stating, 'There was a mark an eighth of an inch wide round deceased's neck. He saw the body at various intervals up to January 4th, and the mark became more apparent as time went on.'[36]

Coroner Wynne Baxter summed up the case, asserting his authority by stating that, while 'Several doctors [were] sent down by the Commissioner of the Metropolitan Police to see the body without his sanction ... he did not wish to make this a personal matter, but certainly it had never happened to him before.'[37] He continued by stating that all five doctors agreed that the cause of death was strangulation, and four of the five were of the opinion that it was homicidal strangulation. On the subject of Bond's evidence, 'he might point out that the Indian doctors had shown that, in cases of murder by Thugs [garrotting by gangs], there was often no mark at all'.[38] The jury took his lead and returned a verdict of 'Murder by person or persons unknown'. A police report finally noted that CID 'does not intend taking any further steps in the matter'.[39] The official view was, and must remain, that Mylett's death was accidental.

Of the last three cases on the police 'Whitechapel Murders' files, the murder of Alice Kinsey, commonly known as McKenzie, displayed the most features of a Ripper murder. However, two eminent police surgeons, Thomas Bond and Doctor George Bagster Phillips, disagreed over whether or not the killer was the 'Whitechapel Murderer', while Coroner Wynne Baxter labelled it a possible copycat crime. Hyam Hyams was at that time secured in Colney Hatch Lunatic Asylum, as he was for the later murder of one Frances Coles.[40] Shortly after 12.50 a.m. on Wednesday 17 July 1889, an officer on his beat, Constable Walter Andrews, found a woman's body on the west side of the pavement on Castle Alley, which ran between Wentworth Street and Whitechapel High Street. She was lying diagonally across the 4 foot pavement beside parked carts and wagons and underneath a lamp post.

He blew his whistle twice to summon his Sergeant, Edward Badham. A veteran of the Annie Chapman and Mary Jane Kelly investigations, Badham reported that he 'noticed a quantity of blood under her head on the footway' and that she was 'laying on her right side with her clothes half up to her waist exposing her abdomen'.[41] The murder's location, victim type and injuries of a cut throat and a long vertical cut down the ribcage and abdomen, from which seven further wounds were scored through the flesh, bore the possible signatures of the Ripper.

The woman's description was circulated as:

> Age about 40 length 5 ft 4 complexion pale hair and eyes brown top of thumb left hand deficient also tooth deficient in upper jaw.
>
> Dress red stuff [meaning a woven woollen cloth] bodice patched under arms and sleeves with marone [*sic*: maroon] one black and one marone stockings brown stuff skirt kilted brown lindsey [*sic*: linsey, or linen-and-wool] petticoat, white chemise and apron, paisley shawl, button boots, all old nothing found on person …
>
> An old clay pipe and a farthing [worth a quarter of a penny] were found under the body.[42]

The Commissioner himself, James Monro, visited the location of the murder and stated his opinion that the killer was the Ripper:

> I need not say that every effort will be made by the Police to discover the murderer, who, I am inclined to believe is identical with the notorious 'Jack the Ripper' of last year.

> It will be seen that in spite of ample Police precautions and vigilance the assassin has again succeeded in committing a murder and getting off without leaving the slightest clue to his identity.[43]

Robert Anderson thought the reverse, however, and quoted what must have been a final view from Monro: 'I am here assuming that the murder of Alice M'Kenzie [*sic*] on the 17th of July 1889, was by another hand. I was absent from London when it occurred, but the Chief Commissioner [Monro] investigated the case on the spot and decided it was an ordinary murder, and not the work of a sexual maniac.'[44]

The extended team who worked on the case was heavily weighted with veterans of the Ripper investigation, counting not only the police but their political masters, the coroner and his assistant, and medical professionals. Like the Ripper murders, the case was notable by its absence of leads. Alice Kinsey was last seen by three acquaintances before midnight, hurrying alone towards Brick Lane and her imminent death at a secluded location.

At the second inquest hearing, Inspector Reid described assessing the body at the crime scene, then searching it for evidence at the mortuary. He commented, 'Her clothing was in a filthy condition, and I should think she was one of the lowest type of prostitutes.'[45] Reid produced the broken clay pipe, a short 'nose warmer', found under Kinsey's body, which was covered with blood, and contained some unburned tobacco.[46] He also found a bronze farthing. When questioned by the coroner, he confirmed that the pavement under the body was dry, and it started to rain at about a quarter to one, placing the murder before that time. When questioned by a juror as to whether coins were found 'in the previous murder cases', Reid said that two farthings were found in the Hanbury Street case, referencing the location of Annie Chapman's murder.[47] In Kinsey's case, he gave his opinion in the press that the farthing was passed off as a sixpence in the dark.[48]

At the third and final hearing, the only witness called was Doctor Phillips, who expanded on testimony he had previously given that the wound in the neck was sufficient to cause death from 'syncope from loss of blood through the divided vessels …'[49] Phillips confirmed that there were two pipes in the case, the first apparently the victim's and the second her killer's: '[He] stated that while he was examining the body another pipe fell from the clothing. It was a clay pipe, and was broken by the fall. It had been used. He had it placed upon the *post-mortem* table, but part of it had disappeared, and although every search had been made, the pieces could not be found.'[50]

Both pipes would be a gift to the modern forensic scientist for traces of saliva and fingerprints. Phillips added a comment about the low degree of skill needed to perform the murder, and the dissimilarity in its *modus operandi* to the Ripper murders, which often featured disembowelling and organ removal: 'He detected in the injuries a knowledge of how effectually to deprive a person of life, and that speedily. The injuries to the abdomen were not similar to those he had seen in the other cases, neither were the injuries to the throat …'[51]

The coroner summed up, giving his opinion that, 'if the crime was not committed by the same person as perpetuated the others, it was clearly an imitation of the other cases …' The jury returned a verdict of 'Murder by some person unknown', recommending that the narrow opening between Castle Alley and Whitechapel High Street be opened up as a thoroughfare.[52]

In his post-mortem examination report, Doctor Phillips specifically discounted Kinsey from the Ripper's canon:

> After careful and long deliberation I cannot satisfy myself on purely anatomical & professional grounds that the Perpetrator of all the 'WhChl. [*sic*: Whitechapel] murders' is one man.
>
> I am on the contrary impelled to a contrary conclusion. This noting the mode of procedure & the character of the mutilations & judging of motive in connection with the latter.[53]

Thomas Bond, by contrast, considered that Kinsey was yet another

Ripper victim. Bond inspected the body on the day after the post-mortem, at the request of Robert Anderson, and reported back to him:

> I see in this murder evidence of similar design to the former Whitechapel murders viz. sudden onslaught on the prostrate woman, the throat skilfully & resolutely cut with subsequent mutilation, each mutilation indicating sexual thoughts & a desire to mutilate the abdomen & sexual organs.
>
> I am of opinion that the murder was performed by the same ['hand' – *deleted*] person who committed the former series of Whitechapel murders.[54]

Bond added that he disagreed with Doctor Phillips that the murderer 'used the knife with his left hand'.[55]

It is hard to determine between the two illustrious police surgeons, whose judgements differed so greatly. Phillips may have been correct that this particular perpetrator was left-handed, a distinctive feature that could have helped to identify him; and Bond that the murder was sexually motivated. Despite the ultimate official conclusion that this was not a Ripper murder, it should be noted that its signature, or *modus operandi,* is reminiscent of the injuries inflicted on Martha Tabram and Polly Nichols. The crime scene was also extremely close to George Yard, where Tabram was killed, and to other 'canonical' murder locations off Whitechapel Road. If it were neither a Ripper murder nor a copycat crime, the killer may just as likely have been a sailor or docker who had contracted a venereal disease from a prostitute like Kinsey and was violent when drunk.[56]

The case of the Pinchin Street torso also features in the police Whitechapel Murders files, yet it does not belong with the Ripper series. The Pinchin Street murder was part of a different series of four, called 'The Thames Torso Murders', which took place in London between 1887 and 1889. Three of the four victims remained unidentified. All were discovered headless, with dismembered limbs and body parts, and some, but not all, of their body parts were found scattered at locations around central London. The *modus operandi* of that series varied hugely from the Ripper's, not only in the method of deconstructing their remains but in a clear demonstration of the killer's mobility across land and water. Robert Anderson's deputy, Melville Macnaghten, lodged an official report, stating: '... these murders had no connection whatever with the Whitechapel horrors. The Rainham mystery in 1887, & the Whitehall mystery (when portions of a woman's body were found under what is now New Scotland Yard) in 1888 were of a similar type to the Thames and Pinchin St crimes'.[57]

The perpetrator of the Torso Murders, like the Ripper, was never caught. In the last of that series, at 5.25 a.m. on Tuesday 10 September 1889, a woman's headless body, with its legs removed and its arms intact, was discovered in a railway arch in Whitechapel.

The arch was located near London Docks at the western end of Pinchin Street, and was the first opening on the right from Backchurch Lane. That location was three minutes' walk away from Leman Street police station, the headquarters of the Ripper investigation, and a similar distance from Berner Street. Speculation began that this was another Ripper murder.

A description of the torso, or 'trunk', was published in the press, in the hope that someone would recognize a missing family member or friend:

> Found, at 5.40 this morning, the trunk of a woman under railway arches in Pinchin-street, Whitechapel. Age about 40; height, 5 ft. 3 in.; hair, dark brown; no clothing except chemise, which is much torn and bloodstained; both elbows discoloured as [if] from habitually leaning on them. *Post-mortem* marks apparently of a rope having been tied round the waist.[58]

On Wednesday 11 September, Commissioner James Monro applied to the Home Office for an increase of 100 more men, 'both uniform

& plain clothes'.[59] An extensive search was under way on land and river for any other parts of the woman's body that might lead to her identification, and the streets were flooded with policemen. Coroner Wynne Baxter held an inquest into the unknown woman's death, which was found to be murder. As with the Ripper, the Torso killer inexplicably stopped killing, and the police lacked sufficient evidence to charge anyone with the crimes.

Monro's estimate of the date of the murder was the night of Sunday 8 September 1889, on the assumption that the body had been stored elsewhere before being deposited in the railway arch.[60] It is worth noting that Hyam Hyams was almost at liberty for the Pinchin Street murder. On 30 August 1889, on the grounds of his improved behaviour, he was discharged from Colney Hatch Lunatic Asylum.[61] At the end of what would prove to be his single week of freedom, he was arrested for stabbing his wife. Hyams was admitted to the City of London's Homerton Workhouse on Bow Road on Saturday 7 September.[62] Two days later, when diagnosed as insane, he was transferred to Stone Lunatic Asylum. He would spend the rest of his life in secure medical facilities.

The final case on the Metropolitan Police Whitechapel Murders files is that of thirty-two-year-old prostitute Frances Coles. Two days before her death, Coles hooked up with a ship's stoker on shore leave, fifty-three-year-old James Thomas 'Tom' Sadler, in an East End pub. Despite the age gap, they had things in common: travelling light, operating solo, and using alcohol for their kicks. They went on a bender around the streets of Whitechapel lasting the best part of thirty hours, repeatedly splitting up then reuniting in a sequence that would end in Coles's death. Their lodgings at Spitalfields Chambers on White's Row was a tangential link between Coles and Annie Millwood.

At 2.15 a.m. on Friday 13 February 1891, new recruit Constable Ernest Thompson was making his first-ever solo round of a beat that took fifteen to twenty minutes to complete. It covered two streets that ran off Leman Street south of its police station, Prescott Street and

Chamber Street, with short stretches on Mansell Street and Leman Street itself forming the short sides of a rectangle. The Great Eastern Railway bridge ran from east to west parallel to Chamber Street, three of its arches connecting Chamber Street with Royal Mint Street. Every time Thompson patrolled Chamber Street, he went up and down each of the railway arches, his route forming the capital letter E.

As he approached the third arch, he could hear footsteps moving away from him, northbound towards Mansell Street. Continuing into the passageway called Swallow Gardens, he found a woman lying on the ground with her throat cut. He saw her open and shut one eye. Thompson blew three times on his whistle to summon help from colleagues,[63] and followed police procedure to stay with the victim if living, until properly relieved. Frances Coles was barely alive. On his arrival, police surgeon Doctor Oxley 'pronounced life extinct'.[64]

Within days, her recent companion Sadler was charged with her murder, but he was released in early March, owing to a lack of evidence.[65] As in the previous case, senior detective Macnaghten concluded that this was not a Ripper murder and opined negatively about Sadler's character, calling him 'a man of ungovernable temper and entirely addicted to drink, and the company of the lowest prostitutes'.[66] Despite the likelihood that Sadler was her killer, Frances Coles was added to the list of unsolved killings attributed to 'Jack the Ripper'.

Of the eleven victims on the police Whitechapel Murders files, one died accidentally, as many as six were killed by the Ripper and four by other men. Both the Metropolitan and City of London Police assigned their best officers to those cases, who despite their utmost efforts were unable to solve them. Yet in the closing days of 1888, Hyam Hyams was removed from the streets and brought to a semblance of justice.

12

THE PERPETRATOR'S INCARCERATION AND DEATH

'The night has been unruly.'

FROM *Macbeth*, BY WILLIAM SHAKESPEARE

On Saturday 29 December 1888, H Division Constable Edward Walker arrested Hyam Hyams and took him into detention for 'behaving erratically' in Leman Street.[1] Hyams went before Franklin Lushington at Thames Magistrates Court on the charge of being a 'wandering lunatic'.[2] Sent to Whitechapel's Baker's Row Workhouse Infirmary, his cause of admission was recorded as *delirium tremens*. His occupation was listed as a 'hawker' and his home address recorded as 217 Jubilee Street in Mile End Old Town. In under two weeks, his DTs having ceased, he was released.[3]

It is a matter of speculation whether, having come to police attention, he was watched throughout the following three months, when he was at liberty between 11 January and 15 April. Certainly, both the Metropolitan and City of London Police Forces had put large numbers of men on plain-clothes duty. Acting City Police Chief Major Henry Smith went to an extreme: 'I put nearly a third of the force into plain clothes, with instructions to do everything which, under ordinary circumstances, a constable should not do … sitting on door-steps, smoking their pipes, hanging about public-houses, and gossiping with all and sundry.'[4]

City Police Detective Inspector Henry 'Harry' Cox gave an

interview to the press on his retirement in December 1906, in which he claimed to have had a Ripper suspect under surveillance. Aged twenty-nine in the period between late 1888 and early 1889,[5] Cox was a highly skilled 'shadower', or 'watcher', both terms meaning a surveillance operative. A published photograph of him shows an unmemorable face, a useful trait for his profession.[6] His noticeably large ears could be covered by a hat or cap.

Cox opened by stating:

> It is only upon certain conditions that I have agreed to deal with the great Whitechapel crimes of fifteen years ago. Much has been written regarding the identity of the man who planned and successfully carried out the outrage. Many writers gifted with a vivid imagination have drawn pictures for the public of the criminal whom the police suspected. All have been woefully wrong ... It is my intention to relate several of my experiences while keeping this fellow under observation ...
>
> We had many people under observations while the murders were being perpetrated, but it was not until the discovery of the body of Mary Jane Kelly had been made that we seemed to get upon the trail. Certain investigations made by several of our cleverest detectives made it apparent to us that a man living in the East End of London was not unlikely to have been connected with the crimes.
>
> To understand the reason we must first of all understand the motive of the Whitechapel crimes. The motive was, there can not be a slightest doubt, revenge. Not merely revenge on the few unfortunate victims of the knife, but revenge on womankind. It was not a lust for blood, as many people have imagined.
>
> The murderer was a misogynist, who at some time or another had been wronged by a woman. And the fact that his victims were of the lowest class proves, I think, that he was not, as has been stated, an educated man who had suddenly gone mad. He belonged to their own class ...[7]

Cox was accurate on the perpetrator's motive and class. The City Police cannot have deduced the killer's identity soon after Eddowes' murder, as any surveillance team would have prevented him from spending four hours alone in a room with Mary Jane Kelly. Regarding the timing of the police breakthrough, the description of Kelly's smartly dressed final companion provided by her acquaintance George Hutchinson might have been crucial. Alternatively, it is just possible that Annie Farmer, attacked two weeks after Mary Jane Kelly, was taken seriously by the police, and taken around the local streets with the plan of sighting her attacker.

However their suspect was detected, Cox provided a profile of him, based on surveillance of a specific unnamed individual for almost three months:

> The man we suspected was about five feet six inches in height, with short, black, curly hair, and he had a habit of taking late walks abroad. He occupied several shops in the East End, but from time to time he became insane, and was forced to spend a portion of his time in an asylum in Surrey.
>
> While the Whitechapel murders were being perpetrated his place of business was in a certain street, and after the last murder [of Mary Jane Kelly] I was on duty in this street for nearly three months.
>
> There were several other officers with me, and I think there can be no harm in stating that the opinion of most of them was that the man they were watching had something to do with the crimes. You can imagine that never once did we allow him to quit our sight. The least slip and another brutal crime might have been perpetrated under our very noses. It was not easy to forget that already one of them had taken place at the very moment when one of our smartest colleagues was passing the top of the dimly lit street [probably the murder of Kate Eddowes].
>
> The Jews in the street soon became aware of our presence.

It was impossible for us to hide ourselves. They became suddenly alarmed, panic-stricken, and I can tell you that at nights we ran a considerable risk. We carried our lives in our hands so to speak, and at last we had to partly take the alarmed inhabitants into our confidence, and so throw them off the scent. We told them we were factory inspectors looking for tailors and cap-makers who employed boys and girls under age, and pointing out the evils accruing from the sweaters' system [exploitation of workers] asked them to co-operate with us in destroying it.

They readily promised so to do, although we knew well that they had no intention of helping us … Day after day we used to sit and chat with them, drinking their coffee, smoking their excellent cigarettes, and partaking of Kosher rum. Before many weeks had passed we were quite friendly with them, and knew that we could carry out our observations unmolested …

We had the use of a house opposite the shop of the man we suspected, and, disguised, of course, we frequently stopped across in the role of customers … The fact, by the way, that the murderer never shifted his ground rather inclines one to the belief that he was a mad, poverty-stricken inhabitant of some slum in the East End.

I shall never forget one occasion when I had to shadow our man during one of his late walks. As I watched him from the house opposite one night, it suddenly struck me that there was a wilder look than usual on his evil countenance, and I felt that something was about to happen. When darkness set in I saw him come forth from the door of his little shop and glance furtively around to see if he were being watched. I allowed him to get right out of the street before I left the house, and then I set off after him. I followed him to Lehman [*sic*] Street, and there I saw him enter a shop which I knew was the abode of a number of criminals well known to the police.

He did not stay long. For about a quarter of an hour I hung

about keeping my eye on the door, and at last I was rewarded by seeing him emerging alone.

He made his way down to St George's in the East End, and there to my astonishment I saw him stop and speak to a drunken woman. I crouched in a doorway and held my breath. Was he going to throw himself right into my waiting arms? He passed on after a moment or two, and on I slunk after him.

As I passed the woman she laughed and shouted something after me, which, however, I did not catch.

My man was evidently of opinion that he might be followed every minute. Now and again he turned his head and glanced over his shoulder, and consequently I had the greatest difficulty in keeping behind him.

I had to work my way along, now with my back to the wall, now pausing and making little runs for a sheltering doorway. Not far from where the model lodging-house stands he met another woman, and for a considerable distance he walked along with her.

Just as I was beginning to prepare myself for a terrible ordeal, however, he pushed her away from him and set off at a rapid pace. In the end he brought me, tired, weary, and nerve-strung back to the street he had left where he disappeared into his own house.

Next morning I beheld him busy as usual. It is indeed very strange that as soon as this madman was put under observation the mysterious crimes ceased, and that very soon he removed from his usual haunts and gave up his nightly prowls. He was never arrested for the reason that not the slightest scrap of evidence could be found to connect him with the crimes.[8]

Cox's suspect is a possible match to Hyam Hyams, and the period of surveillance fits the three months in early 1889, when he was at liberty. Hyams' address at the beginning of that time was most likely 4 Bell Court, a small yard tucked between Bell Lane and Wentworth Street close to his former lodgings at Wentworth Court.[9]

Cox does not specify what type of shop he and his colleagues were frequenting, nor the type of goods they bought from the suspect. Tobacco products, including 'penny smokes', that might be traded by a cigar-maker-turned-salesman like Hyams, would be easily purchased and consumed by the surveillance operatives from a shop run by a member of his extended family.

In an attempt to identify the location described by Cox, it is necessary to return to his police colleague Robert Sagar's version of events. After describing the pursuit of a suspect to King's Block, he went on to comment: 'We had good reason to suspect a certain man who worked in Butchers' Row, Aldgate. We watched him carefully. There was no doubt that this man was insane, and after a time his friends thought it advisable to have him removed to a private asylum. After he was removed, there were no more Ripper atrocities.'[10]

Butchers' Row was the name given to a parade of buildings, numbers 43 to 62, on the south side of Aldgate High Street between the Minories and Mansell Street.[11] Researchers have itemized its buildings and residents without finding any Ripper connection. The north side of Butchers' Row is the bottom of a block that stretches up to Stoney Lane, encompassing the Artizans' Dwellings, where Mark Hyams lived. Mark, Leah and their family remained at 49 North Block until at least 1892,[12] where it is possible that they had shop premises that Hyams helped to mind for them. That small area also included an address associated with Hyam Hyams after 1888 on New Street off Houndsditch, its number variously recorded as No. 26 or 36.[13]

Alternatively, Harry Cox's suspect occupying 'several shops in the East End' could refer to the business premises belonging to Hyams' mother's family, the Mordecais. From Butchers' Row, remaining on the south side of Aldgate High Street, a ten-minute walk eastwards reached 230 Whitechapel Road and Abraham Mordecai. A double left turn out of those premises led on to Plumbers Row. Densely populated by Jewish tailors and others in the clothes industry, it is a better fit than Butchers' Row for an investigation into 'sweating'.

Plumbers Row leads on to Berner Street (if crossing Commercial Road), the site of Elisabeth Stride's murder. For that reason, it arguably fits the following description of a stake-out and suspect provided by Sergeant Stephen White, the officer who had first interviewed grape-seller Matthew Packer. White reported seeing a man close to the scene of one of the Whitechapel Murders, believed to be that of Elisabeth Stride owing to its location in a cul-de-sac, or dead end:

> For five nights we had been watching a certain alley just behind the Whitechapel Road. It could only be entered from where we had two men posted in hiding, and persons entering the alley were under observation by the two men. It was a bitter cold night when I arrived at the scene to take the report of the two men in hiding. I was turning away when I saw a man coming out of the alley. He was walking quickly but noiselessly, apparently wearing rubber shoes, which were rather rare in those days. I stood aside to let the man pass, and as he came under the wall lamp I got a good look at him.
>
> He was about five feet ten inches in height, and was dressed rather shabbily, though it was obvious that the material of his clothes was good. Evidently a man who had seen better days, I thought, but men who have seen better days are common enough down East, and that of itself was not sufficient to justify me in stopping him. His face was long and thin, nostrils rather delicate, and his hair was jet black. His complexion was inclined to be sallow, and altogether the man was foreign in appearance. The most striking thing about him, however, was the extraordinary brilliance of his eyes. They looked like two very luminous glow worms coming through the darkness. The man was slightly bent at the shoulders, though he was obviously quite young – about 33, at the most – and gave one the idea of having been a student or professional man. His hands were snow white, and the fingers long and tapering.

> The man stumbled a few feet away from me, and I made that an excuse for engaging him in conversation. He turned sharply at the sound of my voice, and scowled at me in surly fashion, but he said 'Good night' and agreed with me that it was cold.
>
> His voice was a surprise to me. It was soft and musical, with just a tinge of melancholy in it, and it was the voice of a man of culture – a voice altogether out of keeping with the squalid surroundings of the East End.
>
> As he turned away, one of the police officers came out of the house he had been in, and walked a few paces into the darkness of the alley. 'Hello! what is this?' he cried, and then he called in startled tones to me to come along.
>
> In the East End we are used to shocking sights, but the sight I saw made the blood in my veins turn to ice. At the end of the cul-de-sac, huddled against the wall, there was the body of a woman, and a pool of blood was streaming along the gutter from her body. It was clearly another of those terrible murders. I remembered the man I had seen, and I started after him as fast as I could run, but he was lost to sight in the dark labyrinth of East End mean streets.[14]

Ripper expert Philip Sugden deliberately discounted this description, calling it 'fiction developed out of memories of the Berner Street and Mitre Square murders and of Mrs Mortimer'.[15] Fanny Mortimer was a resident of 36 Berner Street who reported a man with a black bag walking 'very fast' from the direction of Commercial Road, at a time corresponding to the murderer's getaway from Dutfield's Yard. That man was identified by police as local man Leon Goldstein,[16] and discounted as a suspect.

White's suspect was 2½ inches taller than Hyams, although other physical traits might arguably match him. His worn clothes that were originally of good quality could have been sourced from his tailoress sister. It is possible that the man's stumble was caused by him dragging his feet. The description of his unusually refractive eyes can be compared to Hyams' excess of choroidal pigment or melanin, causing yellow or brown spots on the white of the eye. It is debatable whether the suspect's musical lilt was Jewish, but his surly scowl is reminiscent of the suspect's expression as described by Mary Jane Kelly's acquaintance George Hutchinson.

After three months of either genuine freedom or police surveillance, in late March or early April, Hyams again attracted the attention of the authorities. After an attempted assault on his wife that struck his mother, Hyams was first admitted to Baker's Row Workhouse, then transferred to Colney Hatch. His admission papers at Baker's Row were signed by the Doctor Larder who had treated Annie Farmer.[17] Hyams' admission to the workhouse and transfer on to the asylum coincide with a significant reduction in the number of policemen assigned to plain-clothes work in H Division. An order from Commissioner Monro dated 15 March 1889 stood down 'the special police duty in Whitechapel'.

After a brief stay at Baker's Row Workhouse, Hyams was transferred to Colney Hatch Lunatic Asylum. He remained there until the end of August.[18] By the mid-summer of 1889, his wife, thirty-four-year-old Sarah Hyams, and their two children were destitute. On Saturday 13 July 1889, Sarah and their one-year-old daughter Katey were transferred from the City of London's Homerton Workhouse to Mile End Workhouse. Two days later, Sarah and Katey were discharged at their own request.[19] Unlike Katey, who would still have been breast-feeding, her older brother Ike might have been looked after by a relative.

Briefly discharged from Colney Hatch in late August, on Saturday 7 September Hyams was arrested by the City of London Police for stabbing his wife. There is no record of the type of injury sustained by her. Two City policemen took Hyams to Bishopsgate police station, where, like Ripper victim Kate Eddowes, he was briefly placed in a cell, before being admitted to the City of London's Homerton Workhouse.[20] Research into their unique collar numbers has identified Thomas

Cooper as Constable 895 and William Harber as Constable 918.[21] In July 1891, Harber was operating as an undercover detective in a raid on a gambling club, under the direction of Superintendent McWilliam.[22] On that basis, Harber could have been part of an undercover team watching Hyams.

On Monday 9 September, a year and a day after the murder of Annie Chapman, escorted by Constable Cooper, Hyams appeared before Sir Francis Wyatt Truscott at the Guildhall Justice Room. Truscott was father-in-law to City Solicitor Henry Homewood Crawford, who advised the City of London Police on the Eddowes case. Truscott sent Hyams to the City of London Lunatic Asylum at Stone near Dartford, 'as a person of unsound mind'.[23] Reinforcing Hyams' identity as Robert Anderson's suspect, an asylum near Stone was where Ripper researcher Steward Hicks 'alleged that Lady Anderson … once remarked that the Ripper was interned'.[24]

An extract from Donald Swanson's previously referenced 'marginalia' could shed light on what happened to Hyams during the first week of September, when he was temporarily at liberty. It provides a basis in fact for his apparent paranoia, which could have been a reaction to a genuine surveillance operation on him:

> And after this identification which suspect knew, no other murder of this kind took place in London after the suspect had been identified at the Seaside Home where he had been sent by us with difficulty in order to subject him to identification, and he knew he was identified. On suspect's return to his brother's house in Whitechapel he was watched by police (City CID) by day & night.
>
> In a very short time the suspect with his hands tied behind his back, he was sent to Stepney Workhouse and then to Colney Hatch and died soon afterwards …[25]

A natural choice for the Seaside Home is the Police Seaside Home at 51 Clarendon Villas in Hove, which, however, did not open until March

1890. An alternative candidate might be the 'Seaside House' at 55 Marina in St Leonard's-on-Sea, which was a convalescent home of the Royal Hospital for Incurables on West Hill in Putney. It was opened as a 'seaside retreat' in 1885, closing in 1901. The hospital, which is still in use today, specialized in neurological conditions such as epilepsy. Patients who used the Seaside House should have an entry in the hospital's admission case books, which Hyams does not.[26] If Swanson's sentence meant that the Ripper suspect was sent to a 'Seaside Home' in order to be identified by one of its residents, the quandary is three-fold. Not only do the location and the suspect need to be pinpointed, but so also does the individual who carried out that identification.

The marginalia's sentence about the suspect's transfer from one institution to another, if referring to Hyams, was accurate in part, although the truth was more complicated. Hyams was admitted to Stepney's Baker's Row Workhouse and then Colney Hatch. However, in September 1889, his admission to the City of London Workhouse was followed by an admission to Stone Asylum, then a readmission to Colney Hatch. And Hyams did not die soon after his admission to the asylum, but over two decades later. It is possible that his police investigators were ignorant of whether he was alive or dead, or claimed that he was dead to prevent the press from contacting him.

Hyams' medical records in early 1897, the year of the Queen's Diamond Jubilee, reported no improvement, saying he was 'a crafty and dangerous maniac … Violent, abusive and threatening when fitty … Is very destructive … As insane as ever.'[27] It was also the year when my police ancestor Harry Garrett left the Force after twenty-three years' service. In October 1896, he and his 'partner in crime', Constable James Main, were suspended with loss of pay for an unspecified misdemeanour.[28] It was something worse than 'being improperly inside a public house' with his duty armlet or armband on, for which the punishment was a reduction in pay by three shillings a week for six months, and a strict caution. However, it was a lesser offence than being 'drunk and lying on the footway when on duty, and using threatening language at the station', for which the offender was dismissed without pay.[29]

Whatever it was, that misdemeanour led both men to be fined ten shillings, severely reprimanded, cautioned, in Garrett's case removed from Special Duty, and transferred to another Division. Garrett went to Holborn's E Division where, having served a matter of weeks, he resigned and was awarded a No. 2 certificate. The ratings ran from 1 (Excellent) to 5 (Unfit for duty). Garrett's score indicated a service record that was not unblemished, but still very good. His pension for life was £54 1s 8d per annum,[30] an amount which, with a family to support, required him to continue working.

Unlike other police pensioners, Garrett did not volunteer to serve during the Jubilee celebrations. He found other employment as a factory timekeeper, clocking men in and out of their shifts. Garrett, his wife Alice and their five children aged between six and nineteen moved to East Hill in Dartford, Kent, known as the hospital town.[31] They lived one mile west of Stone Lunatic Asylum, which had briefly housed Hyam Hyams between 1889 and 1890. By coincidence, in the 1870s, Alice and her family the Kings lived extremely near Hyams' future doctor at Colney Hatch, Cecil Fowler Beadles, whose father was a General Practitioner on Eltham High Street in Greenwich.[32]

Over the next five years, many of my police ancestor's former colleagues retired or died. H Division's elderly police surgeon Doctor Phillips died in the year of Garrett's retirement. In 1899, Inspector Andrews died by hanging himself. Two years later, Thomas Bond killed himself after a long illness, by jumping from an upstairs window. Also in 1901, Robert Anderson retired as CID Chief and was replaced by Edward Henry, a future Police Commissioner who devised the Henry System of Fingerprint Classification and the Metropolitan Police Fingerprint Bureau, a huge advance in the Force's forensic capability.

Stalwarts of the Ripper investigation, H Division Superintendent Thomas Arnold, Chief Inspector John West, and detectives Henry

Moore, Frederick Abberline, John Littlechild, Edmund Reid and Stephen White had all retired. A handful of the old and bold were still working: CID Superintendent Donald Swanson; his boss CID Chief Sir Melville Macnaghten; and Walter Dew, now an Inspector. Sir Edward Bradford, known as 'zealous, shrewd, and most capable',[33] had replaced James Monro as the Metropolitan Police Commissioner.

Unlike Hyams, who had a deformity of the left elbow, Bradford had lost most of his left arm. Twenty-seven years earlier, he had it amputated above the elbow after being mauled by a tiger on a tiger shoot in India.[34] Bradford's disabled arm did not affect his ability to work. He could even ride using one hand, and when he needed a free hand, he held the reins between his teeth.

Of the City of London Police, now-Superintendent James McWilliam was still leading his team of detectives out of Cloak Lane police station. The officer who never wore a uniform or walked a beat, Detective Inspector Robert Sagar, was still at his command. The last police officer to handle Hyam Hyams, Thomas Cooper, had been promoted to Inspector. Harry Cox had retired in 1896. Major Henry Smith, since knighted, retired as Commissioner in 1901, and was replaced by John Nott-Bower, the father of a same-named later Metropolitan Police Commissioner. In addition to two new Police Commissioners in London, there was a new Home Secretary, Charles Ritchie, a former Member of Parliament for Tower Hamlets. And with the death of Queen Victoria on 22 January 1901, the nation would have a new King, Edward VII.

The new century brought a deterioration in Hyams' health, first noted in February of that year. His medical records stated: 'Has frequent fits and at such times is the most dangerous patient in the ward, also being very destructive dirty and abusive on these occasions. Memory defective, he seems to be altering very gradually and passing to condition of dementia.'[35] By November of that year – when Hyams was aged just forty-eight – a further note was made on file: 'the patient is fast becoming demented'.[36] In addition to his severe seizures, potassium bromide, which he was prescribed as an anticonvulsant and sedative, was also known to hasten the onset of dementia.

The next episode of note was on 5 February 1902, when for the second time in his life, Hyams lost the use of his left arm by breaking his elbow: 'In one of his violent attacks on another patient Levine, Hyams to-day at about 1.30 fell and fractured his olecranon (left). A contracted elbow joint due to an old fracture somewhat complicated matters. The arm was fixed with splints.'[37] He was injected occasionally with hyoscyamine for pain relief and, as with his earlier injury, the bones in his arm 'failed to unite'. Suffering from delusions of 'electricity, torture', he 'attempted to cut off his Penis with a small piece of tin – succeeded only in making a skin incision which was sutured'.[38]

In the early hours of the windy morning of Tuesday 27 January 1903, a fire in a temporary building housing female patients claimed the lives of fifty-one patients and one nurse. Medical Superintendent William Joseph Seward and his staff, in particular the annexe's female attendants, were praised for dragging patients from the burning building and saving dozens of lives. Metropolitan Police Inspector Lambert and eleven of his colleagues were awarded medals by the Society for the Protection of Life from Fire, with Lambert receiving the prestigious silver medal for saving five lives. Lambert said of the fire, which he described as 'terrible ... a shocking sight', that 'it showed what a Britisher will do to save a fellow creature's life'.[39] Their efforts were hindered by the patients' lack of understanding of the danger. Like all inhabitants of Colney Hatch and its surrounding area, Hyams would have been aware of, and possibly distressed by, the fire.

An entry in April 1903 recorded: 'Mental state no change. Health much better.' Then, in September, 'Has had several severe fits of late. After which he is very treacherous.' In December 1905, he seemed physically and mentally weaker, having difficulty walking and 'unable to stand with his eyes shut'. By April 1906, his physical health had improved, but showed 'no mental improvement: at times being exceedingly noisy and maniacal'.[40]

On 6 January 1907, 'during an attack of excitement he broke the distal phalanx [tip] of the first finger of his left hand – this he did by beating his hand on the floor in a paroxysm of passion'.[41] By the 20th, it was recorded, 'Patient has again become maniacal – finger however is weathering the storm fairly well. Health good.'[42] It was observed that he was 'Wet and dirty when excited or fitty',[43] losing control of his bladder and bowels. The year 1910 was characterized by a series of bad fits, as many as seven in a twenty-four-hour period. One entry in his medical records stated, 'He has had 9 diurnal and 4 nocturnal seizures in the last 3 months all of them Major Type [tonic-clonic seizures].'[44] Hyams was kept in bed following his fits, 'very noisy and abusive and excited', and 'in a state of delirium'.[45]

During the last three years of his life, his frequent fits and subsequent bed rest continued to be enumerated. One of the last entries read, 'Demented maniacal very noisy and obscene.'[46] In November 1912, it was noted that he had 'grown somewhat feeble'.[47] On 4 March 1913, he was put to bed and did not get up again. He died at 12.18 a.m. on 22 March 1913, aged fifty-nine, of 'Insanity with Epilepsy'. His death certificate recorded his cause of death as 'Cardio-vascular degeneration of indefinite duration', and 'Exhaustion from Epilepsy many years'.[48] He had been in Colney Hatch for twenty-three years.

The two Sarahs in his life, his long-suffering, loving wife and sister, jointly placed a notice of his death in *The Jewish Chronicle*, calling Hyam a 'beloved husband … deeply mourned by his sorrowing children and relatives'.[49] Shiva, the seven days of mourning after the funeral, was observed at the addresses of both women. Unlike most of his fellow patients, who were buried in New Southgate Cemetery, Hyams' body was buried in the family plot at Plashet Jewish Cemetery in Newham.[50]

Sarah survived him by thirty-one years. She died on 3 November 1944, aged ninety-three, of chronic kidney disease, arteriosclerosis (hardening of the arteries) and old age. On her death certificate, her address was given as 43 North Block, Stoney Lane. It was the same block that offered Hyams a place of refuge after the Mitre Square murder. Her occupation was stated to be: 'Widow of Hyam Hyams, a cigar maker'.[51] Thirty years after his death, Sarah was still being defined by her husband.

In some way, justice was served on Hyam Hyams. If convicted of his crimes, public opinion would have been vehemently in favour of his execution by hanging. But if not hanged, and instead treated as a criminal lunatic who was unfit to plead, Hyams would have been sent to Broadmoor Criminal Lunatic Asylum in Berkshire. Although Broadmoor would have provided a more secure environment, Hyam's lifelong retention at Colney Hatch delivered a similar fate. He was considered to be incurable, was prevented from doing further harm and received the best medical treatment and care that were available at the time. Then, as now, he could never be released. In destroying the lives of others, he had destroyed his own.

CONCLUSION

Robert Anderson was convinced that there was no doubt about the identity of Jack the Ripper. Of all possible suspects, Hyam Hyams best matches the available profiles as the infamous serial killer who terrorized the East End in the late Victorian era. Affected by epilepsy, insanity, alcohol addiction and pain from his injured left arm, he killed six vulnerable women: Martha Tabram, Polly Nichols, Annie Chapman, Elisabeth Stride, Kate Eddowes and Mary Jane Kelly. He also carried out as many as four non-fatal attacks: on Annie Millwood in February 1888; Annie Farmer in November of the same year; and, in 1889, on his mother and wife. The final assault led to his permanent detention, a result less pleasing to police than his conviction for serial murder. Contrary to popular thinking about the Ripper, those attacks were mainly conducted in indoor settings on local women whom he may have known from Whitechapel's streets, pubs, chop houses and lodging houses.

Hyams was particularly violent after epileptic fits, which explains the periodicity of the murders. Severe 'off periods' were marked by the murder of Annie Chapman eight days after that of Polly Nichols, and the double event twenty-two days later, when Elisabeth Stride and Kate Eddowes were killed on the same night. When recalculated to include six murders and four non-fatal attacks, the period of the Ripper's murderous activities extends to one year, six and a half months. Considerably longer than the little-over-two-month spread of the canonical five murders, it spans approximately half of the time frame of the extant police Whitechapel Murders files.

The 'signature' of his crimes developed with the escalation of violence across his murder victims from Martha Tabram to Mary Jane Kelly at locations within an easy walk of his home. His first kill, of Tabram, used a long knife blade to grant him sexual gratification, and occurred within metres of Wentworth Street, the epicentre of his murderous activities. Like his second kill, it was entirely unwitnessed, leaving the police with almost nothing to work on. The murders of Martha Tabram and Polly Nichols provided the template for his future rapid and debilitating attacks: cornering his victim and using his body weight to compensate for his weak arm, partly suffocating her with his right hand before pushing her to the ground and cutting her throat. When killing Elisabeth Stride, he probably knelt on top of her chest to keep her down as he drew out his knife.

With many of his victims, the deepest cuts to the throat, made from left to right, suggested attempts at beheading. He must have laid out the disembowelled intestines of his victims using his right hand, as he placed them to the left side of his victims' bodies. When he had sufficient time, he devoted himself to mutilating his victims, removing their uteri and other organs, in frenzied attacks that escalated over a period of several months. He also derived satisfaction from the posing of their prone bodies, wiping his bloody knife on them, stabbing their private parts and stealing their money and rings.

The evening he spent with Elisabeth Stride was the most witnessed of his crimes, while his soliciting of Kate Eddowes within the hour after Stride's murder was the best witnessed. If the crucial witness Joseph Lawende had been willing to testify, Jack the Ripper's killing spree would have ended. For the first time in history, Jack the Ripper can be identified as Hyam Hyams using distinctive physical characteristics. The murder of Annie Chapman, the Ripper's third kill, was the first where a man with a stiff gait was seen running from the scene of the crime.

Passers-by on the streets, with Thomas Eade, John Thimbleby and George Hutchinson among them, came forward to report sightings of a suspicious man in his mid-thirties with a stiff arm and knees, a peculiar gait and stare. He was of average height and weight, stout and broad-shouldered, with brown hair and a moustache. He favoured dark clothing of varying smartness, and his cutaway coat was noted on several occasions. He spoke colloquial English with a slight hesitancy. A Jewish man, Hyams was described as 'quiet … civil and attentive to his personal appearance', exactly like the mild-mannered clerk he was perceived to be during the double event. Fruiterer Matthew Packer might have sold him grapes on that night, and if it is true that he had a second sighting of the Ripper in October, a golden opportunity to stop him was lost.

Hyams had all of the additional distinctive physical attributes that were reported by eyewitnesses: a hesitancy of speech; an irregular gait with bent knees; sluggish pupils and refractive yellow or brown spots on the whites of his eyes. Those sightings are evidential, placing an identifiable suspect at a Ripper crime location. The City of London Police pursued from Mitre Square 'a well-known man of Jewish appearance'.[1] By the autumn of 1888, Hyams' eccentric behaviour, marked by increasing rage and incoherence, must have made him a well-known figure on Wentworth Street, and beyond that locality, extending to a radius of a couple of miles.

Lucky in his timings, he made two of his great escapes in the double event. While bending over Elisabeth Stride's body planning to cut her further, he was interrupted by the approach of a local man, and escaped without detection. After the murder of Kate Eddowes less than an hour later, he was chased from the scene by the City Police and hid out part way through his escape. His home address of Wentworth Court lay in a direct line from Mitre Square via his brother's apartment at Artizans' Dwellings and the doorway where the physical evidence of a graffito and discarded piece of apron were found. Angry and powerless, he left a chalked message for anyone to find, its intrinsic meaning clear enough: *Look what I've done: I won't be blamed for nothing*. It also posed a defiant challenge: *What are you going to do about it?*

A man at the edge of his physical and mental capabilities, he went the furthest with his last victim, Mary Jane Kelly, slashing her face through her bed sheet as he deconstructed her physical remains. His vices extended to *pica*, the desire to eat non-nutritive objects, and he might have resorted to sexual cannibalism to dispose of the organs he took. Yet when seen accosting her by George Hutchinson, he seemed better than an ordinary punter; flush with money, and able to make a girl laugh. His easy exchange with Kelly might indicate their earlier acquaintance. His earnings from race days made him an attractive prospect to the women he solicited, backed up by an appearance that was smarter than most other punters', affable manners and an unthreatening demeanour.

It is not known when the police started to have a lead on the Ripper. At the very end of 1888, Hyams was first detained by the authorities, when acting strangely under the influence of *delirium tremens*. He might have come to the attention of the police earlier, after the murder of Eddowes, or Kelly, or the later attack on Annie Farmer, as convincing witnesses came forward. Information could have been provided by someone who knew him, a family member, neighbour, 'unfortunate' or acquaintance. Or he may just have been picked up in late December as a wandering lunatic, with his later attacks on his wife instigating further inquiry. He would often have returned home bloodied and bruised, with soiled clothing, after an epileptic fit, or worse. His black coats and trousers would not show the blood, but his hands would. His wife might have suspected him, but she did not report him to the authorities.

A local man with an addiction to alcohol, and perhaps gambling, he walked out of his front door and onwards through a web of East End streets and open spaces, into pubs, clubs and chop houses, up and down Whitechapel Road, into Itchy Park and other churchyards, along lines of market stalls, past street corners and doorways where women could be found. Sexually motivated, his ideal victim type was a woman like his wife, a local woman in her thirties whom he perceived as sexually incontinent, with thousands of her proxies available on the East End streets. Who accosted whom, did he speak first, as with Kelly as he tapped her on the shoulder, or did they sometimes come up to him, to ask him to buy them a drink, or to give them a few pennies?

His victims might have known him, like Elisabeth Stride, who was out on a date with an affable-seeming man. Whether they saw him as congenial or persecuted, they did not fear him. He did not need to target women who had been drinking, or even try to get them drunk, and he did not rape them. He spoke to them nicely, asked politely, and even made Kelly laugh as they hurried back to her place. Wherever they went, indoors or out, it was by mutual agreement. His silent intent, newly formed, was undetectable. It was only with Elisabeth Stride that he was witnessed losing his temper after she rejected his advances, Hyams throwing her to the ground as an onlooker approached.

Jack the Ripper was not a sophisticated operator who deliberately killed in the intervals between policemen's beats, and whose silent invisibility terrified local residents. Nor was he cunning, highly intelligent or organized. Seemingly unthreatening, he was mentally incapable, yet physically able to kill. His knowledge of the streets, while remaining within proximity of his lodgings, helped him to evade capture. By a matter of minutes, or hours in the cases of Martha Tabram and Mary Jane Kelly, he kept ahead of the police who were primed to pursue him.

He knew the East End like the back of his hand: Buck's Row Board School, Mitre Square, his family's premises along Whitechapel Road. He had the extreme good fortune not to be caught red-handed. Unlike in the myths, he did not take a boat to the United States, to continue his killing spree there, or alight into his gentleman's carriage and return to his palace. He roamed short distances close to his home, reducing his risks of detection. For most of the murders, he was safely at home before the streets were searched by police fanning out from the crime scenes.

In the words of Ripper expert Philip Sugden: '[He was] a complete nobody whose name never found its way into the police file … some sad social cripple who lived out his days in obscurity, his true identity a secret now known only to the dead.'[2] That secret is blown by the certainty that the case was solved by the police of the day, who unwittingly directed future researchers to identify their man. Hyam Hyams is a compelling match to the police profile constructed by Robert Anderson, the details of which were confirmed by brother officers in the Metropolitan and City of London Police Forces, alongside numerous eyewitnesses.

Anderson was rightly called 'one of the ablest men ever at the head of the detective service',[3] and the fact that he never wrote his 'Graver Reminiscences'[4] can no longer be regretted. We now know Jack the Ripper's name, where he lived, and some of the factors that motivated his crimes. We can walk in Hyam Hyams' footsteps around the East End streets he haunted as his mental and physical state declined, a killer of the women whom he felt he could blame for everything that was wrong with his life.

EPILOGUE

A relative locates an old family photograph, long awaited, and emails me a copy. In one click, Harry Garrett looks directly back at me with deep-set eyes. Taken in 1925, it is the striking headshot of a man in his early seventies, his chiselled good looks set off by a handlebar moustache and a stylish quiff. When I colourize it online, Garrett's hair shines silver against his freckled tan. His eyebrows and moustache are ash-brown, and his knotted tie comes up light, like bleached linen, under a round, white collar. I note traces of my father in his prominent nose, and the shape of his ears and eyebrows. If you can see a man's life in his face, then Garrett's made him confident, trustworthy and decisive.

Although he does not feature in the surviving papers on the police Whitechapel Murders files, nor is he connected to the Ripper case in any press reports, Garrett had the distinction of performing one act of heroism during his long service. On the night of Thursday 18 October 1888, halfway through the interval between the double event and the final Ripper murder, Garrett had his finest hour in the Force. He coordinated the rescue of eleven people from a serious house fire in Leman Street, charging up flights of smoke-filled stairs to lead, and in the case of an elderly servant, carry them to safety.[1] Rewarded by Commissioner Sir Charles Warren with four shillings for his 'promptitude and courage'[2] while putting his own life at considerable risk, he also received a certificate and a guinea from The Royal Society for the Protection of Life from Fire.[3]

The inhabitants of 96 Leman Street, a Jewish cooperative grocery and general store opposite the police station, were the Landau family. Its illustrious descendants include the neurologist Oliver Sacks,[4] educator Annie Landau, who received the MBE (Member of the Order of the British Empire Medal) as headmistress of the first Jewish school for girls in the newly established State of Israel, and Robert Aumann, joint winner of the Nobel Memorial Prize in Economics in 2005.

Inspired by my police ancestor, who worked on one of the most challenging cases in history, I would have achieved little without accessing the analysis and deductions of hundreds of experts and enthusiasts. Whole communities of researchers have pinpointed where the lamp posts stood on Mitre Square, what type of flower Elisabeth Stride was wearing in her buttonhole, and exactly how short Polly Nichols' stays were. As importantly, they have freely shared their knowledge, and its accumulated store is still growing. I pay tribute to the public-spirited assembly of police and civilians who, over the past 135 years, have assembled a comprehensive dossier against the man who was Jack the Ripper.

TIMELINE

Day	Month	Year	Event
10	January	1888	The author's great-great-grandfather Harry Garrett is transferred to H Division's Leman Street police station on promotion to Sergeant
25	February	1888	Non-fatal attack on Annie Millwood
4	April	1888	Death of Emma Elizabeth Smith, the first alleged victim of Jack the Ripper
7	August	1888	Murder of Martha Tabram
31	August	1888	Murder of Polly Nichols
31	August	1888	Robert Anderson succeeds James Monro as Assistant Commissioner for the CID on the latter's resignation and places Chief Inspector Donald Swanson in overall charge of the 'Whitechapel Murders'
8	September	1888	Murder of Annie Chapman
27	September	1888	First use of the name 'Jack the Ripper' appears in the 'Dear Boss' letter sent to the Central News Agency of London
30	September	1888	Murder of Elisabeth Stride
30	September	1888	Murder of Kate Eddowes
16	October	1888	George Lusk of the Whitechapel Vigilance Committee receives the 'From Hell' letter in a package containing half a human kidney alleged to be that of Kate Eddowes

Timeline

Day	Month	Year	Event
18	October	1888	Harry Garrett and three colleagues rescue eleven members of the Landau family from a fire in Leman Street
9	November	1888	Murder of Mary Jane Kelly
9	November	1888	James Monro succeeds Charles Warren as Metropolitan Police Commissioner, on the latter's resignation
10	November	1888	Police surgeon Mr Thomas Bond produces a criminal profile of 'Jack the Ripper'
21	November	1888	Non-fatal attack on Annie Farmer
20	December	1888	Death of Rose Mylett
29	December	1888	Hyam Hyams arrested as a 'wandering lunatic' and admitted to Baker's Row Workhouse Infirmary
9	April	1889	After a period of liberty between 11 January and early April, Hyams attacks his wife and mother, and is temporarily readmitted to the Workhouse Infirmary
15	April	1889	Hyams transferred to Colney Hatch Lunatic Asylum
17	July	1889	Murder of Alice Kinsey, known as McKenzie
30	August	1889	Hyams discharged from Colney Hatch Lunatic Asylum
7	September	1889	After a brief period of liberty, Hyams assaults his wife and is admitted to the City of London Workhouse, then to Stone Lunatic Asylum
11	September	1889	The Pinchin Street torso is discovered
4	January	1890	Hyams transferred to Colney Hatch Lunatic Asylum for the second time, where he remains until he dies in 1913
13	February	1891	Murder of Frances Coles

ACKNOWLEDGEMENTS

Many people have helped me on my writing journey, most notably my husband Michael, my tutors and classmates at Morley College and Faber Academy, in particular Miranda Doyle, my writing mentor Julia Laflin, my writers' group of Annie Janowitz, Ruth Rosengarten and Julie-ann Rowell, my agent Andrew Lownie, and my editors Louise Dixon and Lucy Stewardson at Michael O'Mara Books. I am also indebted to photographer Julian Calder.

Ripper experts Keith Skinner and Paul Begg provided unflagging support and encouragement. I also thank staff at the Metropolitan Police Heritage Centre, particularly Phillip Barnes-Warden, and also at The National Archives, London Metropolitan Archives and The British Library, who, in addition to responding to my research queries, accommodated my type 1 diabetes.

SOURCES AND BIBLIOGRAPHY

Every reasonable effort has been made to trace copyright holders.

Abbreviations

British Library (BL)
British Newspaper Archive (BNA)
City of London Police (COLP)
General Records Office (GRO)
Home Office (HO)
London Metropolitan Archives (LMA)
Metropolitan Police (MEPO)
The National Archives (TNA)

Select Bibliography

Sir Robert Anderson, *The Lighter Side of My Official Life* (Hodder & Stoughton, 1910)

Paul Begg and John Bennett, *Jack the Ripper CSI: Whitechapel* (Andre Deutsch, 2012)

Paul Begg, Martin Fido and Keith Skinner, *The Complete Jack the Ripper A to Z* (John Blake Publishing, 2010)

Neil R.A. Bell, *Capturing Jack the Ripper* (Amberley Publishing, 2014 and 2016)

Walter Dew, *I Caught Crippen* (Blackie, 1938)

John E. Douglas and Mark Olshaker, *The Cases that Haunt Us* (Pocket Books, 2000 and 2001)

John E. Douglas and Mark Olshaker, *Mindhunter: Inside the FBI's Elite Serial Crime Unit* (Pocket Books, 1995 and 1996)

Stewart P. Evans and Keith Skinner, *The Ultimate Jack the Ripper Sourcebook* (Robinson, 2001)

John Malcolm, *The Whitechapel Murders of 1888: Another Dead End?* (John Malcolm [Cardiff and Swansea], 2020)

Trevor Marriott, *Jack the Ripper: The 21st Century Investigation* (John Blake Publishing, 2005)

M.P. Priestley, *One Autumn in Whitechapel* (Flower and Dean Street Ltd, 2016)

Hallie Rubenhold, *The Five: The Untold Lives of the Women Killed by Jack the Ripper* (Doubleday, 2019)

Donald Rumbelow, *The Complete Jack the Ripper* (Penguin Books Ltd, 2009)

Philip Sugden, *The Complete History of Jack the Ripper* (Da Capo Press, 2002)

M.J. Trow, *Ripper Hunter: Abberline and the Whitechapel Murders* (Wharncliffe, 2012)

PICTURE CREDITS

Plates

Page 1: London Metropolitan Archives (City of London)

Page 2: © National Portrait Gallery, London / photograph by Walter Stoneman (top); portrait from *Days of My Years* by Sir Melville L. Macnaghten, C.B., London 1914 (bottom)

Page 3: Adam Wood / Swanson family (top); portrait of Sir Charles Warren by Alexander Bassano from *Sir Charles Warren and Spion Kop*, London 1902 (bottom)

Page 4: Photograph of Walter Dew from Evans Skinner Crime Archive (top); sketch of Frederick Abberline published in *Toby*, 7 January 1888 (centre); cartoon by Joseph Swain from *Punch, or the London Charivari*, 29 September 1888 / The Cartoon Collector / Print Collector / Getty Images (bottom)

Page 5: © The Wentworth Collection / Mary Evans Picture Library (top); Public Domain / Wikimedia Commons (centre); Public Domain / Wikimedia Commons / Neal Sheldon / Chapman family (bottom)

Page 6: Illustration from *The Pictorial News*, 15 September 1888 (top); Public Domain / Alamy (centre); sketch of Catherine Eddowes from *The Penny Illustrated Paper*, 13 October 1888 (bottom)

Page 7: Public Domain / Wikimedia Commons (top); wood engraving by A. F. Pannemaker after Gustav Doré, 1872 / Wellcome Collection (centre); Public Domain / Wikimedia Commons (bottom)

Page 8: LCC Photograph Library / London Metropolitan Archives / London Picture Library (top); photograph courtesy of the Garrett family (bottom)

In-text pictures

Page 48: © Atlantic Productions

Page 58: *Illustrated Police News* (London, 29 January 1887) / British Library

Page 74: *Illustrated Police News* (London, 8 September 1888) / Lordprice Collection / Alamy

Page 90: Interfoto / Alamy

Page 138: *Illustrated Police News* (London, 6 October 1888) / Lordprice Collection / Alamy

Page 164: Granger / Shutterstock

Page 207: *Famous Crimes, Past and Present* (Vol. II – No. 15) c. 1903 / Pictorial Press Ltd. / Alamy

NOTES

When quoting sources throughout this book, some punctuation has been adjusted to aid readability.

Introduction

1 *Punch*, 29 September 1888
2 H. L. Adam, *The Police Encyclopaedia* (London, ND), Vol. I, pp. xi–xii, quoted from Sugden, *The Complete History of Jack the Ripper*, p. 505
3 Walter Dew, *I Caught Crippen* (Blackie, 1938), p. 87
4 Robert Anderson quoted in TNA: HO 144/221/A49301C, ff. 116–18
5 Sir Melville Macnaghten quoted in TNA: MEPO 3/140, ff. 177–83
6 Inspector Henry Moore quoted in *Aberdeen Evening Express*, 5 November 1889
7 TNA: HO 144/221/A49301C, ff. 195–6, quoted from Stewart P. Evans and Keith Skinner, *The Ultimate Jack the Ripper Sourcebook* (Robinson, 2001), p. 213
8 Both excerpts quoted from LMA: Friern Hospital [Colney Hatch Lunatic Asylum] Patients' Records: Case books – male patients: H12/CH/B/13/037
9 COLP officer Harry Cox quoted in *Thomson's Weekly News*, 1 December 1906
10 LMA: Friern Hospital [Colney Hatch Lunatic Asylum] Patients' Records: Case books – male patients: H12/CH/B/13/069; H12/CH/B/13/071
11 LMA: City of London Mental Hospital [later Stone House Hospital]: Case Book: Male Admissions: CLA/001/B/02/007
12 Ancestry.com: TNA: Metropolitan Police Pension Registers, 1852–1932, No. 12,547 of 7 January 1896
13 GRO: Birth Certificate, 1891, 2nd Quarter, Whitechapel, Volume 1c, p. 352
14 Ancestry.com: TNA: Metropolitan Police Pension Registers, 1852–1932, No. 12,547 of 7 January 1896

1. Whitechapel's vice and villainy

1 Dew, *I Caught Crippen*, p. 85
2 *Cork Weekly News*, 20 October 1888

3 Fiona Rule, *The Worst Street in London* (The History Press, 2018), p. 38
4 TNA: HO 144/220/A49301, ff. 17–18, quoted from Evans and Skinner, *The Ultimate Jack the Ripper Sourcebook*, p. 520
5 *Hendon & Finchley Times*, 27 June 1913
6 Rule, *The Worst Street in London*, p. 41
7 Walter Dew, quoted from *Worthing Gazette*, 19 April 1939
8 G. W. Cornish, *Cornish of the 'Yard': His Reminiscences and Cases* (John Lane, 1935), p. 2
9 *Toronto Daily Mail*, 9 August 1889
10 Dew, *I Caught Crippen*, p. 87
11 Ibid.
12 Ibid.
13 Ibid., pp. 87–8
14 *Dundee Evening Telegraph*, 25 March 1903
15 Dew, *I Caught Crippen*, p. 88
16 Ibid.
17 Ibid.
18 Ibid.
19 *Reynolds's Newspaper*, 16 September 1888
20 TNA: HO 144/221/A49301B, ff. 276–8, quoted from Evans and Skinner, *The Ultimate Jack the Ripper Sourcebook*, p. 306
21 Paul Begg, Martin Fido and Keith Skinner, *The Complete Jack the Ripper A to Z* (John Blake Publishing, 2010), p. 540
22 Ibid., p. 353
23 Arthur Ponsonby Moore-Anderson, *Sir Robert Anderson, KCB, LL.D and Lady Agnes Anderson* (Marshall, Morgan and Scott, 1947), p. 13
24 *Lincolnshire Chronicle*, 28 April 1899
25 Ibid.
26 *Eastern Post*, February 1893, quoted from Begg, Fido and Skinner, *The Complete Jack the Ripper A to Z*, p. 33
27 *East London Observer*, 20 May 1893
28 *Police Review*, 11 July 1913, quoted from Begg, Fido and Skinner, *The Complete Jack the Ripper A to Z*, p. 356
29 *Pall Mall Gazette*, 24 March 1903, quoted from Begg, Fido and Skinner, *The Complete Jack the Ripper A to Z*, p. 7
30 *Tower Hamlets Independent* and *East End Local Advertiser*, 10 February 1912
31 Dew, *I Caught Crippen*, p. 132. The italics are the author's.
32 Ibid., p. 132

33 Ibid., p. 162
34 Evans and Skinner, *The Ultimate Jack the Ripper Sourcebook*, p. 667
35 *Police Review*, 11 July 1913, quoted from Begg, Fido and Skinner, *The Complete Jack the Ripper A to Z*, p. 356
36 TNA: HO 144/221/A49301C, ff. 90–2, quoted from Evans and Skinner, *The Ultimate Jack the Ripper Sourcebook*, pp. 131–2
37 TNA: MEPO 3/140, ff. 235–8, quoted from Evans and Skinner, *The Ultimate Jack the Ripper Sourcebook*, p. 57
38 Ibid.
39 TNA: MEPO 3/140, ff. 24–5, quoted from Evans and Skinner, *The Ultimate Jack the Ripper Sourcebook*, p. 65
40 TNA: MEPO 3/140, ff. 26–8, quoted from Evans and Skinner, *The Ultimate Jack the Ripper Sourcebook*, pp. 66–7
41 TNA: MEPO 3/140, ff. 242–56, quoted from Evans and Skinner, *The Ultimate Jack the Ripper Sourcebook*, pp. 72–3
42 *Lloyd's Weekly London Newspaper*, 9 September 1888
43 TNA: MEPO 3/140, ff. 242–56, quoted from Evans and Skinner, *The Ultimate Jack the Ripper Sourcebook*, pp. 72–3
44 *The British Medical Journal*, 19 January 1918
45 *Lloyd's Weekly London Newspaper*, 16 September 1888
46 LMA: Friern Hospital [Colney Hatch Lunatic Asylum] Patients' Records: Case books – male patients: H12/CH/B/13/036
47 Ancestry.com: TNA: Lunacy Patients Admission Registers, 1846–1913; Class: MH 94; Piece: 6
48 Ancestry.com: TNA: Lunacy Patients Admission Registers, 1846–1913; Class: MH 94; Piece: 30
49 GRO: Death Certificate, 1910, Barnet, 1st Quarter, Volume 3a, p. 191
50 Sir Henry Smith, *From Constable to Commissioner: The Story of Sixty Years Most of Them Misspent* (Chatto and Windus, 1910), pp. 147–8
51 LMA: City of London Police Detective Division: Miscellaneous reports, statements & correspondence on cases, complaints etc.: CLA/048/AD/11/10, 25 September 1888
52 Ancestry.com: TNA: Lunacy Patients Admission Registers, 1846–1913; Class: MH 94; Piece: 6
53 Smith, *From Constable to Commissioner*, p. 148
54 *Sunday Post*, 15 May 1921
55 TNA: MEPO 3/140, ff. 177–83 quoted from Evans and Skinner, *The Ultimate Jack the Ripper Sourcebook*, pp. 645–6
56 Ibid.

57 Ancestry.com: TNA: HO: Calendar of Prisoners, 1868–1929; Reference: TNA: HO 140/130
58 Ancestry.com: TNA: Lunacy Patients Admission Registers, 1846–1913; Class: MH 94; Piece: 30
59 TNA: MEPO 3/140, ff. 177–83, quoted from Evans and Skinner, *The Ultimate Jack the Ripper Sourcebook*, p. 646
60 Ibid.
61 Ibid.
62 Ancestry.com: TNA: Lunacy Patients Admission Registers, 1846–1913; Class: MH 94; Piece: 6
63 Originally proposed by Martin Fido
64 Begg, Fido and Skinner, *The Complete Jack the Ripper A to Z*, pp. 268–74
65 Today's Henriques Street
66 Mile End Old Town Workhouse, Admission & Discharge Books, 1890–1, GLRO (LMA), StBG/ME/114/4–5, all excerpts quoted from Philip Sugden, *The Complete History of Jack the Ripper* (Da Capo Press, 2002), p. 490
67 LMA: Friern Hospital [Colney Hatch Lunatic Asylum] Administration: Visitors' books: H12/CH/B/6/2; Patients' Records: Case books – male patients: H12/CH/B/13/39, quoted from Sugden, *The Complete History of Jack the Ripper*, pp. 491–2
68 GRO: Death Certificate, 1919, Watford, 1st Quarter, Volume 3a, p. 1273
69 Ancestry.com: TNA: 1881 England Census; Class: RG11; Piece: 2108; f. 36; p.17; GSU roll: 1341509
70 *Police Gazette*, 26 October 1888
71 Ancestry.com: TNA: Lunacy Patients Admission Registers, 1846–1913; Class: MH 94; Piece: 30
72 Begg, Fido and Skinner, *The Complete Jack the Ripper A to Z*, p. 390
73 *Sunderland Daily Echo*, 1 September 1888
74 *London Evening Standard*, 12 September 1888
75 Ibid.
76 *Lancashire Evening Post*, 10 September 1888
77 *Northern Echo*, 11 September 1888
78 The *Manchester Courier* and *Lancashire General Advertiser*, 11 September 1888
79 Ancestry.com: LMA: STBG/WH/123/020, London, England, Workhouse Admission and Discharge Records, 1764–1930, Tower Hamlets, Admission Date: 10 Sep 1888; Discharge Date: 9 Oct 1888
80 *Exeter and Plymouth Gazette*, 25 March 1903
81 H. L. Adam, *The Trial of George Chapman* (London: William Hodge, 1930), quoted from Begg, Fido and Skinner, *The Complete Jack the Ripper A to Z*, p. 9

82 *Daily Chronicle*, 23 March 1903, quoted from Begg, Fido and Skinner, *The Complete Jack the Ripper A to Z*, p. 265
83 Chief Inspector John George Littlechild's letter referencing Tumblety dated 23 September 1913 is quoted from Begg, Fido and Skinner, *The Complete Jack the Ripper A to Z*, pp. 301–2
84 Ancestry.com: TNA: HO 140 Home Office: Calendar of Prisoners, 1868–1929; Reference: TNA: HO 140/106
85 Begg, Fido and Skinner, *The Complete Jack the Ripper A to Z*, p. 524
86 The Littlechild letter is quoted from Begg, Fido and Skinner, *The Complete Jack the Ripper A to Z*, pp. 301–2
87 Sir Robert Anderson, *The Lighter Side of My Official Life* (Hodder & Stoughton, 1910), p. 1

2. Hunting CID Chief Robert Anderson's suspect

1 Corporation of London Records Office, Police Box 3.17, No. 197, quoted from Sugden, *The Complete History of Jack the Ripper*, p. 526; *Sunderland Daily Echo and Shipping Gazette*, 2 October 1888
2 *Sunderland Daily Echo and Shipping Gazette*, 2 October 1888
3 *Edinburgh Evening News*, 1 October 1888
4 Today's Durward Street
5 Built over; south of Brushfield Street
6 TNA: HO 144/221/A49301C, ff. 220–3, quoted from Evans and Skinner, *The Ultimate Jack the Ripper Sourcebook*, pp. 400–2
7 Ibid.
8 John E. Douglas and Mark Olshaker, *The Cases that Haunt Us* (Pocket Books, 2000 and 2001), pp. 58–9
9 John E. Douglas, Ann W. Burgess, Allen G. Burgess, and Robert K. Ressler (eds), *Crime Classification Manual: A Standard System for Investigating and Classifying Violent Crimes*, 2nd edn (Jossey-Bass, a Wiley Imprint, 2006)
10 Ibid.
11 Anderson, *The Lighter Side of My Official Life*, p. 134
12 Ibid., pp. 137–8
13 *Eastern Daily Press*, 26 February 1910
14 *The Cambria Daily Leader*, 2 September 1908
15 Anderson, *The Lighter Side of My Official Life*, p. 138
16 Anderson, *The Lighter Side of My Official Life*, pp. 137–9
17 *Shoreditch Observer*, 5 March 1910
18 *Nottingham Evening Post*, 2 December 1901

19 Adam, *The Police Encyclopaedia*, Vol. I, pp. xi–xii, quoted from Sugden, *The Complete History of Jack the Ripper*, p. 487
20 *Daily Chronicle*, 1 September 1908
21 Anderson, *The Lighter Side of My Official Life*, p. 137
22 Smith, *From Constable to Commissioner*, p. 160
23 Ibid., p. 162
24 *The Bridgnorth Journal and South Shropshire Advertiser*, 12 March 1910
25 Sir Melville L. Macnaghten, *Days of My Years* (Edward Arnold, 1914), p. 273
26 Donald Swanson's marginalia is quoted from Begg, Fido and Skinner, *The Complete Jack the Ripper A to Z*, pp. 499–503. The punctuation is the author's.
27 Ibid.
28 *Wales Online*, 14 July 2006
29 The marginalia's handwriting analysis is quoted from Begg, Fido and Skinner, *The Complete Jack the Ripper A to Z*, pp. 501–3
30 LMA: Thames Magistrates Court: Court Register: court 1, part 1: PS/TH/A/01/12
31 LMA: Whitechapel Infirmary: Porters' Admission and Discharge Register: STBG/WH/123/020
32 LMA: City of London Mental Hospital [later Stone House Hospital]: Case Book: Male Admissions: CLA/001/B/02/007
33 LMA: Whitechapel Infirmary: Porters' Admission and Discharge Register: STBG/WH/123/021
34 Ibid.
35 LMA: Friern Hospital [Colney Hatch Lunatic Asylum] Patients' Records: Case books – male patients: H12/CH/B/13/037
36 LMA: Whitechapel Infirmary: Porters' Admission and Discharge Register: STBG/WH/123/021
37 LMA: Homerton Workhouse: Admission and Discharge Register, 1888–1889: CBG/334/012
38 LMA: City of London Mental Hospital [later Stone House Hospital]: Case Book: Male Admissions: CLA/001/B/02/007
39 Ibid.
40 Ibid.
41 Ibid.
42 Ibid.
43 LMA: Friern Hospital [Colney Hatch Lunatic Asylum] Patients' Records: Case books – male patients: H12/CH/B/13/038
44 The *Independent*, 20 November 2006
45 LMA: Friern Hospital [Colney Hatch Lunatic Asylum] Patients' Records:

Case books – male patients: H12/CH/B/13/069. A colourised version is on *One-Armed Jack*'s front cover.

3. Profiling Jack the Ripper

1 All excerpts quoted from LMA: Friern Hospital [Colney Hatch Lunatic Asylum] Patients' Records: Case books – male patients: H12/CH/B/13/038
2 Ibid.
3 Ibid.
4 LMA: Friern Hospital [Colney Hatch Lunatic Asylum] Patients' Records: Case books – male patients: H12/CH/B/13/037
5 Ibid.
6 Ibid.
7 Ibid.
8 Ibid.
9 GRO: Marriage Certificate, 1853, 1st Quarter, St Luke, Volume 01b, p. 655
10 GRO: Birth Certificate, 1853, 3rd Quarter, East London, Volume 1c, p. 9
11 GRO: Birth Certificate, 1853, 4th Quarter, Milton, Kent, Volume 2a, p. 517
12 *Illustrated Weekly News*, 23 August 1862
13 Ibid.
14 Ancestry.com: TNA: Lunacy Patients Admission Registers, 1846–1913; Piece 17: 1859 Jan–1861 Jun
15 GRO: Death Certificate, 1860, Barnet, 4th Quarter, Volume 3a, p. 80
16 GRO: Death Certificate, 1863, East London, 3rd Quarter, Volume 01c, p. 6
17 GRO: Death Certificate, 1863, Whitechapel, 4th Quarter, Volume 1c, p. 244
18 Ancestry.com: TNA: 1871 England Census; Class: RG10; Piece: 509; f. 9; p. 12; GSU roll: 823380
19 GRO: Marriage Certificate, 1877, 4th Quarter, Whitechapel, Volume 1c, p. 875)
20 GRO: Marriage Certificate, 1878, 2nd Quarter, London City, Volume 1c, p. 154; GRO: Birth Certificate, 1851, 1st Quarter, East London, Volume 2, p. 229
21 Mark Hyams was resident at 49 North Block, Stoney Lane, on 11 May 1890, for his daughter Rachel's birth: GRO: Birth Index 1890, 2nd Quarter, London City, Volume 1c, p. 7. He was resident at 67 Brunswick Buildings in 1887, and not at that address in 1888: Ancestry.com: LMA: MR/PER/B/144; London, England; Electoral Registers, 1832–1965; Name: Mark Hyams; Electoral Date: 1887; Street Address: 67 Brunswick Buildings; Ward or Division/Constituency: St Mary, Whitechapel; County or Borough: Tower Hamlets, England
22 Ancestry.com: GRO: England & Wales, Civil Registration Marriage Index,1837–1915, 1878, 1st Quarter, London City, Volume 1c/155

23 Royal London Hospital Archives and Museum: RLHLH/M/1/15
24 *The Globe*, 29 January 1887
25 *Evening News* (London), 28 January 1887
26 Old Bailey Proceedings Online (www.oldbaileyonline.org, version 8.0, 30 September 2022), July 1887, trial of ISRAEL LIPSKI (22) (t18870725-817)
27 *London Daily News*, 12 February 1887
28 GRO: Birth Certificate, 1888, 1st Quarter, Whitechapel, Volume 1c, p. 304
29 LMA: Friern Hospital [Colney Hatch Lunatic Asylum] Patients' Records: Case books – male patients: H12/CH/B/13/037
30 LMA: City of London Mental Hospital [later Stone House Hospital]: Case Book: Male Admissions: CLA/001/B/02/007
31 Hyams' height, weight, hesitancy of speech and sluggish left pupil were recorded at Stone in LMA: City of London Mental Hospital [later Stone House Hospital]: Case Book: Male Admissions: CLA/001/B/02/007; his hair and eye colour were recorded in LMA: Friern Hospital [Colney Hatch Lunatic Asylum] Patients' Records: Case books – male patients: H12/CH/B/13/037
32 Nicholas Connell, *The Annotated I Caught Crippen: Memoirs of Ex-Chief Inspector Walter Dew, C.I.D. of Scotland Yard* (Mango Books, 2019), p. 120
33 Quoted later, those eyewitnesses were: Thomas Eade; John Thimbleby; Stephen White
34 Described under 'Nervous symptoms: his gait is spastic' in LMA: Friern Hospital [Colney Hatch Lunatic Asylum] Patients' Records: Case books – male patients: H12/CH/B/13/069
35 LMA: Friern Hospital [Colney Hatch Lunatic Asylum] Patients' Records: Case books – male patients: H12/CH/B/13/069
36 LMA: City of London Mental Hospital [later Stone House Hospital]: Case Book: Male Admissions: CLA/001/B/02/007
37 Mark Hyams was resident at 32 Tenter Street, Christ Church, Whitechapel, in Ancestry.com: TNA: 1881 England Census; Class: RG11; Piece: 436; f. 99; p. 54; GSU roll: 1341095
38 All excerpts from *London Evening Standard*, 25 October 1881
39 The *Lichfield Mercury*, 22 September 1882. His address is reported as 32 Fenter [*sic*] Street, Fenter [*sic*] Ground, Spitalfields.
40 Ancestry.com: London, England, Electoral Registers, 1832–1965: Abraham Mordecai was at that address in 1888, and continuously from *c.*1871–90
41 Ancestry.com: London, England; Electoral Registers, 1832–1965 for Norah Christmas at that address

42 Emanuel Mordecai was at that address from his 1886 court case, and possibly before, to 1889; Ancestry.com: London, England, Electoral Registers, 1832–1965. He was previously based at his father's premises at 209/210 Whitechapel Road, GRO: Marriage Certificate, 1877, 2nd Quarter, Volume 1c, p. 155
43 Ancestry.com: London, England, Electoral Registers, 1832–1965: Lazarus Mordecai was at that address in 1888
44 *Lloyd's Weekly Newspaper*, 4 April 1886
45 *East London Observer*, 25 February 1888
46 Ibid.
47 *East London Observer*, 10 August 1878
48 All excerpts from ibid.
49 *Canterbury Journal, Kentish Times and Farmers' Gazette*, 18 January 1890
50 *The Salisbury Times*, 17 November 1888
51 *Echo* (London), 15 November 1888
52 LMA: City of London Mental Hospital [later Stone House Hospital]: Case Book: Male Admissions: CLA/001/B/02/007
53 *London Evening Standard*, 12 October 1888
54 Ancestry.com: New York, Passenger and Crew Lists (including Castle Garden and Ellis Island), 1820–1957, Year: 1884; Arrival: New York, New York; Microfilm Serial: M237, 1820–1897; Microfilm Roll: Roll 477; Line: 11; List Number: 703
55 Ancestry.com: LMA: MR/PER/B/144; London, England; Electoral Registers, 1832–1965; Name: Lazarus Hyams; Electoral Date: 1887; Street Address: 259 Brunswick Buildings; Ward or Division/Constituency: St Mary, Whitechapel; County or Borough: Tower Hamlets, England
56 Ancestry.com: Massachusetts, U.S., Town and Vital Records, 1620–1988; Boston Marriages, 1887, Lewis Hyams and Ellen Hambro
57 Ancestry.com: TNA: 1891 England Census; Class: RG12; Piece: 274; f. 55; p. 22; GSU roll: 6095384
58 Ancestry.com: New York, Passenger and Crew Lists (including Castle Garden and Ellis Island), 1820–1957, Year: 1884; Arrival: New York, New York; Microfilm Serial: M237, 1820–1897; Microfilm Roll: Roll 477; Line: 12; List Number: 703
59 Ancestry.com: New York, Passenger and Crew Lists (including Castle Garden and Ellis Island), 1820–1957, Year: 1892; Arrival: New York, New York; Microfilm Serial: M237, 1820–1897; Line: 47; List Number: 15
60 Ancestry.com: New York, U.S., State Census, 1865, Kings, Brooklyn, New York State Archives; Ancestry.com: TNA: 1871 England Census; Class:

RG10; Piece: 520; f. 112; p. 31; GSU roll: 823383; Ancestry.com: TNA: 1881 England Census; Class: RG11; Piece: 444; f. 64; p. 1; GSU roll: 1341096

61 Ancestry.com: New York, U.S., State Census, 1855, Kings, Brooklyn, New York State Archives

62 Ancestry.com: TNA: 1871 England Census; Class: RG10; Piece: 554; f. 7; p. 7; GSU roll: 823397

63 *Dundee Courier*, 16 November 1888

4. The murder of Polly Nichols

1 Hallie Rubenhold, *The Five: The Untold Lives of the Women Killed by Jack the Ripper* (Doubleday, 2019), p. 22

2 GRO: Marriage Certificate, 1864, 1st Quarter, West London, Volume 1c, p. 93

3 *Manchester Courier*, 4 September 1888. Nichols claimed that the affair started after his wife's departure

4 *London Evening Standard*, 3 September 1888 and similar testimony

5 *East London Observer*, 8 September 1888

6 *Edinburgh Evening News*, 3 September 1888

7 *Manchester Courier*, 4 September 1888

8 *Kentish Independent*, 8 September 1888

9 Ibid.

10 TNA: HO 144/221/A49301C, ff. 129–34, quoted from Evans and Skinner, *The Ultimate Jack the Ripper Sourcebook*, p. 33

11 *Aberdeen Free Press*, 1 September 1888

12 *News of the World*, 3 October 1920

13 *East London Observer*, 8 September 1888

14 *Kentish Independent*, 8 September 1888

15 Ibid.

16 Ibid.

17 *Ballinrobe Chronicle and Mayo Advertiser*, 8 September 1888

18 Ibid.

19 Ibid.

20 TNA: HO 144/221/A49301C, ff. 6–7, quoted from Evans and Skinner, *The Ultimate Jack the Ripper Sourcebook*, pp. 38–9

21 *Christchurch Times*, 8 September 1888

22 TNA: MEPO 3/140, ff. 239–41, quoted from Evans and Skinner, *The Ultimate Jack the Ripper Sourcebook*, p. 24

23 TNA: HO 144/221/A49301C, ff. 129–34, quoted from Evans and Skinner, *The Ultimate Jack the Ripper Sourcebook*, p. 31

24 TNA: MEPO 3/140, ff. 177–83 quoted from Evans and Skinner, *The Ultimate Jack the Ripper Sourcebook*, pp. 645–6
25 *Exmouth Journal*, 8 September 1888
26 Ibid.
27 Ibid.
28 *Framlingham Weekly News*, 8 September 1888
29 TNA: MEPO 3/140, ff. 239–41, quoted from Evans and Skinner, *The Ultimate Jack the Ripper Sourcebook*, p. 25
30 *The Beverley Recorder and General Advertiser*, 22 September 1888
31 *Christchurch Times*, 8 September 1888
32 *Echo* (London), 3 September 1888
33 *Congleton & Macclesfield Mercury, and Cheshire General Advertiser*, 22 September 1888
34 *London Evening Standard*, 3 September 1888
35 *Lloyd's Weekly Newspaper*, 9 September 1888
36 *East London Observer*, 8 September 1888
37 Ibid. and *Weekly Dispatch* (London), 9 September 1888
38 *Reynolds's Newspaper*, 23 September 1888
39 *Brecon County Times*, 21 September 1888
40 Ibid.
41 *Lloyd's Weekly Newspaper*, 23 September 1888
42 *Sunderland Daily Echo and Shipping Gazette*, 20 September 1888
43 *London Evening Standard*, 2 October 1888
44 *Echo* (London), 6 September 1888
45 Ibid.
46 TNA: MEPO 3/140, ff. 242–56, quoted from Evans and Skinner, *The Ultimate Jack the Ripper Sourcebook*, p. 70
47 *Birmingham Daily Post*, 24 September 1888
48 Ibid.
49 Ibid.
50 *Taunton Courier and Western Advertiser*, 15 October 1873
51 A. W. Bates, 'Dr Kahn's Museum: Obscene Anatomy in Victorian London', *Journal of the Royal Society of Medicine*, 99(12) (2006), 618–24. doi: 10.1258/jrsm 99.12.618
52 *The Bury and Norwich Post*, and *Suffolk Herald*, 23 December 1873
53 The Shuttleworths were at Ann's Place in 1888: Old Bailey Proceedings Online: www.oldbaileyonline.org, version 8.0, 17 May 2020), September 1888, trial of JAMES SHUTTLEWORTH (53), EZEKIEL LYONS (31) (t18880917-840)

54 Ancestry.com: LMA: London, England, School Admissions and Discharges, 1840–1911 for Rutland Street School, admitted on 21 September 1885, left on 7 May 1886 for Buck's Row; Stepney Jewish School, admitted in November 1889; Settles Street School, admitted 26 October 1891

55 The Wood's Buildings escape route was proposed by M. P. Priestley, *One Autumn in Whitechapel* (Flower and Dean Street Ltd, 2016)

5. The murder of Annie Chapman

1 Held in a private collection

2 *Echo* (London), 10 September 1888

3 *Croydon's Weekly Standard*, 15 September 1888

4 *The Globe*, 19 September 1888

5 *Lloyd's Weekly Newspaper*, 9 September 1888

6 *Morning Post*, 20 September 1888

7 *London Evening Standard*, 10 September 1888

8 The author's account of the witness testimony in all of the inquest hearings is neither comprehensive nor strictly chronological

9 *Tavistock Gazette*, 14 September 1888

10 Ibid.

11 *London Evening Standard*, 12 September 1888

12 *Croydon's Weekly Standard*, 15 September 1888

13 *Diss Express*, 14 September 1888

14 *Tavistock Gazette*, 14 September 1888

15 Ibid.

16 *The Scotsman*, 11 September 1888

17 *Diss Express*, 14 September 1888

18 *London Evening Standard*, 12 September 1888

19 Ibid.

20 *Weekly Dispatch* (London), 16 September 1888

21 *East London Observer*, 15 September 1888

22 *London Evening Standard*, 12 September 1888

23 Ancestry.com: TNA: Metropolitan Police Pension Registers, 1852–1932, No. 13,105 of 5 April 1898

24 Extract from *The Times*, 14 September 1888, in TNA: HO 144/221/A49301C, ff. 16–17, quoted from Evans and Skinner, *The Ultimate Jack the Ripper Sourcebook*, pp. 92–4

25 TNA: MEPO 3/140, ff. 9–11, quoted from Evans and Skinner, *The Ultimate Jack the Ripper Sourcebook*, p. 57

26 *Birmingham Daily Post*, 11 September 1888; *Congleton & Macclesfield Mercury, and Cheshire General Advertiser*, 22 September 1888
27 *Birmingham Mail*, 14 September 1888
28 *The Globe*, 19 September 1888
29 *The Scotsman*, 14 September 1888
30 Dew, *I Caught Crippen*, p. 116
31 *Western Daily Press*, 14 September 1888; *Eastern Evening News*, 14 September 1888; *Morning Post*, 14 September 1888
32 *Morning Post*, 14 September 1888.
33 *Birmingham Mail*, 14 September 1888
34 Ibid.
35 *The Globe*, 19 September 1888
36 *Birmingham Mail*, 14 September 1888
37 *Journal of Forensic Sciences and Criminal Investigation*, 9(5) (June 2018), ISSN: 2476–1311, Review Article. DOI: 10.19080/JFSCI.2018.09.555771
38 *Birmingham Mail*, 14 September 1888
39 Ibid.
40 *The Lancet*, 29 September 1888. DOI: https://doi.org.10.1016/S0140-6736(02)24871-0
41 *Buckingham Express*, 22 September 1888
42 *London Evening Standard*, 19 September 1888
43 Ibid.
44 *Echo* (London), 10 September 1888
45 *Newcastle Daily Chronicle*, 20 September 1888
46 *Pall Mall Gazette*, 15 September 1888
47 Ibid.
48 *Lloyd's Weekly Newspaper*, 23 September 1888
49 *Belfast Newsletter*, 2 October 1888
50 *South Wales Echo*, 27 September 1888
51 *Manchester Evening News*, 1 October 1888
52 *Reynolds's Newspaper*, 23 September 1888
53 *Lloyd's Weekly Newspaper*, 23 September 1888
54 *London Evening Standard*, 18 September 1888
55 *The Times*, 18 September 1888
56 *Peterborough Standard*, 22 September 1888
57 *Lloyd's Weekly Newspaper*, 23 September 1888
58 *Lloyd's Weekly Newspaper*, 9 September 1888
59 *Worcestershire Chronicle*, 29 September 1888

6. The murder of Elisabeth Stride

1 Ancestry.com: Sweden, Emigrants registered in Church Books, 1783–1991, Departure for London 7 February 1866
2 Ancestry.com: England & Wales, Civil Registration Marriage Index, 1837–1915, 1869, 1st Quarter, St Giles, Volume 1b, p. 596
3 LMA: Thames Police Court Ledgers PS/TH/A/01/005, quoted from Rubenhold, *The Five*, p. 205
4 *Daily News* (London), 6 October 1888
5 Ancestry.com: TNA: 1871 England Census; Class: RG10; Piece: 586; f. 35; p. 13; GSU roll: 824898
6 Ancestry.com: TNA: UK Registers of Births, Marriages and Deaths at Sea, 1844–1890; Class: BT 159; Piece: 5
7 Dew, *I Caught Crippen*, p. 134
8 *Evening News* (London), 1 October 1888, quoted from wiki.casebook.org
9 *Dundee Courier*, 1 October 1888
10 *Belfast News–Letter*, 1 October 1888
11 *Taunton Courier and Western Advertiser*, 31 October 1888
12 *Nuneaton Chronicle*, 5 October 1888
13 *The Times*, 2 October 1888, quoted from Evans and Skinner, *The Ultimate Jack the Ripper Sourcebook*, pp. 160–3
14 Ibid.
15 Ibid.
16 *St James's Gazette*, 3 October 1888
17 *The Times*, 2 October 1888, quoted from Evans and Skinner, *The Ultimate Jack the Ripper Sourcebook*, pp. 166–8
18 *Daily News* (London), 4 October 1888
19 *Shields Daily News*, 4 October 1888
20 *Daily News* (London), 4 October 1888
21 *The Times*, 4 October 1888, quoted from Evans and Skinner, *The Ultimate Jack the Ripper Sourcebook*, pp. 176–8
22 *The Times*, 6 October 1888, quoted from Evans and Skinner, *The Ultimate Jack the Ripper Sourcebook*, pp. 181–3
23 *London Evening Standard*, 3 October 1888
24 *The Scotsman*, 6 October 1888
25 *Lloyd's Weekly Newspaper*, 7 October 1888
26 Ibid.
27 *Suffolk and Essex Free Press*, 10 October 1888
28 Ibid.
29 *Reynolds's Newspaper*, 7 October 1888

30 Ibid.
31 *The Times*, 6 October 1888, quoted from Evans and Skinner, *The Ultimate Jack the Ripper Sourcebook*, p. 186
32 *Lloyd's Weekly Newspaper*, 7 October 1888
33 *London Evening Standard*, 24 October 1888
34 *The Times*, 24 October 1888, quoted from Evans and Skinner, *The Ultimate Jack the Ripper Sourcebook*, pp. 192–8
35 Ibid.
36 Ibid.
37 Ibid.
38 Ibid.
39 *Echo* (London), 15 November 1888
40 TNA: MEPO 3/140/221/A49301C, ff. 215–16, quoted from Evans and Skinner, *The Ultimate Jack the Ripper Sourcebook*, pp. 143–4
41 *Bridport News*, 12 October 1888
42 *Leeds Mercury*, 8 October 1888
43 TNA: HO 144/221/A49301C, ff. 148–59, quoted from wiki.casebook.org
44 *Evening News* (London), 31 October 1888
45 Dew, *I Caught Crippen*, p. 142
46 TNA: HO 144/221/A49301C, ff. 148–59, quoted from Evans and Skinner, *The Ultimate Jack the Ripper Sourcebook*, p. 137
47 Ibid., pp. 137–8
48 Old Bailey Proceedings Online (www.oldbaileyonline.org, version 8.0, 30 September 2022), July 1887, trial of ISRAEL LIPSKI (22) (t18870725-817)
49 *London Evening Standard*, 6 October 1888

7. The murder of Kate Eddowes

1 Ancestry.com: LMA; London, England; Reference Number: SOBG/33/6; London, England, Workhouse Admission and Discharge Records, 1659–1930
2 Rubenhold, *The Five*, p. 227
3 Ancestry.com: TNA: 1861 England Census; Class: RG 9; Piece: 1995; f. 9; p. 12; GSU roll: 542900
4 *Weekly Dispatch* (London), 14 October 1888
5 LMA: GBG/250/12 Greenwich Workhouse Admissions and Discharges Registers, quoted from Rubenhold, *The Five*, p. 277
6 LMA: City of London Coroners Inquest 1888–1889: Catherine Eddowes (no. 135): CLA/041/IQ/03/065
7 *Oxford Journal*, 6 October 1888
8 *Daily News* (London) 12 October 1888; *Bridport News*, 12 October 1888

9 *London Evening Standard*, 11 October 1888
10 *Sunderland Daily Echo and Shipping Gazette*, 5 October 1888
11 *Eastern Daily Press*, 5 October 1888
12 *Sunderland Daily Echo and Shipping Gazette*, 5 October 1888
13 *Echo* (London), 11 October 1888
14 *The Times*, 12 October 1888, quoted from Evans and Skinner, *The Ultimate Jack the Ripper Sourcebook*, p. 257
15 *South Wales Daily News*, 5 October 1888
16 *Cheshire Observer*, 6 October 1888
17 *Eastern Evening News*, 4 October 1888
18 Ibid.
19 *London Evening Standard*, 5 October 1888
20 Ibid.
21 Ref. Coroner's Inquest (L), 1888, No. 135, Catherine Eddowes Inquest, 1888 (Corporation of London Record Office), quoted from Evans and Skinner, *The Ultimate Jack the Ripper Sourcebook*, p. 228
22 *The Times*, 5 October 1888, quoted from Evans and Skinner, *The Ultimate Jack the Ripper Sourcebook*, pp. 247–8
23 Ibid.
24 Ibid.
25 Ibid.
26 Ref. Coroner's Inquest (L), 1888, No. 135, Catherine Eddowes Inquest, 1888 (Corporation of London Record Office), quoted from Evans and Skinner, *The Ultimate Jack the Ripper Sourcebook*, pp. 230–1
27 Ibid.
28 Ibid.
29 Ibid.
30 *Eastern Daily Press*, 5 October 1888
31 Ref. Coroner's Inquest (L), 1888, No. 135, Catherine Eddowes Inquest, 1888 (Corporation of London Record Office), quoted from Evans and Skinner, *The Ultimate Jack the Ripper Sourcebook*, p. 229
32 Ibid., p. 230
33 Ibid., pp. 231–2
34 Ibid., p. 232
35 Ibid.
36 Ibid., p. 233
37 *The Globe*, 16 October 1888
38 Ref. Coroner's Inquest (L), 1888, No. 135, Catherine Eddowes Inquest, 1888 (Corporation of London Record Office), quoted from Evans and Skinner, *The Ultimate Jack the Ripper Sourcebook*, p. 236

39 Ibid., p. 237
40 *Evening News* (London), 9 October 1888
41 *The Scotsman*, 12 October 1888
42 Ibid.
43 *Evening News* (London), 9 October 1888
44 *London Evening Standard*, 12 October 1888
45 Ibid.
46 LMA: City of London Coroners Inquest 1888–1889: Catherine Eddowes (no.135): CLA/041/IQ/03/065
47 Ibid.
48 The quoted example is I. Z. Greenberg in *Pall Mall Gazette*, 19 October 1888
49 Ibid.
50 Ibid.
51 *Eastern Evening News*, 12 October 1888
52 Ibid.
53 LMA: City of London Coroners Inquest 1888–1889: Catherine Eddowes (no. 135): CLA/041/IQ/03/065
54 Ibid.
55 Ref. Coroner's Inquest (L), 1888, No. 135, Catherine Eddowes Inquest, 1888 (Corporation of London Record Office), quoted from Evans and Skinner, *The Ultimate Jack the Ripper Sourcebook*, p. 264
56 Ibid.
57 LMA: City of London Coroners Inquest 1888–1889: Catherine Eddowes (no. 135): CLA/041/IQ/03/065
58 Ancestry.com: London, England, Electoral Registers, 1832–1965: in 1892, Mark Hyams was listed as resident at 49 North Block, Artizans, City of London, England
59 *City Press*, 7 January 1905
60 Ibid.
61 Macnaghten, *Days of My Years*, pp. 59–60
62 *Manchester Courier*, 1 October 1888
63 Ancestry.com: LMA; London, England; Electoral Registers, 1832–1965; Name: Lewis Emanuel; Electoral Date: 1890; Street Address: 7 [*sic*: 8] St James's Place; Ward or Division/Constituency: London; County or Borough: City of London, England

8. The police investigation after the 'double event'

1 *Edinburgh Evening News*, 1 October 1888
2 TNA: MEPO 1/48, quoted from Sugden, *The Complete History of Jack the Ripper*, p. 527

3 TNA: HO 144/221/A49301C/8c, quoted from Sugden, *The Complete History of Jack the Ripper*, p. 527
4 TNA: MEPO 2/227, in a clipping from the *Philadelphia Times*, 3 December 1888
5 Ibid.
6 *Eastern Post*, February 1893, quoted from Begg, Fido and Skinner, *The Complete Jack the Ripper A to Z*, pp. 32–3
7 *South Wales Echo*, 1 October 1888
8 Ibid.
9 Ibid.
10 Ibid.
11 *Glasgow Evening Citizen*, 1 October 1888
12 Ibid.
13 Lyttleton Stewart Forbes Winslow, *Recollections of Forty Years* (John Ouseley Ltd, 1910), pp. 251-83
14 *Boston Spa News*, 27 September 1889
15 *Lakes Herald*, 12 October 1888
16 Ibid.
17 *Manchester Courier*, 2 October 1888
18 *St Helens Examiner*, 13 October 1888
19 *Taunton Courier and Western Advertiser*, 10 October 1888
20 From a contemporary photograph, collected by E. K. Larkins and preserved at the Royal London Hospital Archives & Museum, quoted from Sugden, *The Complete History of Jack the Ripper*, p. 129
21 *Tenbury Wells Advertiser*, 23 October 1888
22 Ibid.
23 Smith, *From Constable to Commissioner*, p. 155
24 *London Evening Standard*, 20 October 1888
25 Ibid.
26 Ibid.
27 *Burnley Gazette*, 3 October 1888
28 LMA: Thames Magistrates Court: Court Register: court 1, part 1: PS/TH/A/01/12
29 *Kentish Independent*, 17 November 1888
30 Ibid.
31 TNA: MEPO 3/2890 (undated), quoted from wiki.casebook.org
32 *Leeds Mercury*, 8 November 1888
33 Old Bailey Proceedings Online (www.oldbaileyonline.org, version 8.0, 01 October 2022), December 1876, trial of ISAAC MARKS (37) (t18761211-142)

34 Ibid.
35 Ibid.
36 Ibid.
37 *The Scotsman*, 3 January 1877
38 TNA: HO 144/311/B6288
39 GRO: Marriage Index, 1866, 2nd Quarter, London City, Volume 1c, p. 1301 (corrected by GRO from 224)
40 Ancestry.com: TNA: 1861 England Census; Class: RG 9; Piece: 210; f. 6; p. 6; GSU roll: 542592
41 Ancestry.com: TNA: 1861 England Census; Class: RG 9; Piece: 210; f. 21; p. 36; GSU roll: 542592
42 The Benjamins were there for the 1861 and 1871 censuses: Ancestry.com: TNA: 1871 England Census; Class: RG10; Piece: 412; f. 6; p. 6; GSU roll: 824628. The Davis family were there for the 1861 and 1871 censuses: Ancestry.com: TNA: 1871 England Census; Class: RG10; Piece: 412; f. 20; p. 34; GSU roll: 824628.
43 *London Evening Standard*, 9 January 1884
44 GRO: Marriage Index, 1866, 4th Quarter, London City, Volume 1c, p. 227
45 GRO: Marriage Index, 1883, 4th Quarter, London City, Volume 1c, p. 140
46 The Lewis family and Philip's wife's family the Lyons lived there for decades: Ancestry.com: TNA: 1871 England Census; Class: RG10; Piece: 434; f. 51; p. 11; GSU roll: 823356. The Emanuel family were there for most of the 19th century. Their entries in the 1871 and 1881 censuses: Ancestry.com: TNA: 1871 England Census; Class: RG10; Piece: 434; f. 56; p. 21; GSU roll: 823356; Ancestry.com: TNA: 1881 England Census; Class: RG11; Piece: 381; f. 43; p. 19; GSU roll: 1341082
47 *The Times*, 4 October 1888, quoted from Evans and Skinner, *The Ultimate Jack the Ripper Sourcebook*, pp. 175–6
48 Ibid.
49 *Belfast Weekly News*, 6 October 1888
50 *The Times*, 6 October 1888, quoted from Evans and Skinner, *The Ultimate Jack the Ripper Sourcebook*, pp. 181–3
51 Ibid.
52 *Kentish Independent*, 22 September 1888

9. The murder of Mary Jane Kelly

1 Dew, *I Caught Crippen*, p. 86
2 Raphael Samuel, *East End Underworld: Chapters in the Life of Arthur Harding* (London: Routledge and Kegan Paul, 1981), quoted from Begg, Fido and Skinner, *The Complete Jack the Ripper A to Z*, p. 313
3 LMA: MJ/SPC, NE1888, Box 3, Case Paper 19, quoted from Evans and Skinner, *The Ultimate Jack the Ripper Sourcebook*, pp. 407–17

4 Ibid.
5 *Edinburgh Evening News*, 10 November 1888
6 *The Globe*, 12 November 1888
7 *Nottingham Evening Post*, 14 November 1888
8 *Reynolds's Newspaper*, 18 November 1888
9 LMA: MJ/SPC, NE1888, Box 3, Case Paper 19, quoted from Evans and Skinner, *The Ultimate Jack the Ripper Sourcebook*, pp. 407–17
10 Ibid.
11 *Jersey Independent and Daily Telegraph*, 17 November 1888
12 LMA: MJ/SPC, NE1888, Box 3, Case Paper 19, quoted from Evans and Skinner, *The Ultimate Jack the Ripper Sourcebook*, p. 412
13 *Reynolds's Newspaper*, 18 November 1888
14 *Weekly Dispatch* (London) 18 November 1888
15 *Worcestershire Chronicle*, 17 November 1888
16 *Weekly Dispatch* (London) 18 November 1888
17 Ibid.
18 Ibid.
19 *Reynolds's Newspaper*, 18 November 1888
20 *Weekly Dispatch* (London), 18 November 1888
21 Ibid.
22 Ibid.
23 Ibid.
24 Ibid.
25 Ibid.
26 Ibid.
27 TNA: MEPO 3/3153, ff. 10–18, quoted from Evans and Skinner, *The Ultimate Jack the Ripper Sourcebook*, pp. 382–4
28 TNA: HO 144/221/A49301C, ff. 220–223, quoted from Evans and Skinner, *The Ultimate Jack the Ripper Sourcebook*, p. 401
29 Ibid.
30 LMA: Friern Hospital [Colney Hatch Lunatic Asylum] Patients' Records: Case books – male patients: H12/CH/B/13/038
31 TNA: MEPO 3/140, ff. 227–9, quoted from Evans and Skinner, *The Ultimate Jack the Ripper Sourcebook*, pp. 418–19
32 TNA: MEPO 3/140, ff. 230–2, quoted from Evans and Skinner, *The Ultimate Jack the Ripper Sourcebook*, pp. 419–20
33 *Aberdeen Press and Journal*, 15 November 1888
34 TNA: HO 144/221/A49301C, ff. 220–3, quoted from Evans and Skinner, *The Ultimate Jack the Ripper Sourcebook*, p. 401

35 For example *The Globe*, 14 November 1888
36 *Illustrated Sporting and Dramatic News*, 3 November 1888
37 Ancestry.com: TNA: 1891 England Census; Class: RG12; Piece: 280; f. 106; p. 12
38 *York Herald*, 31 August 1888
39 *Sporting Life*, 8 September 1888
40 *The Globe*, 27 September 1888
41 *The Sportsman* is chosen over *Sporting Life*, as the latter had salmon-pink pages
42 *Sporting Life*, 7 August 1888
43 LMA: Friern Hospital [Colney Hatch Lunatic Asylum] Patients' Records: Case books – male patients: H12/CH/B/13/069

10. The first two murders in the Whitechapel Murders files: Emma Elizabeth Smith and Martha Tabram

1 LMA: St. B.G./Wh/123/19, quoted from Evans and Skinner, *The Ultimate Jack the Ripper Sourcebook*, p. 4
2 Dew, *I Caught Crippen*, p. 94
3 *Lloyd's Weekly Newspaper*, 23 September 1888
4 Ibid.
5 Evans and Skinner, *The Ultimate Jack the Ripper Sourcebook*, p. 3
6 *London Evening Standard*, 7 April 1888
7 LMA: St. B.G./Wh/123/19, quoted from Evans and Skinner, *The Ultimate Jack the Ripper Sourcebook*, p. 4
8 Ibid.
9 Destroyed in the Blitz, its footprint can be seen in today's Altab Ali Park
10 *Worcestershire Chronicle*, 14 April 1888
11 Ibid.
12 *Wigton Advertiser*, 14 April 1888
13 *Morning Advertiser*, 9 April 1888, quoted from Evans and Skinner, *The Ultimate Jack the Ripper Sourcebook*, p. 6
14 *Lloyd's Weekly Newspaper*, 8 April 1888, quoted from Evans and Skinner, *The Ultimate Jack the Ripper Sourcebook*, p. 7
15 *Magnet* (London), 9 April 1888
16 Ibid.
17 Nicholas Connell, *The Annotated I Caught Crippen: Memoirs of Ex-Chief Inspector Walter Dew, C.I.D. of Scotland Yard* (Mango Books, 2019), p. 128
18 *Sporting Life*, 7 August 1888
19 *Sporting Life*, 6 August 1888
20 *The Norwood Review*, Edition #152, copyright The Norwood Society, Registered Charity 285547

21 TNA: MEPO 3/140, f. 34, quoted from Evans and Skinner, *The Ultimate Jack the Ripper Sourcebook*, p. 10
22 *East London Observer*, 11 August 1888
23 Ibid.
24 Ibid.
25 Ibid.
26 Ibid.
27 Ibid.
28 Ibid.
29 Ibid.
30 Ibid.
31 Ibid.
32 *East London Observer*, 25 August 1888
33 Ibid.
34 Ibid.
35 Ibid.
36 Ibid.
37 Ibid.
38 Ibid.
39 Ibid.
40 Ibid.
41 Ibid.
42 Ibid.
43 Ibid.
44 TNA: MEPO 3/140, ff. 36–42, quoted from Evans and Skinner, *The Ultimate Jack the Ripper Sourcebook*, p. 18
45 Ibid., p. 17
46 TNA: MEPO 3/140, ff. 52–9, quoted from Evans and Skinner, *The Ultimate Jack the Ripper Sourcebook*, p. 15
47 Ibid., p. 16
48 Ibid.
49 Ibid.
50 *CS Eye*, April 2014 and *Forensick!*, July 2018, publications by The Chartered Society of Forensic Sciences quoting an article by Robert Milne MFSSoc, FFS, FA IA-IP and including Ian Oldfield's geographical profiling map
51 Douglas and Olshaker, *The Cases that Haunt Us*, p. 58

11. Other possible Ripper victims

1 TNA: HO 144/221/A49301C/8b, quoted from Sugden, *The Complete History*

of Jack the Ripper, p. 487
2 Dew, *I Caught Crippen*, p. 156
3 Douglas and Olshaker, *The Cases that Haunt Us*, p. 70
4 *South Wales Daily News*, 22 November 1888
5 Ibid.
6 *Bury and Norwich Post*, 27 November 1888
7 *South Wales Daily News*, 22 November 1888
8 Ibid.
9 *The Times*, 22 November 1888, quoted from Evans and Skinner, *The Ultimate Jack the Ripper Sourcebook*, p. 423
10 *South Wales Daily News*, 22 November 1888
11 *Abergavenny Chronicle*, 22 November 1888
12 *Belfast News-Letter*, 22 November 1888
13 *Bury and Norwich Post*, 27 November 1888
14 *South Wales Daily News*, 22 November 1888
15 Ibid.
16 Ibid.
17 Ancestry.com: London, England, Workhouse Admission and Discharge Records, 1764–1930, Tower Hamlets, Admission Date: 21 Nov 1888; Discharge Date: 1 Dec 1888: LMA: STBG/WH/123/020
18 LMA: Whitechapel Infirmary: Porters' Admission and Discharge Register: STBG/WH/123/020; STBG/WH/123/021
19 *Bury and Norwich Post*, 27 November 1888
20 *Sporting Life*, 16 November 1888
21 Ancestry.com: London, England, Workhouse Admission and Discharge Records, Tower Hamlets, Admission Date: 25 Feb 1888; Discharge Date: 21 Mar 1888: LMA: STBG/2H/123/020. Her name is the last entry in the Admission Register, suggesting a late admission.
22 *Sheffield Evening Telegraph*, 5 April 1888
23 *Tower Hamlets Independent and East End Local Advertiser*, 7 April 1888
24 Ibid.
25 *Sheffield Evening Telegraph*, 5 April 1888
26 GRO: Death Certificate, 1888, Mile End Old Town, 2nd Quarter, Volume 01C, p. 293
27 *Lloyd's Weekly London Newspaper*, 30 December 1888
28 Ibid.
29 Ibid.
30 TNA: HO 144/221/A49301H, ff. 7–14, quoted from Evans and Skinner, *The Ultimate Jack the Ripper Sourcebook*, pp. 470–1

31 Anderson, *The Lighter Side of My Official Life*, p. 137
32 *Evening Gazette* (Aberdeen), 3 January 1889
33 Ibid.
34 Ibid.
35 *Eastern Morning News*, 10 January 1889
36 Ibid.
37 Ibid.
38 Ibid.
39 TNA: MEPO 3/143, quoted from Evans and Skinner, *The Ultimate Jack the Ripper Sourcebook*, p. 475
40 LMA: Homerton Workhouse: Admission and Discharge Register, 1888–1889: CBG/334/012. Hyams was in continuous detention from 7 September 1889 until his death.
41 TNA: MEPO 3/143, ff. 272–3, quoted from Evans and Skinner, *The Ultimate Jack the Ripper Sourcebook*, p. 497
42 Ibid., p. 498
43 TNA: HO 144/221/A49301I, ff. 5–6, quoted from Evans and Skinner, *The Ultimate Jack the Ripper Sourcebook*, p. 501
44 *Dundee Courier*, 19 July 1889
45 Ibid.
46 Ibid.
47 Ibid.
48 *Warrington Examiner*, 20 July 1889
49 *The People*, 21 July 1889
50 *Northampton Chronicle and Echo*, 14 August 1889
51 *Willesden Chronicle*, 16 August 1889
52 Ibid.
53 TNA: MEPO 3/140, ff. 263–71, quoted from Evans and Skinner, *The Ultimate Jack the Ripper Sourcebook*, p. 510
54 TNA: MEPO 3/140, ff. 259–62, quoted from Evans and Skinner, *The Ultimate Jack the Ripper Sourcebook*, p. 504
55 Ibid.
56 TNA: MEPO 3/140, ff. 263–71, quoted from Evans and Skinner, *The Ultimate Jack the Ripper Sourcebook*, p. 508
57 TNA: MEPO 3/140, ff. 177–83, quoted from Evans and Skinner, *The Ultimate Jack the Ripper Sourcebook*, p. 648
58 *Tiverton Gazette* (*Mid-Devon Gazette*), 17 September 1889
59 TNA: HO 144/221/A49301K, ff. 7–8, quoted from Evans and Skinner, *The Ultimate Jack the Ripper Sourcebook*, p. 554
60 TNA: HO 144/221/A49301K, ff. 1–8, quoted from Evans and Skinner, *The*

Ultimate Jack the Ripper Sourcebook, p. 546

61 LMA: Friern Hospital [Colney Hatch Lunatic Asylum] Patients' Records: Case books – male patients: H12/CH/B/13/037

62 LMA: Homerton Workhouse: Admission and Discharge Register, 1888–1889: CBG/334/012

63 *Sheffield Evening Telegraph*, 16 February 1891

64 TNA: MEPO 3/140, ff. 112–14, quoted from Evans and Skinner, *The Ultimate Jack the Ripper Sourcebook*, p. 609

65 *Western Daily Press*, 18 February 1891

66 TNA: MEPO 3/140, ff. 177–83, quoted from Evans and Skinner, *The Ultimate Jack the Ripper Sourcebook*, p. 648

12. The perpetrator's incarceration and death

1 LMA: Thames Magistrates Court: Court Register: court 1, part 1: PS/TH/A/01/12

2 Ibid.

3 Ancestry,com: London, England, Workhouse Admission and Discharge Records, 1764–1930, Tower Hamlets, Admission Date: 29 Dec 1888; Discharge Date: 11 Jan 1889: LMA: STBG/WH/123/020

4 Smith, *From Constable to Commissioner*, p. 148

5 GRO: Birth Index, 1859, 2nd Quarter, Lambeth, Volume 1d, p. 315

6 *Dundee Courier*, 10 December 1906

7 *Thomson's Weekly News*, 1 December 1906, quoted from Evans and Skinner, *The Ultimate Jack the Ripper Sourcebook*, pp. 703–9

8 Ibid.

9 LMA: Whitechapel Infirmary: Porters' Admission and Discharge Register: STBG/WH/123/021

10 *Reynolds News*, 15 September 1946, quoted from Evans and Skinner, *The Ultimate Jack the Ripper Sourcebook*, p. 702

11 *The Butchers' Row Suspect: Was He Jack the Ripper?*, by Scott Nelson, quoted from casebook.org, reproduced from *Ripperologist* magazine

12 Ancestry.com: London, England, Electoral Registers, 1832–1965: In 1892, Mark Hyams was listed as resident at 49 North Block, Artizans, City of London, England

13 LMA: Homerton Workhouse: Admission and Discharge Register, 1888–1889: CBG/334/012; City of London Mental Hospital [later Stone House Hospital]: Case Book: Male Admissions: CLA/001/B/02/007

14 An article in *The People's Journal*, reprinted in the *Dundee People's Journal*, 27 September 1919

15 Sugden, *The Complete History of Jack the Ripper*, p. 631
16 TNA: HO 144/221/A49301C, ff. 148–59, quoted from Evans and Skinner, *The Ultimate Jack the Ripper Sourcebook*, p. 137
17 LMA: Whitechapel Infirmary: Porters' Admission and Discharge Register: STBG/WH/123/021
18 TNA: HO 144/221/A49301G, ff. 21–2, quoted from Evans and Skinner, *The Ultimate Jack the Ripper Sourcebook*, p. 493
19 Ancestry.com: LMA: London, England, Workhouse Admission and Discharge Records, 1764–1930; Ancestry.com: LMA: Mile End Workhouse Creed Register, 1886–1890
20 LMA: Homerton Workhouse: Admission and Discharge Register, 1888–1889: CBG/334/012
21 Cooper is referenced in LMA: Guildhall Justice Room, City of London, 7 Feb–16 Oct 1889: CLA/005/002/024 and Harber in City of London Police: Personnel Files: Police Officers: CLA/048/AD/01/296
22 *Pall Mall Gazette*, 29 July 1891
23 LMA: Guildhall Justice Room, City of London, 7 Feb–16 Oct 1889: CLA/005/002/024
24 Begg, Fido and Skinner, *The Complete Jack the Ripper A to Z*, p. 205
25 Donald Swanson's marginalia is quoted from Begg, Fido and Skinner, *The Complete Jack the Ripper A to Z*, pp. 499–503. The punctuation is the author's.
26 Email to the author from the Royal Hospital for Neuro-disability dated 6 December 2022
27 LMA: Friern Hospital [Colney Hatch Lunatic Asylum] Patients' Records: Case books – male patients: H12/CH/B/13/038
28 TNA: MEPO 7/58, 1896, 29 October 1896
29 Examples quoted from TNA: MEPO 7 series of Police Orders
30 Ancestry.com: TNA: Metropolitan Police Pension Registers, 1852–1932, No. 12,547 of 7 January 1896
31 Ancestry.com: TNA: 1901 England Census; Class: RG13; Piece: 702; f. 117; p. 15
32 The Kings were at 14 Jubilee Cottages while the Beadles were at an unspecified number on the High Street: Ancestry.com: TNA: 1871 England Census; Class: RG10; Piece: 762; f. 74; p. 8; GSU roll: 824728; Ancestry.com: TNA: 1871 England Census; Class: RG10; Piece: 1018; f. 18; p. 28; GSU roll: 827265.
33 *Penny Illustrated Paper*, 3 July 1897
34 *Pall Mall Gazette*, 21 August 1902
35 LMA: Friern Hospital [Colney Hatch Lunatic Asylum] Patients' Records: Case books – male patients: H12/CH/B/13/069
36 Ibid.

37 Ibid.
38 Ibid.
39 *West Somerset Free Press*, 4 July 1903
40 All excerpts from LMA: Friern Hospital [Colney Hatch Lunatic Asylum] Patients' Records: Case books – male patients: H12/CH/B/13/069
41 Ibid.
42 Ibid.
43 Ibid.
44 Ibid.
45 Ibid.
46 LMA: Friern Hospital [Colney Hatch Lunatic Asylum] Patients' Records: Case books – male patients: H12/CH/B/13/071
47 Ibid.
48 GRO: Death Certificate, 1913, Barnet, 2nd Quarter, Volume 03a, p. 521; his death certificate stated his age wrongly as fifty-seven
49 *The Jewish Chronicle*, 28 March 1913
50 The United Synagogue burial database at theus.org.uk
51 GRO: Death Certificate, 1944, London City, 4th Quarter, Volume 01c, p. 7

Conclusion

1 *City Press*, 7 January 1905
2 Sugden, *The Complete History of Jack the Ripper*, p. 564
3 *Mid Sussex Times*, 30 April 1901
4 *The Sketch*, 9 November 1910

Epilogue

1 *The Star*, 18 October 1888
2 TNA: MEPO 7/50, 1888, 27 October 1888; TNA: MEPO 7/51, 1889, 19 January 1889
3 LMA: Society for the Protection of Life from Fire, 1882–1904: Minutes of general meetings and committees: CLC/014/MS34980/004
4 The Landaus feature in Oliver Sacks, *Uncle Tungsten: Memories of a Chemical Boyhood* (Picador, 2012)

INDEX

Index

ANNIE CHAPMAN
MARY JANE KELLY
HYAMS' LODGINGS
MARTHA TABRAM
GOULSTON STREET GRAFFITO
KATE EDDOWES